REVELATIONS OF DIVINE MERCY

REVELATIONS OF
DIVINE MERCY

Daily Readings from the Diary
of Blessed Faustina Kowalska

REV. GEORGE W. KOSICKI, C.S.B.

CHARIS

Servant Publications
Ann Arbor, Michigan

Charis Books is an imprint of Servant Publications designed to serve Roman Catholics.

Unless otherwise indicated, Scripture quotations are from the Revised Standard Version of the Bible, © 1946, 1952, 1971 by the Division of Christian Education of the National Council of Churches of Christ in the USA. Used by permission.

Readings are excerpted from the English translation of Blessed Faustina Kowalska's diary, entitled *Divine Mercy in My Soul*, © 1987 by Congregation of Marians. Used by permission. All rights reserved.

Published by Servant Publications
P.O. Box 8617
Ann Arbor, Michigan 48107

Cover design: Janice Hendrick, Good Visuals, Ann Arbor, MI

96 97 98 99 00 10 9 8 7 6 5 4 3 2 1

Printed in the United States of America
ISBN 0-89283-977-5

Library of Congress Cataloging-in-Publication Data

Faustyna, Siostra, 1905-1938
Revelations of divine mercy : daily readings from the diary of Blessed Faustina Kowalska / [compiled by] George Kosicki.
    p. cm.
ISBN 0-89283-977-5
1. Devotional calendars—Catholic Church.   2. Catholic Church—Prayer-books and devotions—English.   3. Faustyna, Siostra 1905-1938.   I. Kosicki, George W., 1928- . II. Title.
BX2170.C56F38   1996
271'.9202—dc20   96-25435
                                                                    CIP

"Faithfulness to the inspirations
of the Holy Spirit—that is the shortest
route to holiness"
(Diary, 291).

CONTENTS

Introduction

The Diary of Blessed Faustina is much more than a collection of private revelations, events, prayers, and impressions of a Polish nun. It is an extraordinary teaching on how to live the spiritual life, written in simple language that engages and challenges the reader.

It has the highest recommendations. In the introduction to the Diary, Andrew Cardinal Deskur writes:

> The theology alone which is found in the Diary awakens in the reader a conviction of its uniqueness; and if one considers the contrast between Sister Faustina's education and the loftiness of her theology, the contrast alone indicates the special influence of Divine Grace.

Further, the Church has given it a special recommendation in the introduction to the Office of Readings for the feast of Blessed Faustina (October 5): "Her spiritual Diary is counted among the outstanding works of mystical literature."

But the Diary as written presents a problem for many readers. The subject matter is jumbled, especially in the first notebook (paragraphs 1-521), which she rewrote by memory after she burned the first text. Most entries have no date and do not follow the subject matter of the previous entry.

Revelations of Divine Mercy: Daily Readings from the Diary of Blessed Faustina Kowalska is a response to the request to gather the topics of her Diary into themes. This became possible to do as a result of the *Study Guide to the Diary of Blessed Faustina Kowalska* (Marian Helpers, Stockbridge, MA), which is an index of the Diary under some ninety themes. The advantage of this present book is that it gathers the major themes to provide daily reading for a month at a time. The same theme continued for a month gives the advantage of an in-depth insight into Sr. Faustina's spiritual life.

Special thanks are extended to Christine Kruszyna for her careful and faithful work in preparing the Thematic Diary and the Daily Readings from the Diary.

Editor's Note: All parenthetical notations within the text, unless otherwise noted, correspond to the numbered passages of Blessed Faustina's original diary.

How to Use This Book

This book is an excellent basic resource for those who wish to study the spiritual life of Blessed Faustina. The introductory material contains insights into both the life of Blessed Faustina and the Divine Mercy devotion.

This book will also greatly benefit you, the reader, as a daily devotional. Read a selection in the morning or in the evening to feed both the heart and mind. The treasures contained in the Diary are cumulative: the more we read, study, and pray, the richer the insights become.

Study and prayer groups can profitably use this book as the main text of their reading, sharing, and prayer on the spiritual life of Blessed Faustina. Such a group might meet monthly to discuss the previous month's theme, using the "Practice, Prayer, and Promise" listed at the end of each monthly introduction as a springboard for discussion and application. These gathered themes can also be useful when making retreats.

With great spiritual profit we can learn from "the great apostle of Divine Mercy in our time" (John Paul II, April 10, 1994).

THE LIFE OF BLESSED FAUSTINA AND THE ORIGIN OF THE DIVINE MERCY DEVOTION

On February 22, 1931, a young Polish nun, Sr. Faustina Kowalska, saw a vision of Jesus with rays of mercy streaming from the area of His Heart. He told her to have an image painted to represent this vision and to sign it, "Jesus, I trust in You!" Calling her the Apostle and Secretary of His Mercy, He ordered her to begin writing a diary so others would come to know and trust in Him.

In a series of revelations that followed between 1931 and Sr. Faustina's death in 1938, Jesus taught the young nun that His mercy is unlimited and available even to the greatest sinners. He revealed special ways for people to respond to His mercy in their lives, and He gave her several promises for those who would trust in His mercy and show mercy to others.

By 1938, devotion to the Divine Mercy had already begun to spread throughout Eastern Europe. In July of 1940, Fr. Joseph Jarzebowski, a Polish Marian priest fleeing from war-torn Poland, prayed to the merciful Savior to help him escape, vowing to spend the rest of his life spreading the Divine Mercy devotion. He arrived safely on American soil in May, 1941, and Marian communities in Detroit and Washington, D.C. were soon distributing Mercy of God materials.

In 1944, a group of Marians opened a new house and apostolate on Eden Hill in Stockbridge, Massachusetts and began spreading the devotion on a large scale. By 1953, the Marian apostolate on Eden Hill had become the international center for the Divine Mercy devotion, distributing more than twenty-five million pieces of mercy literature per year. In 1960, with donations from all over the world, the Marians on Eden Hill completed construction of a shrine to the Mercy of God.

The shrine has now become the National Shrine of the Divine Mercy, and the apostolate has become the Marian Helpers Center, a modern religious publishing house spreading devotion to the Mercy of God and to Mary Immaculate.

As Sr. Faustina herself predicted (378), the Divine Mercy devotion, according to the forms she proposed, was initially banned by the Holy See because of misleading translations. In 1978 the ban was lifted, according to the Vatican Congregation, because of the careful, informed intervention of then Archbishop of Cracow, Cardinal Karol Wojtyla. (For more information see footnote 89 in the Diary, or *The Divine Mercy Message and Devotion*, produced by the Marian Helpers, p. 15-19.)

The process for the beatification of Sr. Faustina was begun in 1966. On March 7, 1992, in the presence of the Holy Father, the Congregation for the Causes of Saints promulgated the Decree of Heroic Virtues, by which the Church acknowledges that Sr. Faustina practiced all the Christian virtues to a heroic degree. On December 21, 1992, a healing through Sr. Faustina's intercession was declared a miracle. On the Sunday after Easter, April 18, 1993 (Mercy Sunday), Sr. Faustina was solemnly beatified in Rome by Pope John Paul II. She is now officially known as Blessed Faustina Kowalska.

THE MYSTERY OF MERCY

Blessed Faustina is the great Apostle of Divine Mercy. That is the way Pope John Paul II referred to her. And it is from this perspective that we can approach her Diary and delve into the "Mystery of Mercy."

The "Mystery of Mercy" is how both John Paul II and Blessed Faustina refer to God's mercy. The meaning of the word "mystery" as used here is more than a detective's search for clues that lead to an answer. As used here, the search into the "Mystery of Mercy" will lead us deeper and deeper into the very Heart of God. The more we discover about the mystery of God, the more we will find that there is still more to discover. The most profound mystery that we will discover is "Christ in [us], the hope of glory" (Col 1:27). Christ is Mercy Incarnate (John Paul II, *Rich in Mercy*, par. 2-3).

The daily selections of the Diary of Blessed Faustina are arranged under the major themes related to Divine Mercy so that they can be reflected upon systematically and delved into more fully. Each of the monthly themes features one facet of the sparkling diamond of God's great mercy. These combined themes form a commentary on the spiritual life or even a whole course for a year of spiritual formation. These reflections have been keyed with parenthetical notations to Blessed Faustina's Diary, *Divine Mercy in My Soul.*

WHY BLESSED FAUSTINA?

Why should we study the diary of a simple nun? Each person is a unique presence of Christ; each saint expresses that presence in an extraordinary way. Christ is present as mercy in Blessed Faustina as in no other person. She is a model of mercy. Saints also serve as intercessors for us at the Throne of God. Blessed Faustina now continues her ministry in heaven, interceding for mercy for souls. What a great sister we have in heaven!

In the Office of Readings for the Liturgy of the Hours (October 5), the Church describes for us the value of studying the Diary of Blessed Faustina: "She left behind a spiritual Diary which is numbered among the outstanding works of mystical literature." This evaluation of her Diary places her writing among the doctors of the Church.

WHAT IS MERCY?

Mercy is God's very goodness that pours itself out in creating us, redeeming us after we have sinned, and sanctifying us. It is a pure gift of perfect love—we cannot merit it, but we need to receive it by turning to Him with trust and with thanksgiving.

As love is of the very nature of God, so is mercy. The goodness that comes from the depths of His being is tender and compassionate. It has been described as coming from His "bowels" but could be better described as coming from His "heart-womb."

St. Augustine and St. Thomas Aquinas described mercy as the greatest attribute of God, as do both Blessed Faustina and Pope John Paul II.

Many languages have a word for mercy that combines love or compassion and heart, such as the Latin word for mercy, *misericordia,* that is *miser* (pity or compassion) and *cor* (heart). No single English word is adequate to describe this mercy, so many multiple words are used, such as *tender-kindness, loving-mercy, faithful-love, committed-love, everlasting-love,* and *heartfelt-love.*

Blessed Faustina speaks of the mercy of God in a variety of ways: as "the *merciful* God," focusing on His attribute of mercy; as "*the* Divine Mercy," focusing on His essence; as "an *ocean* of mercy, without limit," focusing on the power and radiance of His mercy.

THE MESSAGE

The message of Divine Mercy is that God is Mercy. He is love itself poured out for us, and He wants no one to escape that merciful love.

The message is that God wants us to turn to Him with trust and repentance while there is still time, before He comes as the just Judge. This turning with trust to Him who is Mercy itself is the only source of peace for mankind. Turning to and imploring God's mercy is the answer to the troubled world. There is no escaping that answer.

The Response of Trust and Conversion. What God most wants of us is to turn to Him with *trust.* And the first act of trust is to *receive* His mercy. To trust God is to rely on Him who is Mercy itself. The Lord wants us to live with trust in Him in all circumstances. We trust Him because He is God, and He loves us and cares for us.

His mercy is always available to us, no matter what we have done or what state we are in, even if our sins are as black as night and we are filled with fears and anxieties. "The greater the sinner, the greater the right he has to My mercy" (723).

But there is more we can do. As Catholics, as Christians, we can go to the Sacrament of Reconciliation and be reconciled to God and to man. The Lord wants us to live reconciled with Him and with one another.

The Response of Mercy Toward Others. Not only are we to *receive* His mercy, but we are to *use* it, being merciful to others by our actions, by our words, and by our prayers; in other words, by practicing the Corporal and Spiritual Works of Mercy.

The Corporal Works of Mercy are feeding the hungry, giving drink to the thirsty, clothing the naked, sheltering the travelers, comforting the prisoners, visiting the sick, and burying the dead. The Spiritual Works of Mercy include teaching the ignorant, praying for the living and the dead, correcting sinners, counseling those in doubt, consoling the sorrowful, bearing wrongs patiently, and forgiving wrongs willingly.

The Divine Mercy and the Gospel. The Divine Mercy message— which is Jesus Himself—is at the heart of the gospel. In the New Testament Jesus exhorts us to "be merciful even as your Father is merciful" (Lk 6:36). Jesus sets the highest goal for us and expects us to obtain it by His merciful love: "Blessed are the merciful for they shall obtain mercy" (Mt 5:7). When He comes again, He will judge us on our mercy toward one another: "Truly, I say to you, as you did it to one of the least of my brethren, you did it to me" (Mt 25:40, NAB).

Mercy—The Message and Response Through the Ages. The message and response of mercy is not something new. In the past, God spoke a message of mercy through the patriarchs and prophets—through Noah, Abraham, Moses, Elijah, and many others. In the last days God has spoken to us by His Son, Jesus Christ, who is Mercy Incarnate.

The message of mercy presents the truth and the call of the gospel to our present age. This message of mercy is proclaimed by Pope John Paul II, in his encyclical *Rich in Mercy*, as the message of our age.

...the Church must consider it one of her principle duties—at every stage of history and especially in our modern age—*to proclaim and to introduce into life* the mystery of mercy, supremely revealed in Jesus Christ (14).

DEVOTION TO THE DIVINE MERCY

Our Lord not only taught Blessed Faustina the fundamentals of trust, and of mercy to others, but He also revealed special ways to live out the response to His mercy. These we call the *devotion to the Divine Mercy*. The word "devotion" means fulfilling our vows. It is a commitment of our lives to the Lord who is Mercy.

By giving our lives to the Divine Mercy—Jesus Christ Himself—we become instruments of His mercy to others, and so we can live out the command of the Lord, "Be merciful even as your Father is merciful" (Lk 6:36).

Through Blessed Faustina, Our Lord gave us special means of drawing on His mercy: a Feast of Mercy, an Image of the Divine Mercy, a Chaplet of Divine Mercy, a novena, and a prayer at the three o'clock hour—the hour of His death. These special means (devotions) are not ends in themselves, but are intended to help us lead a life more committed to the Lord. (Of course, they are not to replace the Sacraments of Eucharist and Reconciliation, which have been given to the whole Church.)

The devotions described by Blessed Faustina in her Diary are unique in that they are designed and taught by the Lord for our spiritual growth. They are designed so that we may become a "living devotion," as Blessed Faustina virtually became a "living chaplet of Divine Mercy" (482), a "living Eucharist" (483), and a "living image of mercy" (163).

The Feast of the Divine Mercy. Our Lord asked Blessed Faustina to pray and work towards establishing a Feast of the Divine Mercy on the Sunday after Easter. He told her:

On that day the very depths of My tender mercy are open. I pour out a whole ocean of graces upon souls who approach the fount of My mercy. The soul that will go to Confession and receive Holy Communion shall obtain complete forgiveness of sins and punishment. (699)

Mercy Sunday was to become a day to celebrate the paschal mystery with a focus on God's covenant of mercy. It would be a day of complete forgiveness and pardon, like the day of atonement in the Old Testament (see Leviticus 16). On that day all our sins and the punishment due to them would receive atonement.

The message Blessed Faustina received has become reality. On Mercy Sunday, April 23, 1995, Pope John Paul II celebrated Holy Mass and enthroned the Divine Mercy Image at the Divine Mercy Center established for the Diocese of Rome in the Church of the Holy Spirit in Sassia.

We can celebrate this "Mercy Sunday" by going to Confession in preparation (preferably before that Sunday) and by receiving Communion, preparing ourselves to receive the presence of Our Lord with great expectancy. We can honor the mercy of the Lord by venerating the Image of the Divine Mercy and by our prayers and works of mercy.

The Image of the Divine Mercy. Jesus appeared to Blessed Faustina with rays of red and pale light streaming from the area around His heart. His right hand was raised in blessing, recalling the scene of Easter Sunday night (see John 20:19-23).

He asked Blessed Faustina to have this vision painted and signed with the words, "Jesus, I trust in You!" He offered this Image to remind people to trust in His mercy, and to come to Him for mercy:

I am offering people a vessel with which they are to keep coming for graces to the fountain of mercy. That vessel is this image with the signature: "Jesus, I trust in You." (327)

Jesus explained that the rays represented the blood and water which flowed from His pierced side, and He taught Blessed Faustina the prayer:

O Blood and Water, which gushed forth from the Heart of Jesus as a fount of mercy for us, I trust in You!   (84)

Our Lord told Blessed Faustina that He wanted this Image be venerated first in the Sisters' Chapel, then throughout the world (47).

The Chaplet of the Divine Mercy. Our Lord taught Blessed Faustina a prayer for mercy that she was to pray "unceasingly." He told her that, if she prayed in this way, her prayers would have great power for the conversion of sinners (687), for peace for the dying (1541), and even for controlling nature (1128). This prayer became known as the Chaplet of the Divine Mercy.

We, too, can pray this chaplet, using ordinary rosary beads of five decades. We begin with the Our Father, the Hail Mary, and the Apostles' Creed. Then on the large beads we pray:

Eternal Father, I offer you the Body and Blood, Soul and Divinity of Your Dearly Beloved Son, Our Lord, Jesus Christ, in atonement for our sins and those of the whole world.

On the small beads we pray:

For the sake of His sorrowful Passion, have mercy on us and on the whole world.

And at the end, we pray three times:

Holy God, Holy Mighty One, Holy Immortal One, have mercy on us and on the whole world.   (476)

The Novena Before the Feast. In preparation for the Feast of the Divine Mercy, the Lord asked Blessed Faustina to make a novena (nine days) of prayer from Good Friday to the following Saturday.

> **I desire that during these nine days you bring souls to the fount of My mercy, that they may draw therefrom strength and refreshment and whatever graces they need in the hardships of life, and especially at the hour of death.** (1209)

These nine days of prayer before the Feast of Mercy are like the nine days of prayer in the Upper Room before the day of Pentecost (see Acts 1:14). For each of the nine days, our Lord gave Blessed Faustina a different intention:

- *Day One:* all mankind, especially sinners
- *Day Two:* the souls of priests and religious
- *Day Three:* all devout and faithful souls
- *Day Four:* those who do not believe in God and those who do not yet know Jesus
- *Day Five:* the souls who have separated themselves from the Church
- *Day Six:* the meek and humble souls and the souls of little children
- *Day Seven:* the souls who especially venerate and glorify His mercy
- *Day Eight:* the souls detained in purgatory
- *Day Nine:* souls who have become lukewarm

We, too, can make a novena of prayer for these intentions and others, especially by praying the Chaplet of the Divine Mercy. This novena can also be prayed any time during the year.

The Three O'Clock Hour. In His revelations to Blessed Faustina, Jesus asked for special, daily remembrance at three o'clock, the very hour He died for us on the cross:

> **At three o'clock, implore My mercy, especially for sinners; and if only for a brief moment, immerse yourself in My Passion, particularly in My abandonment at the moment of agony. This is the hour of great mercy for the whole world. I will allow you to enter into My mortal sorrow. In this hour, I will refuse nothing to the soul that makes a request of Me in virtue of My Passion.** (1320)

At 3:00 each afternoon we can pray:

> You expired, Jesus, but the source of life gushed forth for souls, and the ocean of mercy opened up for the whole world. O Fount of Life, unfathomable Divine Mercy, envelop the whole world and empty Yourself out upon us. (1319)

> O Blood and Water, which gushed forth from the Heart of Jesus as a fount of mercy for us, I trust in You! (84)

THE MISSION OF BLESSED FAUSTINA IS OURS

The Mission of Mercy is the mission of Jesus Christ and of His Church, and so it is our mission, too.

In our times this Mission of Mercy has come to a new focus in the life of Blessed Faustina, the Secretary and Apostle of Divine Mercy. By looking to her and her mission we can be inspired to learn the scope and purpose of our own mission.

Blessed Faustina writes that she strives for the greatest possible perfection—for sanctity, which is union with God—so that she may be useful to the Church (1475, 1505). The union of her heart with the Heart of Jesus is the foundation of her Mission of Mercy. By and through this union of hearts she is the Apostle of His Mercy. Because of this union of hearts, she had a profound knowledge of the Merciful Heart of Jesus, and could write freely about it.

Glorifying His Mercy. In one of the most powerful entries in her Diary, Blessed Faustina describes her mission. She wants to glorify the Lord's mercy by being transformed into a reflection of His compassionate Heart:

> My Jesus, penetrate me through and through so that I might be able to reflect You in my whole life. Divinize me so that my deeds may have supernatural value. Grant that I may have love, compassion, and mercy for every soul without exception. O my Jesus, each of Your saints reflects one of Your virtues; I desire to reflect Your compassionate heart, full of mercy; I want to glorify it. Let Your mercy, O Jesus, be impressed upon my heart and soul like a seal, and this will be my badge in this and the future life. Glorifying Your mercy is the exclusive task of my life.
>
> (1242)

> I want to be completely transformed into Your Mercy and to be Your living reflection.... O my Jesus, transform me into Yourself, for You can do all things. (163)

Blessed Faustina accomplished her mission of glorifying the Lord's mercy by becoming the living image of mercy. In her Diary she describes many ways in which to glorify the Lord's mercy, among them: trust; thanksgiving; praise of His mercy; proclaiming His mercy; prayer for mercy; submitting to God's will; offering prayer, work, and suffering; faithfully fulfilling His desires; fighting for the kingdom; receiving Holy Eucharist; venerating the Image of the Divine Mercy; and celebrating the Feast of Divine Mercy.

Blessed Faustina was aware that her mission was only to begin on earth, that it was to continue in heaven (281, 1242, 1325, 1729). What a blessing for those of us who need God's mercy and need to grow in its knowledge and experience to make mercy our mission.

Making Mercy Our Mission. The example of Blessed Faustina demonstrates how we are to make mercy our mission. With her whole being she plunged into the infinite mercy of God with abandonment to His will and trust in His mercy. She offered her life as an oblation in union with Christ crucified for the salvation of souls. Now we have her as our intercessor in heaven, where she continues her mission of mercy. And so it is with confidence we pray:

Blessed Faustina, you told us that your mission would continue after your death and that you would not forget us.

Our Lord also granted you a great privilege, telling you to "distribute graces as you will, to whom you will, and when you will."

Relying on this, I ask your intercession for the graces I need, especially _____.

Help me, above all, to trust in Jesus as you did, and thus to glorify His mercy every moment of my life.

MERCY

January

IN THIS FIRST MONTH of readings on God's mercy, the Diary of Blessed Faustina records for us four special aspects of mercy:

- **The nature of God's mercy:** The nature and quality of God's mercy is described as *inconceivable, inexhaustible, an ocean without limit, an abyss, tender, infinite,* and *compassionate.*

- **The vessels of mercy:** The Image, the Feast, and the Chaplet are three of the devotions the Lord Himself designed. By these devotions we are to become the living images of mercy.

- **Her Mission of Mercy:** The mission of Blessed Faustina was to *practice* mercy, to *proclaim* mercy, and to *plead* for mercy for the whole world. Blessed Faustina tells us if we live in the spirit of mercy, we shall obtain mercy.

- **The merciful Heart of Jesus.** The merciful Heart of Jesus, pierced as a fount of mercy for us, was a special focal point of Blessed Faustina's devotion.

Each of these aspects have a special meaning for us because they apply to those of us who want to grow in deeper union with the merciful Lord. Watch for these four elements, among others, as you reflect on the daily readings and apply them to your own life.

FOR THIS MONTH:

Practice: Venerate the Image of the Merciful Savior. Hang it in a prominent place, or carry a card of the Image with you (47).

Prayer: Offer the Chaplet of Divine Mercy each day (476, 1541).

Promise: "God has made us sharers in His mercy and even more than that, dispensers of that mercy..." (539).

JANUARY 1

O Eternal Love, You command Your Sacred Image to be painted
And reveal to us the inconceivable fount of mercy,
You bless whoever approaches Your rays,
And a soul all black will turn into snow.

O sweet Jesus, it is here [in the picture] You established the
    throne of Your mercy
To bring joy and hope to sinful man.
From Your open Heart, as from a pure fount,
Flows comfort to a repentant heart and soul.

May praise and glory for this Image
Never cease to stream from man's soul.
May praise of God's mercy pour from every heart,
Now, and at every hour, and forever and ever....   (1)

February 22, 1931. In the evening, when I was in my cell, I saw
the Lord Jesus clothed in a white garment. One hand [was]
raised in the gesture of blessing, the other was touching the
garment at the breast. From beneath the garment, slightly
drawn aside at the breast, there were emanating two large rays,
one red, the other pale. In silence I kept my gaze fixed on the
Lord; my soul was struck with awe, but also with great joy. After
a while, Jesus said to me, **Paint an image according to the pattern you see, with the signature: Jesus, I trust in You. I desire
that this image be venerated, first in your chapel, and** [then]
throughout the world.   (47)

**I promise that the soul that will venerate this image will not
perish. I also promise victory over** [its] **enemies already here
on earth, especially at the hour of death. I Myself will defend
it as My own glory.**   (48)

JANUARY 2

When I told this to my confessor.... [h]e told me, "Certainly, paint God's image in your soul." When I came out of the confessional, I again heard words such as these: **My image already is in your soul. I desire that there be a Feast of Mercy. I want this image, which you will paint with a brush, to be solemnly blessed on the first Sunday after Easter; that Sunday is to be the Feast of Mercy.** (49)

I desire that priests proclaim this great mercy of Mine towards souls of sinners. Let the sinner not be afraid to approach Me. The flames of mercy are burning Me—clamoring to be spent; I want to pour them out upon these souls.

Jesus complained to me in these words, **Distrust on the part of souls is tearing at My insides. The distrust of a chosen soul causes Me even greater pain; despite My inexhaustible love for them they do not trust Me. Even My death is not enough for them. Woe to the soul that abuses these** [gifts]. (50)

When I spoke about this to Mother Superior [Rose, telling her] that God had asked this of me, she answered that Jesus should give some sign so that we could recognize Him more clearly.

When I asked the Lord Jesus for a sign as a proof "that You are truly my God and Lord and that this request comes from You," I heard this interior voice, **I will make this all clear to the Superior by means of the graces which I will grant through this image.** (51)

JANUARY 3

Write this: before I come as the just Judge, I am coming first as the King of Mercy. Before the day of justice arrives, there will be given to people a sign in the heavens of this sort:

All light in the heavens will be extinguished, and there will be great darkness over the whole earth. Then the sign of the cross will be seen in the sky, and from the openings where the hands and the feet of the Savior were nailed will come forth great lights which will light up the earth for a period of time. This will take place shortly before the last day. (83)

O Blood and Water, which gushed forth from the Heart of Jesus as a fount of mercy for us, I trust in You! (84)

On Friday, after Holy Communion, I was carried in spirit before the throne of God. There I saw the heavenly Powers which incessantly praise God. Beyond the throne I saw a brightness inaccessible to creatures, and there only the Incarnate Word enters as Mediator. When Jesus entered this light, I heard these words, **Write down at once what you hear: I am the Lord in My essence and am immune to orders or needs. If I call creatures into being—that is the abyss of My mercy.** And at that very moment I found myself, as before, in our chapel at my kneeler, just as Mass had ended. I already had these words written. (85)

JANUARY 4

During adoration I felt God close to me. A moment later I saw Jesus and Mary. At the sight of them I was filled with joy, and I asked the Lord, "What is Your will, Jesus, concerning the matter about which my confessor told me to ask You?" Jesus replied, **It is My will that he should remain here and that he should not take the initiative of dispensing himself.** I asked Jesus whether the inscription could be: "Christ King of Mercy." He answered, **I am King of Mercy,** but He did not say "Christ." **I desire that this image be displayed in public on the first Sunday after Easter. That Sunday is the Feast of Mercy. Through the Word Incarnate I make known the bottomless depth of My mercy.** (88)

Strangely, all things came about just as the Lord had requested. In fact, it was on the first Sunday after Easter [April, 1935] that the image was publicly honored by crowds of people for the first time. For three days it was exposed and received public veneration. Since it was placed at the very top of a window at Ostra Brama [Shrine of Our Lady above the "Eastern Gate" to the city of Vilnius], it could be seen from a great distance. At Ostra Brama, during these three days, the closing of the Jubilee of the Redemption of the World was being celebrated, marking the nineteen hundred years that have passed since the Passion of our Savior. I see now that the work of Redemption is bound up with the work of mercy requested by the Lord. (89)

JANUARY 5

November, 1932. Today I arrived in Warsaw for the third probation. After a cordial meeting with the dear Mothers, I went into the small chapel for a moment. Suddenly God's presence filled my soul, and I heard these words, **My daughter, I desire that your heart be formed after the model of My merciful Heart. You must be completely imbued with My mercy.**

Dear Mother Directress [Margaret] at once asked me whether I had had a retreat that year, and I said no. "Then you must first have a retreat of at least three days." Thanks be to God there was at Walendow an eight-day retreat in which I could take part. But difficulties arose in regard to my leaving for this retreat. A certain person opposed my going very much, and it already [appeared that] I was not to go. After dinner, I went into the chapel for a five-minute adoration. Suddenly I saw the Lord Jesus, who said to me, **My daughter, I am preparing many graces for you, which you will receive during this retreat which you will begin tomorrow.** I answered, "Jesus, the retreat has already begun, and I am not supposed to go." And He said to me, **Get ready for it, because you will begin the retreat tomorrow. And as for your departure, I will arrange that with the superiors.** And in an instant, Jesus disappeared. (167)

JANUARY 6

O Most Holy Trinity! As many times as I breathe, as many times as my heart beats, as many times as my blood pulsates through my body, so many thousand times do I want to glorify Your mercy.

I want to be completely transformed into Your mercy and to be Your living reflection, O Lord. May the greatest of all divine attributes, that of Your unfathomable mercy, pass through my heart and soul to my neighbor.

Help me, O Lord, that my eyes may be merciful, so that I may never suspect or judge from appearances, but look for what is beautiful in my neighbors' souls and come to their rescue.

Help me, that my ears may be merciful, so that I may give heed to my neighbors' needs and not be indifferent to their pains and moanings.

Help me, O Lord, that my tongue may be merciful, so that I should never speak negatively of my neighbor, but have a word of comfort and forgiveness for all. (163a)

JANUARY 7

Help me, O Lord, that my hands may be merciful and filled with good deeds, so that I may do only good to my neighbors and take upon myself the more difficult and toilsome tasks.

Help me, that my feet may be merciful, so that I may hurry to assist my neighbor, overcoming my own fatigue and weariness. My true rest is in the service of my neighbor.

Help me, O Lord, that my heart may be merciful so that I myself may feel all the sufferings of my neighbor. I will refuse my heart to no one. I will be sincere even with those who, I know, will abuse my kindness. And I will lock myself up in the most merciful Heart of Jesus. I will bear my own suffering in silence. May Your mercy, O Lord, rest upon me.

You yourself command me to exercise the three degrees of mercy. The first: the act of mercy, of whatever kind. The second: the word of mercy—if I cannot carry out a work of mercy, I will assist by my words. The third: prayer—if I cannot show mercy by deeds or words, I can always do so by prayer. My prayer reaches out even there where I cannot reach out physically. O my Jesus, transform me into Yourself, for you can do all things. (163b)

JANUARY 8

Renewal of vows. From the moment I woke up in the morning, my spirit was totally submerged in God, in that ocean of love. I felt that I had been completely immersed in Him. During Holy Mass, my love for Him reached a peak of intensity. After the renewal of vows and Holy Communion, I suddenly saw the Lord Jesus, who said to me with great kindness, **My daughter, look at My merciful Heart.** As I fixed my gaze on the Most Sacred Heart, the same rays of light, as are represented in the image as blood and water, came forth from it, and I understood how great is the Lord's mercy. And again Jesus said to me with kindness, **My daughter, speak to priests about this inconceivable mercy of Mine. The flames of mercy are burning Me—clamoring to be spent; I want to keep pouring them out upon souls; souls just don't want to believe in My goodness.** Suddenly Jesus disappeared. But throughout that whole day my spirit remained immersed in God's tangible presence, despite the buzz and chatter that usually follow a retreat. It did not disturb me in the least....   (177)

JANUARY 9

During Advent, a great yearning for God arose in my soul. My spirit rushed toward God with all its might. During that time, the Lord gave me much light to know His attributes.

The first attribute which the Lord gave me to know is His holiness. His holiness is so great that all the Powers and Virtues tremble before Him. The pure spirits veil their faces and lose themselves in unending adoration, and with one single word they express the highest form of adoration; that is—Holy... The holiness of God is poured out upon the Church of God and upon every living soul in it, but not in the same degree. There are souls who are completely penetrated by God, and there are those who are barely alive.

The second kind of knowledge which the Lord granted me concerns His justice. His justice is so great and penetrating that it reaches deep into the heart of things, and all things stand before Him in naked truth, and nothing can withstand Him.

The third attribute is love and mercy. And I understood that the greatest attribute is love and mercy. It unites the creature with the Creator. This immense love and abyss of mercy are made known in the Incarnation of the Word and in the Redemption [of humanity], and it is here that I saw this as the greatest of all God's attributes.   (180)

JANUARY 10

Jesus, living Host, You are my Mother, You are my all! It is with simplicity and love, with faith and trust that I will always come to You, O Jesus! I will share everything with You, as a child with its loving mother, my joys and sorrows—in a word, every-thing....   (230)

Holy Hour. During this hour of adoration, I saw the abyss of my misery; whatever there is of good in me is Yours, O Lord. But because I am so small and wretched, I have a right to count on Your boundless mercy....   (237)

Jesus, I trust in You; I trust in the ocean of Your mercy. You are a Mother to me....   (249)

I feel certain that my mission will not come to an end upon my death, but will begin. O doubting souls, I will draw aside for you the veils of heaven to convince you of God's goodness, so that you will no longer continue to wound with your distrust the sweetest Heart of Jesus. God is Love and Mercy.(281)

JANUARY 11

1934. Once, when I returned to my cell, I was so tired that I had to rest a moment before I started to undress, and when I was already undressed, one of the sisters asked me to fetch her some hot water. Although I was tired, I dressed quickly and brought her the water she wanted, even though it was quite a long walk from the cell to the kitchen, and the mud was ankle-deep. When I re-entered my cell, I saw the ciborium with the Blessed Sacrament, and I heard this voice, **Take this ciborium and bring it to the tabernacle.** I hesitated at first, but when I approached and touched it, I heard these words, **Approach each of the sisters with the same love with which you approach Me; and whatever you do for them, you do it for Me.** A moment later, I saw that I was alone....   (285)

August 9, 1934. Night adoration on Thursdays. I made my hour of adoration from eleven o'clock till midnight. I offered it for the conversion of hardened sinners, especially for those who have lost hope in God's mercy. I was reflecting on how much God had suffered and on how great was the love He had shown for us, and on the fact that we still do not believe that God loves us so much. O Jesus, who can understand this? What suffering it is for our Savior! How can He convince us of His love if even His death cannot convince us? I called upon the whole of heaven to join me in making amends to the Lord for the ingratitude of certain souls.   (319)

JANUARY 12

When, on one occasion, my confessor told me to ask the Lord Jesus the meaning of the two rays in the image, I answered, "Very well, I will ask the Lord." During prayer I heard these words within me: **The two rays denote Blood and Water. The pale ray stands for the Water, which makes souls righteous. The red ray stands for the Blood which is the life of souls...**

These two rays issued forth from the very depths of My tender mercy when My agonized Heart was opened by a lance on the Cross.

These rays shield souls from the wrath of My Father. Happy is the one who will dwell in their shelter, for the just hand of God shall not lay hold of him. I desire that the first Sunday after Easter be the Feast of Mercy. (299)

JANUARY 13

Ask of My faithful servant [Father Sopocko] **that, on this day, he tell the whole world of My great mercy; that whoever approaches the Fount of Life on this day will be granted complete remission of sins and punishment.**

Mankind will not have peace until it turns with trust to My mercy.

Oh, how much I am hurt by a soul's distrust! Such a soul professes that I am Holy and Just, but does not believe that I am Mercy and does not trust in My Goodness. Even the devils glorify My Justice but do not believe in My Goodness.

My Heart rejoices in this title of Mercy. (300)

Proclaim that mercy is the greatest attribute of God. All the works of My hands are crowned with mercy. (301)

JANUARY 14

January 10, 1935. In the evening during benediction, such thoughts as these began to distress me: Is not perhaps all this that I am saying about God's great mercy just a lie or an illusion...? And I wanted to think about this for a while, when I heard a strong and clear inner voice saying, **Everything that you say about My goodness is true; language has no adequate expression to extol My goodness.** These words were so filled with power and so clear that I would give my life in declaring they came from God. I can tell this by the profound peace that accompanied them at that time and that still remains with me. This peace gives me such great strength and power that all difficulties, adversities, sufferings, and death itself are as nothing. This light gave me a glimpse of the truth that all my efforts to bring souls to know the mercy of the Lord are very pleasing to God. And from this springs such great joy in my soul that I do not know whether it could be any greater in heaven. Oh, if souls would only be willing to listen, at least a little, to the voice of conscience and the voice—that is, the inspirations—of the Holy Spirit! I say "at least a little," because once we open ourselves to the influence of the Holy Spirit, He Himself will fulfill what is lacking in us. (359)

JANUARY 15

On one occasion, Jesus gave me to know that when I pray for intentions that people... entrust to me, He is always ready to grant His graces, but souls do not always want to accept them:

My Heart overflows with great mercy for souls, and especially for poor sinners. If only they could understand that I am the best of Fathers to them and that it is for them that the Blood and Water flowed from My Heart as from a fount overflowing with mercy. For them I dwell in the tabernacle as King of Mercy. I desire to bestow My graces upon souls, but they do not want to accept them. You, at least, come to Me as often as possible and take these graces they do not want to accept. In this way you will console My Heart. Oh, how indifferent are souls to so much goodness, to so many proofs of love! My Heart drinks only of the ingratitude and forgetfulness of souls living in the world. They have time for everything, but they have no time to come to Me for graces.   (367a)

JANUARY 16

So I turn to you, you—chosen souls, will you also fail to understand the love of My Heart? Here, too, My Heart finds disappointment; I do not find complete surrender to My love. So many reservations, so much distrust, so much caution. To comfort you, let Me tell you that there are souls living in the world who love Me dearly. I dwell in their hearts with delight. But they are few. In convents, too, there are souls that fill My Heart with joy. They bear My features; therefore the Heavenly Father looks upon them with special pleasure. They will be a marvel to Angels and men. Their number is very small. They are a defense for the world before the justice of the Heavenly Father and a means of obtaining mercy for the world. The love and sacrifice of these souls sustain the world in existence. The infidelity of a soul specially chosen by Me wounds My Heart most painfully. Such infidelities are swords which pierce My Heart....   (367b)

On Friday during Mass when my soul was flooded with God's happiness, I heard these words in my soul: **My mercy has passed into souls through the divine-human Heart of Jesus as a ray from the sun passes through crystal.** I felt in my heart and understood that every approach to God is brought about by Jesus, in Him and through Him. (528)

JANUARY 17

O my Jesus, You know, You alone know well that my heart knows no other love but You! All my virginal love is drowned eternally in You, O Jesus! I sense keenly how Your divine Blood is circulating in my heart; I have not the least doubt that Your most pure love has entered my heart with Your most sacred Blood. I am aware that You are dwelling in me, together with the Father and the Holy Spirit, or rather I am aware that it is I who am living in You, O incomprehensible God! I am aware that I am dissolving in You like a drop in an ocean. I am aware that You are within me and all about me, that You are in all things that surround me, in all that happens to me. O my God, I have come to know You within my heart, and I have loved You above all things that exist on earth or in heaven. Our hearts have a mutual understanding, and no one of humankind will comprehend this. (478)

All my nothingness is drowned in the sea of Your mercy. With the confidence of a child, I throw myself into Your arms, O Father of Mercy, to make up for the unbelief of so many souls who are afraid to trust in You. Oh, how very few souls really know You! How ardently I desire that the Feast of Mercy be known by souls! Mercy is the crown of Your works; You provide for all with the love of a most tender mother. (505)

JANUARY 18

Friday, September 13, 1935. In the evening, when I was in my cell, I saw an Angel, the executor of divine wrath. He was clothed in a dazzling robe, his face gloriously bright, a cloud beneath his feet. From the cloud, bolts of thunder and flashes of lightning were springing into his hands; and from his hand they were going forth, and only then were they striking the earth. When I saw this sign of divine wrath which was about to strike the earth, and in particular a certain place, which for good reasons I cannot name, I began to implore the Angel to hold off for a few moments, and the world would do penance. But my plea was a mere nothing in the face of the divine anger. Just then I saw the Most Holy Trinity. The greatness of Its majesty pierced me deeply, and I did not dare to repeat my entreaties. At that very moment I felt in my soul the power of Jesus' grace, which dwells in my soul. When I became conscious of this grace, I was instantly snatched up before the Throne of God. Oh, how great is our Lord and God and how incomprehensible His holiness! I will make no attempt to describe this greatness, because before long we shall all see Him as He is. I found myself pleading with God for the world with words heard interiorly.

As I was praying in this manner, I saw the Angel's helplessness: he could not carry out the just punishment that was rightly due for sins. Never before had I prayed with such inner power as I did then. (474)

JANUARY 19

The words with which I entreated God are these: **Eternal Father, I offer You the Body and Blood, Soul and Divinity of Your dearly beloved Son, Our Lord Jesus Christ for our sins**

and those of the whole world; for the sake of His sorrowful Passion, have mercy on us. (475)

The next morning, when I entered chapel, I heard these words interiorly: **Every time you enter the chapel, immediately recite the prayer which I taught you yesterday.** When I had said the prayer, in my soul I heard these words: **This prayer will serve to appease My wrath. You will recite it for nine days, on the beads of the rosary, in the following manner: First of all, you will say one OUR FATHER and HAIL MARY and the I BELIEVE IN GOD. Then on the OUR FATHER beads you will say the following words: "Eternal Father, I offer You the Body and Blood, Soul and Divinity of Your dearly beloved Son, Our Lord Jesus Christ, in atonement for our sins and those of the whole world." On the HAIL MARY beads you will say the following words: "For the sake of His sorrowful Passion have mercy on us and on the whole world." In conclusion, three times you will recite these words: "Holy God, Holy Mighty One, Holy Immortal One, have mercy on us and on the whole world."** (476)

JANUARY 20

Almost every feast of the Church gives me a deeper knowledge of God and a special grace. That is why I prepare myself for each feast and unite myself closely with the spirit of the Church. What a joy it is to be a faithful child of the Church! Oh, how much I love the Holy Church and all those who live in it! I look upon them as living members of Christ, who is their Head. I burn with love with those who love; I suffer with those who suffer. I am consumed with sorrow at the sight of those who are cold and ungrateful; and I then try to have such a love for God that it will make amends for those who do not love Him, those who feed their Savior with ingratitude at its worst. (481)

O my God, I am conscious of my mission in the Holy Church. It is my constant endeavor to plead for mercy for the world. I unite myself closely with Jesus and stand before Him as an atoning sacrifice on behalf of the world. God will refuse me nothing when I entreat Him with the voice of His Son. My sacrifice is nothing in itself, but when I join it to the sacrifice of Jesus Christ, it becomes all-powerful and has the power to appease divine wrath. God loves us in His Son; the painful Passion of the Son of God constantly turns aside the wrath of God.   (482)

JANUARY 21

The mercy of the Lord I will sing forever,
Before all the people will I sing it,
For it is God's greatest attribute
And for us an unending miracle.

  You gush forth from the Divine Trinity,
  But from one single womb filled with love.
  The mercy of the Lord will be revealed in the soul
  In all its fullness, when the veil falls.

From the fountain of Your mercy, O Lord,
Flows all happiness and life,
And thus, all creatures and the whole of creation
Sing out in ecstasy a song of mercy.

  The bowels of God's mercy are opened for us
  Through the life of Jesus, stretched on the Cross.
  O sinner, you must not doubt or despair,
  But trust in mercy, for you also can become holy.

Two streams in the form of rays
Have gushed forth from the Heart of Jesus,
Not for Angels, nor Cherubim, nor Seraphim,
But for the salvation of sinful man.   (522)

JANUARY 22

As God has made us sharers in His mercy and even more than that, dispensers of that mercy, we should therefore have great love for each soul, beginning with the elect and ending with the soul that does not yet know God. By prayer and mortification, we will make our way to the most uncivilized countries, paving the way for the missionaries. We will bear in mind that a soldier on the front line cannot hold out long without support from the rear forces that do not actually take part in the fighting but provide for all his needs; and that such is the role of prayer, and that therefore each one of us is to be distinguished by an apostolic spirit.   (539)

And always and in everything, their intention should be pure, for every sort of mixed motive is displeasing to God. They should accuse themselves of all external transgressions, and ask the superior for a penance. They should do this in a spirit of humility.

They should love one another with a sublime love, with a pure love, seeing God's likeness in every sister. Love should be the special characteristic of this little community, so they must not close up their hearts, but embrace the whole world, rendering mercy to every soul through prayer, according to their calling. If we live in this spirit of mercy, we ourselves will obtain mercy.
(550)

JANUARY 23

On one occasion, I saw Jesus in a bright garment; this was in the greenhouse. [He said to me,] **Write what I say to you. My delight is to be united with you. With great desire, I wait and long for the time when I shall take up My residence sacramentally in your convent. My spirit will rest in that convent and I will bless its neighborhood in a special way. Out of love for you all, I will avert any punishments which are rightly meted out by My Father's justice. My daughter, I have inclined My heart to your requests. Your assignment and duty here on earth is to beg for mercy for the whole world. No soul will be justified until it turns with confidence to My mercy, and this is why the first Sunday after Easter is to be the Feast of Mercy. On that day, priests are to tell everyone about My great and unfathomable mercy. I am making you the administrator of My mercy. Tell the confessor that the Image is to be on view in the church and not within the enclosure in that convent. By means of this Image I shall be granting many graces to souls; so let every soul have access to it.** (570)

JANUARY 24

On a certain occasion, the Lord said to me, **I am more deeply wounded by the small imperfections of chosen souls than by the sins of those living in the world.** It made me very sad that chosen souls make Jesus suffer, and Jesus told me, **These little imperfections are not all. I will reveal to you a secret of My Heart: what I suffer from chosen souls. Ingratitude in return for so many graces is My Heart's constant food, on the part of [such] a chosen soul. Their love is lukewarm, and My Heart cannot bear it; these souls force Me to reject them. Others distrust My goodness and have no desire to experience that sweet intimacy in their own hearts, but go in search of Me, off in the** distance, and do not find Me. This distrust of My goodness hurts Me very much. If My death has not convinced you of My love, what will? Often a soul wounds Me mortally, and then no one can comfort Me. They use My graces to offend Me. There are souls who despise My graces as well as all the proofs of My love. They do not wish to hear My call, but proceed into the abyss of hell. The loss of these souls plunges Me into deadly sorrow. God though I am, I cannot help such a soul because it scorns Me; having a free will, it can spurn Me or love Me. You, who are the dispenser of My mercy, tell all the world about My goodness, and thus you will comfort My Heart.   (580)

JANUARY 25

O my Jesus, I implore You by the goodness of Your most sweet Heart, let Your anger diminish and show us Your mercy. May Your wounds be our shield against Your Father's justice. I have come to know You, O God, as the source of mercy that vivifies and nourishes every soul. Oh, how great is the mercy of the Lord; it surpasses all His other qualities! Mercy is the greatest attribute of God; everything that surrounds me speaks to me of this. Mercy is the life of souls; His compassion is inexhaustible. O Lord, look on us and deal with us according to Your countless mercies, according to Your great mercy. (611)

Father Andrasz told me that it would be a good thing to have in God's Church a group of souls who would beg for His mercy, because in fact we are all in need of that mercy. After these words, an extraordinary light filled my soul. Oh, how good is the Lord!   (623)

O my Jesus, Your goodness surpasses all understanding, and no one will exhaust Your mercy. Damnation is for the soul who wants to be damned; but for the one who desires salvation, there is the inexhaustible ocean of the Lord's mercy to draw from. How can a small vessel contain the unfathomable ocean? (631)

JANUARY 26

As I was preparing for confession, I said to Jesus, hidden in the Blessed Sacrament, "Jesus, I beg You to speak to me through the mouth of this priest. And this will be a sign to me, because he does not know at all that You want me to establish that Congregation of Mercy. Let him say something to me about this mercy."

When I approached the confessional and started my confession, the priest interrupted me and started telling me about the great mercy of God, and he spoke more forcefully about it than I had ever heard anyone speak before. And he asked me, "Do you know that the mercy of the Lord is greater than all His works, that it is the crown of His works?" And I listened attentively to these words which the Lord was speaking through the mouth of the priest. Although I believe that it is always God who speaks through the lips of the priest in the confessional, I experienced it in a special way on that occasion.

Although I did not reveal anything of the divine life that is in my soul, and only accused myself of my offenses, the priest himself told me very much of what was in my soul and put me under obligation to be faithful to the inspirations of God. He said to me, "You are going through life with the Mother of God, who faithfully responded to every divine inspiration." O my Jesus, who can ever comprehend Your goodness? (637)

JANUARY 27

O incomprehensible God, how great is Your mercy! It surpasses the combined understanding of all men and Angels. All the Angels and all humans have emerged from the very depths of Your tender mercy. Mercy is the flower of love. God is love, and mercy is His deed. In love it is conceived; in mercy it is revealed. Everything I look at speaks to me of God's mercy. Even God's very justice speaks to me about His fathomless mercy, because justice flows from love.   (651)

Now I understand that confession is only the confessing of one's sins, and spiritual guidance is a different thing altogether. But this is not what I want to speak about. I want to tell about a strange thing that happened to me for the first time. When the confessor started talking to me, I did not understand a single word. Then I saw Jesus Crucified and He said to me, **It is in My Passion that you must seek light and strength.** After the confession, I meditated on Jesus' terrible Passion, and I understood that what I was suffering was nothing compared to the Savior's Passion, and that even the smallest imperfection was the cause of this terrible suffering. Then my soul was filled with very great contrition, and only then I sensed that I was in the sea of the unfathomable mercy of God. Oh, how few words I have to express what I am experiencing! I feel I am like a drop of dew engulfed in the depths of the bottomless ocean of divine mercy.   (654)

JANUARY 28

O my Jesus, how immensely I rejoice at the assurance You have given me that the Congregation will come into being. I no longer have the least shadow of a doubt about this, and I see how great is the glory which it will give to God. It will be the reflection of God's greatest attribute; that is, His divine mercy. Unceasingly, they will intercede for divine mercy for themselves and for the whole world. And every act of mercy will flow from God's love, that love with which they will be filled to overflowing. They will strive to make their own this great attribute of God, and to live by it and to bring others to know it and to trust in the goodness of the Lord. This Congregation of Divine Mercy will be in God's Church like a beehive in a magnificent garden, hidden and meek. The sisters will work like bees to feed their neighbors' souls with honey, while the wax will flame for the glory of God.   (664)

During Holy Mass, I offered myself completely to the heavenly Father through the sweetest Heart of Jesus; let Him do as He pleases with me. Of myself I am nothing, and in my misery I have nothing of worth; so I abandon myself into the ocean of Your mercy, O Lord.   (668)

JANUARY 29

On one occasion, I saw the throne of the Lamb of God and before the throne three Saints: Stanislaus Kostka, Andrew Bobola, and Prince Casimir, who were interceding for Poland. All at once I saw a large book which stands before the throne, and it was given to me to read. The book was written in blood. Still, I could not read anything but the name, Jesus. Then I heard a voice which said to me, **Your hour has not yet come.** Then the book was taken away from me, and I heard these words: **You will bear witness to My infinite mercy. In this book are written the names of the souls that have glorified My mercy.** I was overwhelmed with joy at the sight of such great goodness of God.   (689)

O Jesus, I understand that Your mercy is beyond all imagining, and therefore I ask You to make my heart so big that there will be room in it for the needs of all the souls living on the face of the earth. O Jesus, my love extends beyond the world, to the souls suffering in purgatory, and I want to exercise mercy toward them by means of indulgenced prayers. God's mercy is unfathomable and inexhaustible, just as God himself is unfathomable. Even if I were to use the strongest words there are to express this mercy of God, all this would be nothing in comparison with what it is in reality. O Jesus, make my heart sensitive to all the sufferings of my neighbor, whether of body or of soul. O my Jesus, I know that You act toward us as we act toward our neighbor.

My Jesus, make my heart like unto Your merciful Heart. Jesus, help me to go through life doing good to everyone.   (692)

JANUARY 30

On one occasion, I heard these words: **My daughter, tell the whole world about My inconceivable mercy. I desire that the Feast of Mercy be a refuge and shelter for all souls, and especially for poor sinners. On that day the very depths of My tender mercy are open. I pour out a whole ocean of graces upon those souls who approach the fount of My mercy. The soul that will go to Confession and receive Holy Communion shall obtain complete forgiveness of sins and punishment. On that day all the divine floodgates through which grace flows are opened. Let no soul fear to draw near to Me, even though its sins be as scarlet. My mercy is so great that no mind, be it of man or of Angel, will be able to fathom it throughout all eternity. Everything that exists has come forth from the very depths of My most tender mercy. Every soul in its relation to**

**Me will contemplate My love and mercy throughout eternity.
The Feast of Mercy emerged from My very depths of tenderness. It is My desire that it be solemnly celebrated on the first
Sunday after Easter. Mankind will not have peace until it turns
to the Fount of My Mercy.** (699)

JANUARY 31

At present, the topic of my particular examen is my union
with the Merciful Christ. This practice gives me unusual
strength; my heart is always united with the One it desires, and
its actions are regulated by mercy, which flows from love.(703)

Today I received a letter from Father Sopocko. I learned that
he intends to publish a holy card of the Merciful Christ. He
asked me to send him a certain prayer which he wants to put
on the back, if he receives the Archbishop's approbation. Oh,
what great joy fills my heart that God has let me see this work
of His mercy! How great is this work of the Most High God! I
am but His instrument. Oh, how ardently I desire to see this
Feast of the Divine Mercy which God is demanding through
me. But if it is the will of God that it be celebrated solemnly
only after my death, even so I rejoice in it already, and I celebrate it interiorly with my confessor's permission. (711)

LOVE

February

"LOVE'S SECOND NAME IS MERCY," writes Pope John Paul II (*Rich in Mercy, par.* 7). Mercy is love present in the modern world, more powerful than evil, more powerful than sin and death.

In this month's readings on the theme of love of God, you will discover a special dimension of Blessed Faustina's life—her fierce love of God. Some of her most beautiful and mystical writing records her attempts to describe her experience of that love.

FOR THIS MONTH:

Practice: Love the Lord your God with all your heart, with all your soul, with all your mind, and with all your strength (Mk 12:30). To help you to grow in love read the Gospel of John, chapters 13 through 17—slowly in meditative portions each day, repeating as needed.

Prayer: O Wound of Mercy, Heart of Jesus, hide me in Your depths as a drop of Your own blood, and do not let me out forever! Lock me in Your depths, and do You Yourself teach me to love You!... Lord, You can make my soul capable of understanding completely who You are.... Bring me into an intimacy with You so far as it is possible for human nature to be brought (1631).

Promise: I want to give myself to souls and to fill them with My love, but few there are who want to accept all the graces My love has intended for them. (1017)

God so loved the world that He gave His only Son.... (Jn 3:16).

FEBRUARY 1

O my Jesus, You are the life of my life. You know only too well that I long for nothing but the glory of Your Name and that souls come to know Your goodness. Why do souls avoid You, Jesus?—I don't understand that. Oh, if I could only cut my heart into tiny pieces and in this way offer to You, O Jesus, each piece as a heart whole and entire, to make up in part for the hearts that do not love You! I love You, Jesus, with every drop of my blood, and I would gladly shed my blood for You to give You a proof of the sincerity of my love.

O God, the more I know You the less I can comprehend You, but this "non-comprehension" lets me realize how great You are! And it is this impossibility of comprehending You which enflames my heart anew for You, O Lord. From the moment when You let me fix the eyes of my soul on You, O Jesus, I have been at peace and desired nothing else. I found my destiny at the moment when my soul lost itself in You, the only object of my love. In comparison with You, everything is nothing. Sufferings, adversities, humiliations, failures, and suspicions that have come my way are splinters that keep alive the fire of my love for You, O Jesus.... (57)

FEBRUARY 2

Though these [dark nights of the soul] are frightening things, the soul should not be too fearful, because God will never test us beyond what we are able to bear. On the other hand, He may never send us such sufferings, but I write this because, if it pleases the Lord to let a soul pass through such sufferings, it should not be afraid but, insofar as this depends on the soul itself, it should remain faithful to God. God will do a soul no harm, because He is Love itself, and in this unfathomable love has called it into being. However, when I was so tormented, I myself did not understand this. (106)

Pure love is capable of great deeds, and it is not broken by difficulty or adversity. As it remains strong in the midst of great difficulties, so too it perseveres in the toilsome and drab life of each day. It knows that only one thing is needed to please God: to do even the smallest things out of great love—love, and always love.

Pure love never errs. Its light is strangely plentiful. It will not do anything that might displease God. It is ingenious at doing what is more pleasing to God, and no one will equal it. It is happy when it can empty itself and burn like a pure offering. The more it gives of itself, the happier it is. But also, no one can sense dangers from afar as can love; it knows how to unmask and also knows with whom it has to deal. (140)

FEBRUARY 3

No one can comprehend what my heart feels when I meditate on the fact that God unites me with Himself through the vows. God makes known to me, even now, the immensity of the love He already had for me before time began; and as for me, I have just begun to love Him, in time. His love was [ever] great, pure, and disinterested, and my love for Him comes from the fact that I am beginning to know Him. The more I come to know Him, the more ardently, the more fiercely I love Him, and the more perfect my acts become. Meanwhile, each time I call to mind that in a few days I am to become one with the Lord through perpetual vows, a joy beyond all description floods my soul. From the very first time that I came to know the Lord, the gaze of my soul became drowned in Him for all eternity. Each time the Lord draws close to me and my knowledge of Him grows deeper, a more perfect love grows within my soul. (231)

Prayer during the Mass on the day of the perpetual vows. Today I place my heart on the paten where Your Heart has been placed, O Jesus, and today I offer myself together with You to God, Your Father and mine, as a sacrifice of love and praise. Father of Mercy, look upon the sacrifice of my heart, but through the wound in the Heart of Jesus. (239)

FEBRUARY 4

Jesus told me that I please Him best by meditating on His sorrowful Passion, and by such meditation much light falls upon my soul. He who wants to learn true humility should reflect upon the Passion of Jesus. When I meditate upon the Passion of Jesus, I get a clear understanding of many things I could not comprehend before. I want to resemble You, O Jesus,— You crucified, tortured, and humiliated. Jesus, imprint upon my heart and soul Your own humility. I love You, Jesus, to the point of madness, You who were crushed with suffering as described by the prophet [cf. Isaiah 53:2-9], as if he could not see the human form in You because of Your great suffering. It is in this condition, Jesus, that I love You to the point of madness. O eternal and infinite God, what has love done to You?... (267)

When Jesus ravished me by His beauty and drew me to Himself, I then saw what in my soul was displeasing to Him and made up my mind to remove it, cost what it may; and aided by the grace of God I did remove it at once. This magnanimity pleased the Lord, and from that moment God started granting me higher graces. In my interior life I never reason; I do not analyze the ways in which God's Spirit leads me. It is enough for me to know that I am loved and that I love. Pure love enables me to know God and understand many mysteries. (293)

FEBRUARY 5

O Supreme Good, I want to love You as no one on earth has ever loved You before! I want to adore You with every moment of my life and unite my will closely to Your holy will. My life is not drab or monotonous, but it is varied like a garden of fragrant flowers, so that I don't know which flower to pick first, the lily of suffering or the rose of love of neighbor or the violet of humility. I will not enumerate these treasures in which my every day abounds. It is a great thing to know how to make use of the present moment. (296)

Great love can change small things into great ones, and it is only love which lends value to our actions. And the purer our love becomes, the less there will be within us for the flames of suffering to feed upon, and the suffering will cease to be a suffering for us; it will become a delight! By the grace of God, I have received such a disposition of heart that I am never so happy as when I suffer for Jesus, whom I love with every beat of my heart. (303a)

FEBRUARY 6

Once when I was suffering greatly, I left my work and escaped to Jesus and asked Him to give me His strength. After a very short prayer I returned to my work filled with enthusiasm and joy. Then, one of the sisters [probably Sister Justine] said to me, "You must have many consolations today, Sister; you look so radiant. Surely, God is giving you no suffering, but only consolations."

"You are greatly mistaken, Sister," I answered, "for it is precisely when I suffer much that my joy is greater; and when I suffer less, my joy also is less." However, that soul was letting me recognize that she does not understand what I was saying. I tried to explain to her that when we suffer much we have a great chance to show God that we love Him; but when we suffer little we have less occasion to show God our love; and when we do not suffer at all, our love is then neither great nor pure. By the grace of God, we can attain a point where suffering will become a delight to us, for love can work such things in pure souls. (303b)

FEBRUARY 7

Although You take the form of a little Child, I see in You the immortal, infinite Lord of lords, whom pure spirits adore, day and night, and for whom the hearts of the Seraphim burn with the fire of purest love. O Christ, O Jesus, I want to surpass them in my love for You! I apologize to you, O pure spirits, for my boldness in comparing myself to you. I, this chasm of misery, this abyss of misery; and You, O God, who are the incomprehensible abyss of mercy, swallow me up as the heat of the sun swallows up a drop of dew! A loving look from You will fill up any abyss. I feel immensely happy at the greatness of God. Seeing God's greatness is more than enough to make me happy throughout all eternity! (334)

I know now that nothing can put a stop to my love for You, Jesus, neither suffering, nor adversity, nor fire, nor the sword, nor death itself. I feel stronger than all these things. Nothing can compare with love. I see that the smallest things done by a soul that loves God sincerely have an enormous value in the eyes of His Saints. (340)

FEBRUARY 8

True love is measured by the thermometer of suffering. Jesus, I thank You for the little daily crosses, for opposition to my endeavors, for the hardships of communal life, for the mis-interpretation of my intentions, for humiliations at the hands of others, for the harsh way in which we are treated, for false suspicions, for poor health and loss of strength, for self-denial, for dying to myself, for lack of recognition in everything, for the upsetting of all my plans.

Thank You, Jesus, for interior sufferings, for dryness of spirit, for terrors, fears, and incertitudes, for the darkness and the deep interior night, for temptations and various ordeals, for torments too difficult to describe, especially for those which no one will understand, for the hour of death with its fierce struggle and all its bitterness.

I thank You, Jesus, You who first drank the cup of bitterness before You gave it to me, in a much milder form. I put my lips to this cup of Your holy will. Let all be done according to Your good pleasure; let that which Your wisdom ordained before the ages be done to me. I want to drink the cup to its last drop, and seek not to know the reason why. In bitterness is my joy, in hopelessness is my trust. In You, O Lord, all is good, all is a gift of Your paternal Heart. I do not prefer consolations over bit-terness or bitterness over consolations, but thank You, O Jesus, for everything! It is my delight to fix my gaze upon You, O incomprehensible God!...

O Uncreated Beauty, whoever comes to know You once cannot love anything else. I can feel the bottomless abyss of my soul, and nothing will fill it but God himself. I feel that I am drowned in Him like a single grain of sand in a bottomless ocean. (343)

FEBRUARY 9

In the fundamental meditation about the goal; that is, of choosing love: the soul must love; it has need of loving. The soul must divert the stream of its love, but not into the mud or into a vacuum, but into God. How I rejoice when I reflect on this, for I feel clearly that He Himself is in my heart. Just Jesus alone! I love creatures insofar as they help me to become united with God. I love all people because I see the image of God in them. (373)

Only love has meaning; it raises up our smallest actions into infinity. (502)

My Jesus, truly I would not know how to live without You—my spirit is welded to Yours. No one can really understand this; one must first live in You in order to recognize You in others. (503)

I desire, O my Jesus, to suffer and burn with the flame of Your love in all the circumstances of my life. I am Yours, completely Yours, and I wish to disappear in You, O Jesus, I wish to be lost in Your divine beauty. You pursue me with Your love, O Lord; You penetrate my soul like a ray of the sun and change its darkness into Your light. I feel very vividly that I am living in You as one small spark swallowed up by the incomprehensible fire with which You burn, O inconceivable Trinity! No greater joy is to be found than that of loving God. Already here on earth we can taste the happiness of those in heaven by an intimate union with God, a union that is extraordinary and often quite incomprehensible to us. One can attain this very grace through simple faithfulness of soul.   (507)

FEBRUARY 10

Once, I suddenly saw Jesus in great majesty, and He spoke these words to me: **My daughter, if you wish, I will this instant create a new world, more beautiful than this one, and you will live there for the rest of your life.** I answered, "I don't want any worlds. I want You, Jesus. I want to love You, with the same love that You have for me. I beg You for only one thing: to make my heart capable of loving you. I am very much surprised at Your offer, my Jesus; what are those worlds to me? Even if You gave me a thousand of them, what are they to me? You know very well, Jesus, that my heart is dying of longing for You. Everything that is not You is nothing to me."—At that moment, I could no longer see anything, but a strange force took over my soul, a strange fire sprang up in my heart, and I entered into a kind of agony for Him. Then I heard these words: **With no other soul do I unite myself as closely and in such a way as I do with you, and this because of the deep humility and ardent love which you have for Me.**   (587)

Love casts out fear. Since I came to love God with my whole being and with all the strength of my heart, fear has left me. Even if I were to hear the most terrifying things about God's justice, I would not fear Him at all, because I have come to know Him well. God is Love, and His Spirit is Peace. I see now that my deeds which have flowed from love are more perfect than those which I have done out of fear. I have placed my trust in God and fear nothing. I have given myself over to His holy will; let Him do with me as He wishes, and I will still love Him.   (589)

FEBRUARY 11

Intimate communion of a soul with God. God approaches a soul in a special way, known only to Himself and to the soul. No one perceives this mysterious union. Love presides in this union, and everything is achieved by love alone. Jesus gives Himself to the soul in a gentle and sweet manner, and in His depths there is peace. He grants the soul many graces and makes it capable of sharing His eternal thoughts. And frequently, He reveals to it His divine plans.   (622)

Tonight God's presence is pervading me, and in an instant I come to know the great holiness of God. Oh, how the greatness of God overwhelms me! I then come to know the whole depth of my nothingness. This is a great torment, for this knowledge is followed by love. The soul bounds forward vehemently toward God, and the two loves come face to face: the Creator and the creature; one little drop seeks to measure itself with the ocean. At first, the little drop wants to enclose the infinite ocean within itself; but at the same moment, it knows itself to be just one small drop, and thus it is vanquished, and it passes completely into God like a drop into the ocean. At first, this moment is a torment, but so sweet that, on experiencing it, the soul is happy.   (702)

FEBRUARY 12

O my Jesus, I understand well that, just as illness is measured with a thermometer, and a high fever tells us of the seriousness of the illness, so also, in the spiritual life, suffering is the thermometer which measures the love of God in a soul. (774)

And God has given me to understand that there is but one thing that is of infinite value in His eyes, and that is love of God; love, love, and once again, love; and nothing can compare with a single act of pure love of God. Oh, with what inconceivable favors God gifts a soul that loves Him sincerely! Oh, how happy is the soul who already here on earth enjoys His special favors! And of such are the little and humble souls. (778)

O Love, O queen! Love knows no fear. It passes through all the choirs of Angels that stand on guard before His throne. It will fear no one. It reaches God and is immersed in Him as in its sole treasure. The Cherubim, who guards paradise with flaming sword, has no power over it. O pure love of God, how great and unequaled you are! Oh, if souls only knew your power! (781)

FEBRUARY 13

Jesus, my Love, today gave me to understand how much He loves me, although there is such an enormous gap between us, the Creator and the creature; and yet, in a way, there is something like equality: love fills up the gap. He Himself descends to me and makes me capable of communing with Him. I immerse myself in Him, losing myself as it were; and yet, under His loving gaze, my soul gains strength and power and an awareness that it loves and is especially loved. It knows that the Mighty One protects it. Such prayer, though short, benefits the soul greatly, and whole hours of ordinary prayer do not give the soul that light which is given by a brief moment of this higher form of prayer. (815)

I have come to understand today that even if I did not accomplish any of the things the Lord is demanding of me, I know that I shall be rewarded as if I had fulfilled everything, because He sees the intention with which I begin, and even if He called me to Himself today, the work would not suffer at all by that, because He Himself is the Lord of both the work and the worker. My part is to love Him to folly; all works are nothing more than a tiny drop before Him. It is love that has meaning and power and merit. He has opened up great horizons in my soul—love compensates for the chasms. (822)

FEBRUARY 14

In the evening, a great longing took possession of my soul. I took the pamphlet with the Image of the Merciful Jesus on it and pressed it to my heart, and the following words burst forth from my soul: "Jesus, Eternal Love, I live for You, I die for You, and I want to become united with You." Suddenly I saw the Lord in His inexpressible beauty. He looked at me graciously and said, **My daughter, I too came down from heaven out of love for you; I lived for you, I died for you, and I created the heavens for you.** And Jesus pressed me to His Heart and said to me, **Very soon now; be at peace, My daughter.** When I was alone, my soul was set afire with the desire to suffer until the moment when the Lord would say, "Enough." And even if I were to live for thousands of years, I see in the light of God that that is but one moment. Souls...[unfinished thought]. (853)

During the morning meditation, I felt an aversion and a repugnance for all created things. Everything pales before my eyes; my spirit is detached from all things. I desire only God himself, and yet I must live. This is a martyrdom beyond description. God imparts Himself to the soul in a loving way and draws it into the infinite depths of His divinity, but at the same time He leaves it here on earth for the sole purpose that it might suffer and die of longing for Him. And this strong love is so pure that God Himself finds pleasure in it; and self-love has no access to its deeds, for here everything is totally saturated with bitterness, and thus is totally pure. Life is a continuous dying, painful and terrible, and at the same time it is the depth of true life and of inconceivable happiness and the strength of the soul; and because of this, [the soul] is capable of great deeds for the sake of God.   (856)

FEBRUARY 15

Jesus, You have given me to know and understand in what a soul's greatness consists: not in great deeds but in great love. Love has its worth, and it confers greatness on all our deeds. Although our actions are small and ordinary in themselves, because of love they become great and powerful before God.
                                                              (889)

Love is a mystery that transforms everything it touches into things beautiful and pleasing to God. The love of God makes a soul free. She is like a queen; she knows no slavish compulsion; she sets about everything with great freedom of soul, because the love which dwells in her incites her to action. Everything that surrounds her makes her know that only God Himself is worthy of her love. A soul in love with God and immersed in Him approaches her duties with the same dispositions as she does Holy Communion and carries out the simplest tasks with great care, under the loving gaze of God. She is not troubled if, after some time, something turns out to be less successful. She remains calm, because at the time of the action she had done what was in her power. When it happens that the living presence of God, which she enjoys almost constantly, leaves her, she then tries to continue living in lively faith. Her soul understands that there are periods of rest and periods of battle. Through her will, she is always with God. Her soul, like a knight, is well trained in battle; from afar it sees where the foe is hiding and is ready for battle. She knows she is not alone—God is her strength.   (890)

FEBRUARY 16

Sometimes there are whole hours when my soul is lost in wonder at seeing the infinite majesty of God abasing Itself to the level of my soul. Unending is my interior astonishment that the Most High Lord is pleased in me and tells me so Himself. And I immerse myself even deeper in my nothingness, because I know what I am of myself. Still I must say that I, in return, love my Creator to folly with every beat of my heart and with every nerve; my soul unconsciously drowns, drowns... in Him. I feel that nothing will separate me from the Lord, neither heaven nor earth, neither the present nor the future. Everything may change, but love never, never; it is always the same. He, the Immortal Mighty One, makes His will known to me that I may love Him very specially, and He Himself makes my soul capable of the kind of love with which He wants me to love Him. I bury myself more and more in Him, and I fear nothing....

In pure love, there is room for everything: the highest praise and the deepest adoration, yet the soul is immersed in Him in deepest peace through love; and the words of people, speaking from the exterior, have no effect upon that soul. What they tell the soul about God is but a pale shadow in comparison to its own experience of Him; and it is often surprised how other people can be struck with admiration at what someone else says about God when, for this soul, it is nothing special, as it knows that what can be put into words is not yet that great. So this soul listens to everything with respect, but has its own special life in God. (947)

FEBRUARY 17

Although it is not easy to live in constant agony,
To be nailed to the cross of various pains,
Still, I am inflamed with love by loving,
And like a Seraph I love God, though I am but weakness.

Oh, great is the soul that, midst suffering,
Stands faithfully by God and does His will
And remains uncomforted midst great rainbows and storms,
For God's pure love sweetens her fate.

It is no great thing to love God in prosperity
And thank Him when all goes well,
But rather to adore Him midst great adversities
And love Him for His own sake and place one's hope
    in Him.

When the soul is in the shadows of Gethsemane,
All alone in the bitterness of pain,
It ascends toward the heights of Jesus,
And though ever drinking bitterness—it is not sad.

When the soul does the will of the Most High God,
Even amidst constant pain and torments,
Having pressed its lips to the chalice proffered,
It becomes mighty, and nothing will daunt it.

Though tortured, it repeats: Your will be done,
Patiently awaiting the moment of its transfiguration,
For, though in deepest darkness, it hears the voice of Jesus:
 You are Mine,
And this it will know fully when the veil falls. (955)

FEBRUARY 18

The Lord said to me, **I want to give Myself to souls and to fill them with My love, but few there are who want to accept all the graces My love has intended for them. My grace is not lost; if the soul for whom it was intended does not accept it, another soul takes it.** (1017)

I understand the spiritual espousal of a soul with God, which has no exterior manifestation. It is a purely interior act between the soul and God. This grace has drawn me into the very burning center of God's love. I have come to understand His Trinitarian Quality and the absolute Oneness of His Being. This grace is different from all other graces. It is so extremely spiritual that my inaccurate description knows not how to express even a shade of it. (1020)

I have such a strong desire to hide myself that I would like to live as though I did not exist. I feel a strange inner urge to hide myself as deeply as possible so as to be known only to the Heart of Jesus. I want to be a quiet little dwelling place for Jesus to rest in. I shall admit nothing that might awaken my

Beloved. My concealment gives me a chance to commune constantly and exclusively with my Bridegroom. I commune with creatures insofar as it is pleasing to Him. My heart has come to love the Lord with the full force of love, and I know no other love, because it is from the beginning that my soul has sunk deeply in the Lord as in its only treasure. (1021)

FEBRUARY 19

Today, I received some oranges. When the sister had left, I thought to myself, "Should I eat the oranges instead of doing penance and mortifying myself during Holy Lent? After all, I am feeling a bit better." Then I heard a voice in my soul: **My daughter, you please Me more by eating the oranges out of obedience and love of Me than by fasting and mortifying yourself of your own will. A soul that loves Me very much must, ought to live by My will. I know your heart, and I know that it will not be satisfied by anything but My love alone.** (1023)

O my Jesus, give me wisdom, give me a mind great and enlightened by Your light, and this only, that I may know You better, O Lord. For the better I get to know You, the more ardently will I love You, the sole object of my love. In You my soul drowns, in You my heart dissolves. I know not how to love partially, but only with the full strength of my soul and the total ardor of my heart. You Yourself, O Lord, have enkindled this love of mine for You; in You my heart has drowned forever.

(1030)

My heart is languishing for God. I desire to become united with Him. A faint fear pierces my soul and at the same time a kind of flame of love sets my heart on fire. Love and suffering are united in my heart. (1050)

FEBRUARY 20

April 16, 1937. Today, as God's Majesty swept over me, my soul understood that the Lord, so very great though He is, delights in humble souls. The more a soul humbles itself, the greater the kindness with which the Lord approaches it. Uniting Himself closely with it, He raises it to His very throne. Happy is the soul whom the Lord Himself defends. I have come to know that only love is of any value; love is greatness; nothing, no works, can compare with a single act of pure love of God.

(1092)

Today, during a catechetical lecture [by Father Theodore], I was given a confirmation of what I had understood interiorly and lived by for quite some time; namely, that if a soul loves God sincerely and is intimately united with Him, then, even though such a soul may be living in the midst of difficult external circumstances, nothing can disturb its interior life; and in the midst of corruption, it can remain pure and unsullied; because the great love of God gives it strength for battle, and God also protects in a special way, even in a miraculous way, a soul that loves Him sincerely.

(1094)

Oh, how sweet it is to have in the depth of one's soul that which the Church tells us we must believe. When my soul is immersed in love, I solve the most intricate questions clearly and quickly. Only love is able to cross over precipices and mountain peaks. Love, once again, love.

(1123)

FEBRUARY 21

A light from the morning meditation: Whatever You do with me, Jesus, I will always love You, for I am Yours. Little matter whether You leave me here or put me somewhere else; I am always Yours.

It is with love that I abandon myself to Your most wise decrees, O God, and Your will, O Lord, is my daily nourishment. You, who know the beatings of my heart, know that it beats for You alone, my Jesus. Nothing can quench my longing for You. I am dying for You, Jesus. When will You take me into Your dwelling place [cf. John 14:1-3]? (1145)

As long as we live, the love of God grows in us. Until we die, we ought to strive for the love of God. I have learned and experienced that souls living in love are distinguished in this: that they are greatly enlightened concerning the things of God, both in their own souls and in the souls of others. And simple souls, without an education, are outstanding for their knowledge. (1191)

Today, I have heard these words: **My daughter, delight of My Heart, it is with pleasure that I look into your soul. I bestow many graces only because of you. I also withhold My punishments only because of you. You restrain Me, and I cannot vindicate the claims of My justice. You bind My hands with your love.** (1193)

FEBRUARY 22

Profound silence engulfs my soul. Not a single cloud hides the sun from me. I lay myself entirely open to its rays, that His love may effect a complete transformation in me. I want to come out of this retreat a saint, and this, in spite of everything; that is to say, in spite of my wretchedness, I want to become a saint, and I trust that God's mercy can make a saint even out of such misery as I am, because I am utterly in good will. In spite of all my defeats, I want to go on fighting like a holy soul and to comport myself like a holy soul. I will not be discouraged by anything, just as nothing can discourage a soul who is holy. I want to live and die like a holy soul, with my eyes fixed on You, Jesus, stretched out on the Cross, as the model for my actions. I used to look around me for examples and found nothing which sufficed, and I noticed that my state of holiness seemed to falter. But from now on, my eyes are fixed on You, O Christ, who are for me the best of guides. I am confident that You will bless my efforts. (1333)

In the meditation on sin, the Lord gave me to know all the malice of sin and the ingratitude that is contained in it. I feel within my soul a great aversion for even the smallest sin. However, the eternal truths I have been meditating on do not bring even a shadow of disturbance or unrest into my soul. And although I take them very much to heart, my contemplation is not thereby interrupted. In this contemplation, it is not transports of the heart that I experience, but a depth of peace and a wonderful silence. Although my love is great, I experience an extraordinary equilibrium. Even receiving the Eucharist causes no feeling, but brings me to a depth of union where my love and God's love are fused together as one.

(1334)

FEBRUARY 23

Where there is genuine virtue, there must be sacrifice as well; one's whole life must be a sacrifice. It is only by means of sacrifice that souls can become useful. It is my self-sacrifice which, in my relationship with my neighbor, can give glory to God, but God's love must flow through this sacrifice, because everything is concentrated in this love and takes its value from it.

(1358)

I am coming out of this retreat thoroughly transformed by God's love. My soul is beginning a new life, earnestly and courageously; although outwardly my life will not change, and no one will notice it, nevertheless, pure love is [now] the guide of my life and, externally, it is mercy which is its fruit. I feel that I have been totally imbued with God and, with this God, I am going back to my everyday life, so drab, tiresome, and wearying, trusting that He whom I feel in my heart will change this drabness into my personal sanctity.   (1363)

O Eternal Love, who enkindles a new life within me, a life of love and of mercy, support me with Your grace, so that I may worthily answer Your call, so that what You Yourself have intended to accomplish in souls through me might indeed be accomplished.

My God, I see the radiance of eternal dawn. My whole soul bounds toward You, O Lord; nothing any longer holds me back, nothing ties me to earth. Help me, O Lord, to bear the rest of my days with patience. The sacrifice of my love burns incessantly before Your Majesty, but so silently that only Your divine eye sees it, O God, and no other creature is capable of perceiving it.   (1365)

FEBRUARY 24

The retreat has come to an end, those beautiful days of communing alone with the Lord Jesus. I made this retreat in the way Jesus wanted me to make it, and as He had told me to on the first day of the retreat; that is, in the deepest peace, I meditated on God's blessings. I have never made a retreat like this before. My soul was more profoundly strengthened by this peace than it would have been by any tremors or emotions. In the rays of love, I saw everything as it really is.

Coming out of this retreat, I feel thoroughly transformed by God's love. (1370)

My Jesus, You know that from my earliest years I have wanted to become a great saint; that is to say, I have wanted to love You with a love so great that there would be no soul who has hitherto loved You so. At first these desires of mine were kept secret, and only Jesus knew of them. But today I cannot contain them within my heart; I would like to cry out to the whole world, "Love God, because He is good and great is His mercy!" (1372)

O most gracious Lord, how merciful it is on Your part to judge each one according to his conscience and his discernment, and not according to people's talk. My spirit delights and feeds more and more on Your wisdom, which I am getting to know more and more deeply. And in this, the vastness of Your mercy becomes more and more manifest to me. O my Jesus, the effect of all this knowledge on my soul is that I am being transformed into a flame of love towards You, my God. (1456)

FEBRUARY 25

Today, the love of God is transporting me into the other world. I am all immersed in love; I love and feel that I am loved, and with full consciousness I experience this. My soul is drowning in the Lord, realizing the great Majesty of God and its own littleness; but through this knowledge my happiness increases... This awareness is so vivid in the soul, so powerful and, at the same time, so sweet. (1500)

Everlasting love, pure flame, burn in my heart ceaselessly and deify my whole being, according to Your infinite pleasure by which You summoned me into existence and called me to take part in Your everlasting happiness. O merciful Lord, it is only out of mercy that You have lavished these gifts upon me. Seeing all these free gifts within me, with deep humility I worship Your incomprehensible goodness. Lord, my heart is filled with amazement that You, absolute Lord, in need of no one, would nevertheless stoop so low out of pure love for us. I can never help being amazed that the Lord would have such an intimate relationship with His creatures. That again is His unfathomable goodness. Every time I begin this meditation, I never finish it, because my spirit becomes entirely drowned in Him. What a delight it is to love with all the force of one's soul and to be loved even more in return, to feel and experience this with the full consciousness of one's being. There are no words to express this. (1523)

FEBRUARY 26

At that moment, love for Jesus was enkindled so strongly in my heart that, offering myself for ungrateful souls, I immersed myself completely in Him. When I came to my senses, the

Lord allowed me to taste a little of the ingratitude which flooded His Heart. This experience lasted for a short while.

(1538)

The Lord said to me, **I am delighted with your love. Your sincere love is as pleasing to My Heart as the fragrance of a rosebud at morningtide, before the sun has taken the dew from it. The freshness of your heart captivates Me; that is why I unite Myself with you more closely than with any other creature...**

(1546)

O Everlasting Love, Jesus, who have enclosed
    Yourself in the Host,
And therein hide Your divinity and conceal Your
    beauty,
You do this in order to give Yourself, whole and
    entire, to my soul
And in order not to terrify it with Your greatness.

O Everlasting Love, Jesus, who have shrouded
    Yourself with bread,
Eternal Light, incomprehensible Fountain of joy
    and happiness,
Because You want to be heaven on earth to me,
That indeed You are, when Your love, O God,
    imparts itself to me.

(1569)

FEBRUARY 27

Hail to You, Eternal Love, my Sweet Jesus, who have condescended to dwell in my heart! I salute You, O glorious Godhead who have deigned to stoop to me, and out of love for me have so emptied Yourself as to assume the insignificant form of bread. I salute You, Jesus, never-fading flower of humanity. You are all there is for my soul. Your love is purer than a lily, and Your presence is more pleasing to me than the fragrance of a hyacinth. Your friendship is more tender and subtle than the scent of a rose, and yet it is stronger than death. O Jesus, incomprehensible beauty, it is with pure souls that You communicate best, because they alone are capable of heroism and sacrifice. O sweet, rose-red blood of Jesus, ennoble my blood and change it into Your own blood, and let this be done to me according to Your good pleasure. (1575)

O my Jesus, if You Yourself do not soothe the longing of my soul, then no one can either comfort or soothe it. Your every approach arouses new raptures of love in my soul, but also a new agony; because, despite all Your approaches to my soul, even the most exceptional, I am still loving You from a distance, and my heart dies in an ecstasy of love; because this is still not the complete and eternal union, although You commune with me so very often unveiled [as if face to face]; nevertheless, You thereby open in my soul and heart an abyss of love and desire for You, my God, and this bottomless abyss, this total desiring of God, cannot be completely filled on this earth. (1600)

FEBRUARY 28

O Wound of Mercy, Heart of Jesus, hide me in Your depths as a drop of Your own blood, and do not let me out forever! Lock me in Your depths, and do You Yourself teach me to love You! Eternal Love, do You Yourself form my soul that it be made capable of returning Your love. O living Love, enable me to love You forever. I yearn to eternally reciprocate Your love. O Christ, a single gaze from You is dearer to me than a thousand worlds, than all heaven itself. Lord, You can make my soul capable of understanding completely who You are. I know and I believe that You can do all things; if You have deigned to give Yourself to me so generously, then I know that You can be even more generous. Bring me into an intimacy with You so far as it is possible for human nature to be brought... (1631)

O Christ, suffering for You is the delight of my heart and my soul. Prolong my sufferings to infinity, that I may give You a proof of my love. I accept everything that Your hand will hold out to me. Your love, Jesus, is enough for me. I will glorify You in abandonment and darkness, in agony and fear, in pain and bitterness, in anguish of spirit and grief of heart. In all things may You be blessed. My heart is so detached from the earth, that You Yourself are enough for me. There is no longer any moment in my life for self concern. (1662)

FEBRUARY 29

After Holy Mass, I went out to the garden to make my meditation, since there were not yet any patients in the garden at this time, and so I felt at ease. As I was meditating on the blessings of God, my heart was burning with a love so strong that it seemed my breast would burst. Suddenly Jesus stood before me and said, **What are you doing here so early?** I answered, "I am thinking of You, of Your mercy and Your goodness toward us. And You, Jesus, what are You doing here?" **I have come out to meet you, to lavish new graces on you. I am looking for souls who would like to receive My grace.** (1705)

O my Jesus, You know that I desire to love You with a love that no soul has ever before loved You with. I would like the whole world to be transformed into love for You, my Betrothed. You feed me with the honey and milk of Your Heart. From my earliest years, You reared me for Yourself alone, so that I would know how to love You now. You know that I love You, because You alone know the depth of the sacrifice I offer You each day.

(1771)

MERCY

March

As you begin a second month of reflections on the mercy of God, you will read about some of the same facets of Divine Mercy already described in January—the power of the Chaplet of Divine Mercy, praying for all mankind, especially for sinners, and proclaiming the message of God's mercy to the whole world—but each of them with a new force and new insights. Then you will also discover *new facets* of this sparkling diamond as Blessed Faustina sheds new light on God's mercy, among them:

- **The Novena to the Divine Mercy** is the fourth vessel of mercy revealed by Our Lord. The novena is offered in preparation for the Feast of Mercy.

- **The Great Hour of Mercy,** at three o'clock, is the fifth vessel of Mercy. It is the time to recall the death of our Lord, and to implore mercy especially for sinners.

Reflection on the facets of mercy in the Diary will enrich your knowledge of the Divine Mercy and deepen your love for Him. When one particular statement or entry from Blessed Faustina's Diary strikes you—stay with it. Dwell on it and ponder it. Underline it or write it down in your journal. Let the word spark other insights and foster your prayer and praise of the Divine Mercy. There is no need to hurry on. Feed on the word as long as you draw nourishment from it.

FOR THIS MONTH:

Practice: Choose and do a work of mercy each day—by deed, by word, and by prayer (742).

Prayer: At 3:00 P.M. pray especially for sinners (1320).

Promise: My love and mercy know no bounds (718).

MARCH 1

After Holy Communion, I heard these words:—**You see what you are of yourself, but do not be frightened at this. If I were to reveal to you the whole misery that you are, you would die of terror. However, be aware of what you are. Because you are such great misery, I have revealed to you the whole ocean of My mercy. I seek and desire souls like yours, but they are few. Your great trust in Me forces Me to continuously grant you graces. You have great and incomprehensible rights over My Heart, for you are a daughter of complete trust. You would not have been able to bear the magnitude of the love which I have for you if I had revealed it to you fully here on earth. I often give you a glimpse of it, but know that this is only an exceptional grace from Me. My love and mercy know no bounds.** (718)

In this retreat, I shall keep you continually close to My Heart, that you may better know My mercy, that mercy which I have for people and especially for poor sinners. (730)

MARCH 2

Today, I received a letter from Father Sopocko. I learned from it that God Himself is conducting this whole affair. And as the Lord has begun it, so will He continue to carry it along. And the greater the difficulties which I see, the more am I at peace. Oh, if in this whole matter the glory of God and the profit to souls were not greatly served, Satan would not be opposing it so much. But he senses what he is going to lose because of it. I have now learned that Satan hates mercy more than anything else. It is his greatest torment. Still, the word of God will not pass away; God's utterance is living; difficulties will not suppress the works of God, but show that they are God's... (764)

MARCH 3

I must be on my guard, especially today, because I am becoming over-sensitive to everything. Things I would not pay any attention to when I am healthy bother me today. O my Jesus, my shield and my strength, grant me Your grace that I may emerge victorious from these combats. O my Jesus, transform me into Yourself by the power of Your love, that I may be a worthy tool in proclaiming Your mercy. (783)

MARCH 4

When I entered my solitude, I heard these words: **At the hour of their death, I defend as My own glory every soul that will say this chaplet; or when others say it for a dying person, the indulgence is the same. When this chaplet is said by the bedside of a dying person, God's anger is placated, unfathomable mercy envelops the soul, and the very depths of My tender mercy are moved for the sake of the sorrowful Passion of My Son.**

Oh, if only everyone realized how great the Lord's mercy is and how much we all need that mercy, especially at that crucial hour! (811)

O bright and clear day on which all my dreams will be fulfilled; O day so eagerly desired, the last day of my life! I look forward with joy to the last stroke the Divine Artist will trace on my soul, which will give my soul a unique beauty that will distinguish me from the beauty of other souls. O great day, on which divine love will be confirmed in me. On that day, for the first time, I shall sing before heaven and earth the song of the Lord's fathomless mercy. This is my work and the mission which the Lord has destined for me from the beginning of the world. That the song of my soul may be pleasing to the Holy Trinity, do You, O Spirit of God, direct and form my soul Yourself. I arm myself with patience and await Your coming, O merciful God, and as to the terrible pains and fear of death, at this moment more than at any other time, I trust in the abyss of Your mercy and am reminding You, O merciful Jesus, sweet Savior, of all the promises You have made to me.   (825)

MARCH 5

While I was saying the chaplet, I heard a voice which said, **Oh, what great graces I will grant to souls who say this chaplet; the very depths of My tender mercy are stirred for the sake of those who say the chaplet. Write down these words, My daughter. Speak to the world about My mercy; let all mankind recognize My unfathomable mercy. It is a sign for the end times; after it will come the day of justice. While there is still time, let them have recourse to the fount of My mercy; let them profit from the Blood and Water which gushed forth for them.** O human souls, where are you going to hide on the day of God's anger? Take refuge now in the fount of God's mercy. O what a great multitude of souls I see! They worshiped the Divine Mercy and will be singing the hymn of praise for all eternity.

(848)

Today the Lord's gaze shot through me suddenly, like lightning. At once, I came to know the tiniest specks in my soul, and knowing the depths of my misery, I fell to my knees and begged the Lord's pardon, and with great trust I immersed myself in His infinite mercy. Such knowledge does not depress me nor keep me away from the Lord, but rather it arouses in my soul greater love and boundless trust. The repentance of my heart is linked to love. These extraordinary flashes from the Lord educate my soul. O sweet rays of God, enlighten me to the most secret depth, for I want to arrive at the greatest possible purity of heart and soul. (852)

MARCH 6

O my Jesus, You are giving me back my health and life; give me also strength for battle, because I am unable to do anything without You. Give me strength, for You can do all things. You see that I am a frail child, and what can I do: I know the full power of Your mercy, and I trust that You will give me everything Your feeble child needs. (898)

Today, during the Passion Service, I saw Jesus being tortured and crowned with thorns and holding a reed in His hand. Jesus was silent as the soldiers were bustling about, vying with each other in torturing Him. Jesus said nothing, but just looked at me, and in that gaze I felt His pain, so terrible that we have not the faintest idea of how much He suffered for us before He was crucified. My soul was filled with pain and longing; in my soul, I felt great hatred for sin, and even the smallest infidelity on my part seemed to me like a huge mountain for which I must expiate by mortification and penance. When I see Jesus tormented, my heart is torn to pieces, and I think: what will become of sinners if they do not take advantage of the Passion of Jesus? In His Passion, I see a whole sea of mercy. (948)

MARCH 7

Eternal God, in whom mercy is endless and the treasury of compassion inexhaustible, look kindly upon us and increase Your mercy in us, that in difficult moments we might not despair nor become despondent, but with great confidence submit ourselves to Your holy will, which is Love and Mercy itself.   (950)

O incomprehensible and limitless Mercy Divine,
To extol and adore You worthily, who can?
Supreme attribute of Almighty God,
You are the sweet hope for sinful man.

Into one hymn yourselves unite, stars, earth, and sea, and in one accord, thankfully and fervently sing of the incomprehensible Divine Mercy.   (951)

Jesus looked at me and said, **Souls perish in spite of My bitter Passion. I am giving them the last hope of salvation; that is, the Feast of My Mercy. If they will not adore My mercy, they will perish for all eternity. Secretary of My mercy, write, tell souls about this great mercy of Mine, because the awful day, the day of My justice, is near.**   (965)

Today I heard these words: **Pray for souls that they be not afraid to approach the tribunal of My mercy. Do not grow weary of praying for sinners. You know what a burden their souls are to My Heart. Relieve My deathly sorrow; dispense My mercy.**   (975)

MARCH 8

This evening, a certain young man was dying; he was suffering terribly. For his intention, I began to say the chaplet which the Lord had taught me. I said it all, but the agony continued. I wanted to start the Litany of the Saints, but suddenly I heard the words, **Say the chaplet.** I understood that the soul needed the special help of prayers and great mercy. And so I locked myself in my room and fell prostrate before God and begged for mercy upon that soul. Then I felt the great majesty of God and His great justice. I trembled with fear, but did not stop begging the Lord's mercy for that soul. Then I took the cross off my breast, the crucifix I had received when making my vows, and I put it on the chest of the dying man and said to the Lord, "Jesus, look on this soul with the same love with which You looked on my holocaust on the day of my perpetual vows, and by the power of the promise which You made to me in respect to the dying and those who would invoke Your mercy on them, [grant this man the grace of a happy death]." His suffering then ceased, and he died peacefully. Oh, how much we should pray for the dying! Let us take advantage of mercy while there is still time for mercy. (1035)

MARCH 9

I realize more and more how much every soul needs God's mercy throughout life and particularly at the hour of death. This chaplet mitigates God's anger, as He himself told me.

(1036)

I am immensely happy, although I am the least of all; and I would not change anything of what God has given me. I would not want to change places even with a Seraph, as regards the interior knowledge of God which He Himself has given me. The intimate knowledge I have of the Lord is such as no creature can comprehend, particularly, the depth of His mercy that envelops me. I am happy with everything You give me.

(1049)

In the morning, during Mass, I heard these words: **Tell the superior that I want adoration to take place here for the intention of imploring mercy for the world.** (1070)

MARCH 10

The flames of mercy are burning me. I desire to pour them out upon human souls. Oh, what pain they cause Me when they do not want to accept them!

My daughter, do whatever is within your power to spread devotion to My mercy. I will make up for what you lack. Tell aching mankind to snuggle close to My merciful Heart, and I will fill it with peace.

Tell [all people], My daughter, that I am Love and Mercy itself. When a soul approaches Me with trust, I fill it with such an abundance of graces that it cannot contain them within itself, but radiates them to other souls. (1074)

Souls who spread the honor of My mercy I shield through their entire lives as a tender mother her infant, and at the hour of death I will not be a Judge for them, but the Merciful Savior. At that last hour, a soul has nothing with which to defend itself except My mercy. Happy is the soul that during its lifetime immersed itself in the Fountain of Mercy, because justice will have no hold on it. (1075)

MARCH 11

June 4. Today is the Feast of the Most Sacred Heart of Jesus. During Holy Mass, I was given the knowledge of the Heart of Jesus and of the nature of the fire of love with which He burns for us and of how He is an Ocean of Mercy. Then I heard a voice: **Apostle of My mercy, proclaim to the whole world My unfathomable mercy. Do not be discouraged by the difficulties you encounter in proclaiming My mercy. These difficulties that affect you so painfully are needed for your sanctification and as evidence that this work is Mine. My daughter, be diligent in writing down every sentence I tell you concerning My mercy, because this is meant for a great number of souls who will profit from it.** (1142)

We resemble God most when we forgive our neighbors. God is Love, Goodness, and Mercy...

Every soul, and especially the soul of every religious, should reflect My mercy. My Heart overflows with compassion and mercy for all. The heart of My beloved must resemble Mine; from her heart must spring the fountain of My mercy for souls; otherwise I will not acknowledge her as Mine. (1148)

MARCH 12

God's floodgates have been opened for us. Let us want to take advantage of them before the day of God's justice arrives. And that will be a dreadful day! (1159)

Today during the Angelus, the Lord gave me an understanding of God's incomprehensible love for people. He lifts us up to His very Godhead. His only motives are love and fathomless mercy. Though You make known the mystery to us through an Angel, You Yourself carry it out. (1172)

Whatever Jesus did, He did well. He went along, doing good. His manner was full of goodness and mercy. His steps were guided by compassion. Toward His enemies He showed goodness, kindness, and understanding, and to those in need help and consolation.

I have resolved to mirror faithfully these traits of Jesus in myself during this month, even if this costs me much. (1175)

MARCH 13

O Lord, my Love, I thank You for this day on which You have allowed me to draw a wealth of graces from the fountain of Your unfathomable mercy. O Jesus, not only today, but at every moment, I draw from Your unfathomable mercy everything that the soul and body could want. (1178)

Jesus. **From all My wounds, like from streams, mercy flows for souls, but the wound in My Heart is the fountain of unfathomable mercy. From this fountain spring all graces for souls. The flames of compassion burn Me. I desire greatly to pour them out upon souls. Speak to the whole world about My mercy.**
(1190)

MARCH 14

Jesus, I trust in You.
Novena to the Divine Mercy
which Jesus instructed me to write down and make before the
Feast of Mercy. It begins on Good Friday.

**I desire that during these nine days you bring souls to the
fountain of My mercy, that they may draw therefrom strength
and refreshment and whatever grace they need in the hardships of life, and especially at the hour of death.**

**On each day you will bring to My Heart a different group of
souls, and you will immerse them in this ocean of My mercy,
and I will bring all these souls into the house of My Father.
You will do this in this life and in the next. I will deny nothing
to any soul whom you will bring to the fount of My mercy. On
each day you will beg My Father, on the strength of My bitter
Passion, for graces for these souls.**

I answered, "Jesus, I do not know how to make this novena or
which souls to bring first into Your Most Compassionate
Heart." Jesus replied that He would tell me which souls to
bring each day into His Heart.   (1209)

MARCH 15

First Day
**Today, bring to Me all mankind, especially all sinners, and
immerse them in the ocean of My mercy. In this way you will
console Me in the bitter grief into which the loss of souls
plunges Me.**   (1210)

Most Merciful Jesus, whose very nature it is to have compassion on us and to forgive us, do not look upon our sins but upon our trust which we place in Your infinite goodness. Receive us all into the abode of Your Most Compassionate Heart, and never let us escape from it. We beg this of You by Your love which unites You to the Father and the Holy Spirit.

Oh omnipotence of Divine Mercy,
Salvation of sinful people,
You are a sea of mercy and compassion;
You aid those who entreat You with humility.

Eternal Father, turn Your merciful gaze upon all mankind and especially upon poor sinners, all enfolded in the Most Compassionate Heart of Jesus. For the sake of His sorrowful Passion, show us Your mercy, that we may praise the omnipotence of Your mercy forever and ever. Amen.   (1211)

MARCH 16

Second Day

Today bring to me the souls of priests and religious, and immerse them in My unfathomable mercy. It was they who gave Me the strength to endure My bitter Passion. Through them, as through channels, My mercy flows out upon mankind.   (1212)

Most Merciful Jesus, from whom comes all that is good, increase Your grace in men and women consecrated to Your service, that we may perform worthy works of mercy; and that all who see them may glorify the Father of Mercy who is in heaven.

The fountain of God's love
Dwells in pure hearts,
Bathed in the Sea of Mercy,
Radiant as stars, bright as the dawn.

Eternal Father, turn Your merciful gaze upon the company [of chosen ones] in Your vineyard—upon the souls of priests and religious; and endow them with the strength of Your blessing. For the love of the Heart of Your Son in which they are enfolded, impart to them Your power and light, that they may be able to guide others in the way of salvation and with one voice sing praise to Your boundless mercy for ages without end. Amen.   (1213)

MARCH 17

Third Day

Today bring to Me all devout and faithful souls, and immerse them in the ocean of My mercy. These souls brought Me consolation on the Way of the Cross. They were that drop of consolation in the midst of an ocean of bitterness.   (1214)

Most Merciful Jesus, from the treasury of Your mercy, You impart Your graces in great abundance to each and all. Receive us into the abode of Your Most Compassionate Heart and never let us escape from it. We beg this of You by that most wondrous love for the heavenly Father with which Your Heart burns so fiercely.

The miracles of mercy are impenetrable.
Neither the sinner nor just one will fathom them.
When You cast upon us an eye of pity,
You draw us all closer to Your love.

Eternal Father, turn Your merciful gaze upon faithful souls, as upon the inheritance of Your Son. For the sake of His sorrowful Passion, grant them Your blessing and surround them with Your constant protection. Thus may they never fail in love or lose the treasure of the holy faith, but rather, with all the hosts of Angels and Saints, may they glorify Your boundless mercy for endless ages. Amen. (1215)

MARCH 18

Fourth Day

Today bring to Me those who do not believe in God and those who do not yet know Me. I was thinking also of them during My bitter Passion, and their future zeal comforted My Heart. Immerse them in the ocean of My mercy. (1216)

Most compassionate Jesus, You are the Light of the whole world. Receive into the abode of Your Most Compassionate Heart the souls of those who do not believe in God and of those who as yet do not know You. Let the rays of Your grace enlighten them that they, too, together with us, may extol Your wonderful mercy; and do not let them escape from the abode which is Your Most Compassionate Heart.

> May the light of Your love
> Enlighten the souls in darkness;
> Grant that these souls will know You
> And, together with us, praise Your mercy.

Eternal Father, turn Your merciful gaze upon the souls of those who as yet do not know You, but who are enclosed in the Most Compassionate Heart of Jesus. Draw them to the light of the Gospel. These souls do not know what great happiness it is to love You. Grant that they, too, may extol the generosity of Your mercy for endless ages. Amen. (1217)

MARCH 19

Fifth Day

Today bring to Me the souls of those who have separated themselves from My Church, and immerse them in the ocean of My mercy. During My bitter Passion they tore at My Body and Heart; that is, My Church. As they return to unity with the Church, My wounds heal, and in this way they alleviate My Passion. (1218)

Most Merciful Jesus, Goodness Itself, You do not refuse light to those who seek it of You. Receive into the abode of Your Most Compassionate Heart the souls of those who have separated themselves from Your Church. Draw them by Your light into the unity of the Church, and do not let them escape from the abode of Your Most Compassionate Heart; but bring it about that they, too, come to glorify the generosity of Your mercy.

Even for those who have torn the garment of your unity,
A fount of mercy flows from Your Heart.
The omnipotence of Your mercy, O God
Can lead these souls also out of error.

Eternal Father, turn Your merciful gaze upon the souls of those who have separated themselves from Your Church who have squandered Your blessings and misused Your graces by obstinately persisting in their errors. Do not look upon their errors, but upon the love of Your own Son and upon His bitter Passion, which He underwent for their sake, since they, too, are enclosed in the Most Compassionate Heart of Jesus. Bring it about that they also may glorify Your great mercy for endless ages. Amen. (1219)

MARCH 20

Sixth Day

Today bring to me the meek and humble souls and the souls of little children, and immerse them in My mercy. These souls most closely resemble My Heart. They strengthened Me during My bitter agony. I saw them as earthly Angels, who would keep vigil at My altars. I pour out upon them whole torrents of grace. Only the humble soul is able to receive My grace. I favor humble souls with My confidence. (1220)

Most Merciful Jesus, You Yourself have said, "Learn from Me for I am meek and humble of heart." Receive into the abode of Your Most Compassionate Heart all meek and humble souls and the souls of little children. These souls send all heaven into ecstasy and they are the heavenly Father's favorites. They are a sweet-smelling bouquet before the throne of God; God Himself takes delight in their fragrance. These souls have a permanent abode in Your Most Compassionate Heart, O Jesus, and they unceasingly sing out a hymn of love and mercy.(1221)

> A truly gentle and humble soul
> Already here on earth the air of paradise breathes,
> And in the fragrance of her humble heart
> The Creator Himself delights. (1222)

Eternal Father, turn Your merciful gaze upon meek souls, upon humble souls, and upon the souls of little children who are enfolded in the abode which is the Most Compassionate

Heart of Jesus. These souls bear the closest resemblance to Your Son. Their fragrance rises from the earth and reaches Your very throne. Father of mercy and of all goodness, I beg You by the love You bear these souls and by the delight You take in them: Bless the whole world, that all souls together may sing out the praises of Your mercy for endless ages. Amen.

(1223)

MARCH 21

Seventh Day

Today bring to me the souls who especially venerate and glorify My mercy, and immerse them in My mercy. These souls sorrowed most over My Passion and entered most deeply into My Spirit. They are living images of My Compassionate Heart. These souls will shine with a special brightness in the next life. Not one of them will go into the fire of hell. I shall particularly defend each one of them at the hour of death. (1224)

Most Merciful Jesus, whose Heart is Love Itself, receive into the abode of Your Most Compassionate Heart the souls of those who particularly extol and venerate the greatness of Your mercy. These souls are mighty with the very power of God Himself. In the midst of all afflictions and adversities they go forward, confident of Your mercy. These souls are united to Jesus and carry all mankind on their shoulders. These souls will not be judged severely, but Your mercy will embrace them as they depart from this life.

A soul who praises the goodness of her Lord
Is especially loved by Him.
She is always close to the living fountain
And draws graces from Mercy Divine.

Eternal Father, turn Your merciful gaze upon the souls who glorify and venerate Your greatest attribute, that of Your fathomless mercy, and who are enclosed in the Most Compassionate Heart of Jesus. These souls are a living Gospel; their hands are full of deeds of mercy, and their spirit, overflowing with joy, sings a canticle of mercy to You, O Most High! I beg You O God: Show them Your mercy according to the hope and trust they have placed in You. Let there be accomplished in them the promise of Jesus, who said to them, **I Myself will defend as My own glory, during their lifetime, and especially at the hour of their death, those souls who will venerate My fathomless mercy.** (1225)

MARCH 22

Eighth Day

Today bring to Me the souls who are in the prison of Purgatory, and immerse them in the abyss of My mercy. Let the torrents of My Blood cool down their scorching flames. All these souls are greatly loved by Me. They are making retribution to My justice. It is in your power to bring them relief. Draw all the indulgences from the treasury of My Church and offer them on their behalf. Oh, if you only knew the torments they suffer, you would continually offer for them the alms of the spirit and pay off their debt to My justice. (1226)

Most Merciful Jesus, You Yourself have said that You desire mercy; so I bring into the abode of Your Most Compassionate Heart the souls in Purgatory, souls who are very dear to You, and yet, who must make retribution to Your justice. May the streams of Blood and Water which gushed forth from Your Heart put out the flames of the purifying fire, that in that place, too, the power of Your mercy may be praised.

From that terrible heat of the cleansing fire
Rises a plaint to Your mercy,
And they receive comfort, refreshment, relief
In the stream of mingled Blood and Water.

Eternal Father, turn Your merciful gaze upon the souls suffering in Purgatory, who are enfolded in the Most Compassionate Heart of Jesus. I beg You, by the sorrowful Passion of Jesus Your Son, and by all the bitterness with which His most sacred Soul was flooded: Manifest Your mercy to the souls who are under Your just scrutiny. Look upon them in no other way but only through the Wounds of Jesus, Your dearly beloved Son; for we firmly believe that there is no limit to Your goodness and compassion. (1227)

MARCH 23

Ninth Day

Today bring to Me souls who have become lukewarm, and immerse them in the abyss of My mercy. These souls wound My Heart most painfully. My soul suffered the most dreadful loathing in the Garden of Olives because of lukewarm souls. They were the reason I cried out: "Father, take this cup away from Me, if it be Your will." For them, the last hope of salvation is to flee to My mercy. (1228)

Most Compassionate Jesus, You are Compassion Itself. I bring lukewarm souls into the abode of Your Most Compassionate Heart. In this fire of Your pure love let these tepid souls, who like corpses, filled You with such deep loathing, be once again set aflame. O Most Compassionate Jesus, exercise the omnipotence of Your mercy and draw them into the very ardor of Your love, and bestow upon them the gift of holy love, for nothing is beyond Your power.

Fire and ice cannot be joined,
Either the fire dies, or the ice melts.
But by Your mercy, O God,
You can make up for all that is lacking.

Eternal Father, turn Your merciful gaze upon lukewarm souls, who are nonetheless enfolded in the Most Compassionate Heart of Jesus. Father of Mercy, I beg You by the bitter Passion of Your Son and by His three-hour agony on the Cross: Let them, too, glorify the abyss of Your mercy... (1229)

MARCH 24

O God, show me Your mercy
According to the compassion of the Heart of Jesus.
Hear my sighs and entreaties,
And the tears of a contrite heart.

O Omnipotent, ever-merciful God,
Your compassion is never exhausted.
Although my misery is as vast as the sea,
I have complete trust in the mercy of the Lord.

O Eternal Trinity, yet ever-gracious God,
Your compassion is without measure.
And so I trust in the sea of Your mercy,
And sense You, Lord, though a veil holds me aloof.

May the omnipotence of Your mercy, O Lord.
Be glorified all over the world.
May its veneration never cease.
Proclaim, my soul, God's mercy with fervor. (1298)

Eternal Love, Depth of Mercy, O Triune Holiness, yet One God, whose bosom is full of love for all, as a good Father You scorn no one. O Love of God, Living Fountain, pour Yourself out upon us, Your unworthy creatures. May our misery not hold back the torrents of Your love, for indeed, there is no limit to Your mercy.   (1307)

MARCH 25

When I make the Way of the Cross, I am deeply moved at the twelfth station. Here I reflect on the omnipotence of God's mercy which passed through the Heart of Jesus. In this open wound of the Heart of Jesus I enclose all poor humans... and those individuals whom I love, as often as I make the Way of the Cross. From that Fount of Mercy issued the two rays; that is, the Blood and the Water. With the immensity of their grace they flood the whole world....   (1309)

O my Jesus, now everything is clear to me, and I understand all that has just happened. I somehow felt and asked myself what sort of a poor man is this who radiates such modesty. From that moment on, there was stirred up in my heart an even purer love toward the poor and the needy. Oh, how happy I am that my superiors have given me such a task! I understand that mercy is manifold; one can do good always and everywhere and at all times. An ardent love of God sees all around itself constant opportunities to share itself through deed, word, and prayer. Now I understand the words which You spoke to me, O Lord, some time ago.   (1313)

MARCH 26

You expired, Jesus, but the source of life gushed forth for souls, and the ocean of mercy opened up for the whole world. O Fount of Life, unfathomable Divine Mercy, envelop the whole world and empty Yourself out upon us.   (1319)

At three o'clock, implore My mercy, especially for sinners; and, if only for a brief moment, immerse yourself in My Passion, particularly in My abandonment at the moment of agony. This is the hour of great mercy for the whole world. I will allow you to enter into My mortal sorrow. In this hour, I will refuse nothing to the soul that makes a request of Me in virtue of My Passion....   (1320)

As I was meditating on the sin of the Angels and their immediate punishment, I asked Jesus why the Angels had been punished as soon as they had sinned. I heard a voice: **Because of their profound knowledge of God. No person on earth, even though a great saint, has such knowledge of God as an Angel has.** Nevertheless, to me who am so miserable, You have shown Your mercy, O God, and this, time and time again. You carry me in the bosom of Your mercy and forgive me every time that I ask Your forgiveness with a contrite heart.   (1332)

MARCH 27

As I was praying before the Blessed Sacrament and greeting the five wounds of Jesus, at each salutation I felt a torrent of graces gushing into my soul, giving me a foretaste of heaven and absolute confidence in God's mercy.   (1337)

O merciful God, You do not despise us, but lavish Your graces on us continuously. You make us fit to enter Your kingdom, and in Your goodness You grant that human beings may fill the places vacated by the ungrateful Angels. O God of great mercy, who turned Your sacred gaze away from the rebellious Angels and turned it upon contrite man, praise and glory be to Your unfathomable mercy, O God who does not despise the lowly heart. (1339)

My Jesus, let my sacrifice burn before Your throne in all silence, but with the full force of love, as I beg You to have mercy on souls. (1342)

MARCH 28

When I entered the chapel for a moment in the evening, I felt a terrible thorn in my head. This lasted for a short time, but the pricking was so painful that in an instant my head dropped onto the communion rail. It seemed to me that the thorn had thrust itself into my brain. But all this is nothing; it is all for the sake of souls, to obtain God's mercy for them. (1399)

Christ, give me souls. Let anything You like happen to me, but give me souls in return. I want the salvation of souls. I want souls to know Your mercy. I have nothing left for myself, because I have given everything away to souls, with the result that on the day of judgment I will stand before You empty-handed, since I have given everything away to souls. Thus You will have nothing on which to judge me, and we shall meet on that day: Love and mercy... (1426)

Today during confession, breaking the wafer with me spiritually, he [my confessor] gave me the following wishes: "Be as faithful as you can to the grace of God; secondly, beg God's mercy for yourself and for the whole world, because we are all in great need of God's mercy." (1432)

MARCH 29

After I had gone into the refectory, during the reading, my whole being found itself plunged in God. Interiorly, I saw God looking at us with great pleasure. I remained alone with the Heavenly Father. At that moment, I had a deeper knowledge of the Three Divine Persons, whom we shall contemplate for all eternity and, after millions of years, shall discover that we have just barely begun our contemplation. Oh, how great is the mercy of God, who allows man to participate in such a high degree in His divine happiness! At the same time, what great pain pierces my heart [at the thought] that so many souls have spurned this happiness. (1439)

Write, speak of My mercy. Tell souls where they are to look for solace; that is, in the Tribunal of Mercy [the Sacrament of Reconciliation]. **There the greatest miracles take place [and] are incessantly repeated. To avail oneself of this miracle, it is not necessary to go on a great pilgrimage or to carry out some external ceremony; it suffices to come with faith to the feet of My representative and to reveal to him one's misery, and the miracle of Divine Mercy will be fully demonstrated. Were a soul like a decaying corpse so that from a human standpoint, there would be no [hope of] restoration and everything would already be lost, it is not so with God. The miracle of Divine Mercy restores that soul in full. Oh, how miserable are those who do not take advantage of the miracle of God's mercy!...**

(1448)

MARCH 30

Jesus, lover of human salvation, draw all souls to the divine life. May the greatness of Your mercy be praised here on earth and in eternity. O great lover of souls, who in Your boundless compassion opened the salutary fountains of mercy so that weak souls may be fortified in this life's pilgrimage, Your mercy runs through our life like a golden thread and maintains in good order the contact of our being with God. For He does not need anything to make Him happy; so everything is solely the work of His mercy. My senses are transfixed with joy when God grants me a deeper awareness of that great attribute of His; namely, His unfathomable mercy. (1466)

Jesus, hide me in Your mercy and shield me against everything that might terrify my soul. Do not let my trust in Your mercy be disappointed. Shield me with the omnipotence of Your mercy, and judge me leniently as well. (1480)

MARCH 31

O incomprehensible God, my heart dissolves in joy that You have allowed me to penetrate the mysteries of Your mercy! Everything begins with Your mercy and ends with Your mercy. (1506)

All grace flows from mercy, and the last hour abounds with mercy for us. Let no one doubt concerning the goodness of God; even if a person's sins were as dark as night, God's mercy is stronger than our misery. One thing alone is necessary: that the sinner set ajar the door of his heart, be it ever so little, to let in a ray of God's merciful grace, and then God will do the rest. But poor is the soul who has shut the door on God's mercy, even at the last hour. It was just such souls who plunged

Jesus into deadly sorrow in the Garden of Olives; indeed, it was from His Most Merciful Heart that divine mercy flowed out. (1507)

My daughter, tell souls that I am giving them My mercy as a defense. I Myself am fighting for them and am bearing the just anger of My Father. (1516)

TRUST

April

"Trust in My Mercy" is the oft-repeated word of our Lord to Blessed Faustina. Our Lord tells her to distinguish herself by trusting in His mercy. He tells her to encourage souls to trust in His mercy, especially sinners.

Notice that the word of our Lord is not just "trust" but "trust in *My Mercy*." It is not an abstract trust but trust in a person who is mercy—Jesus. The phrase that Jesus asked to be signed on each image of the Merciful Savior is "Jesus, I Trust in You." It is our trust placed in the person of Jesus, who is mercy personified and incarnate (see John Paul II, *Rich in Mercy*, par. 2), that is the key issue.

When we trust we make an act of our will. It is a decision and not a feeling. It is a decision to rely on the truth that Jesus is God, that He is all powerful, that He loves us, that He knows us and cares for us.

FOR THIS MONTH:

Practice: Do not worry (five times in Mt 6:25-34). Dismiss all anxiety (Phil 4:6).

Prayer: Jesus, I trust in You! (47, 239).

Promise: When a soul approaches Me with trust, I fill it with such an abundance of graces that it cannot contain them within itself, but radiates them to other souls (1074).

APRIL 1

When I look into the future, I am frightened,
But why plunge into the future?
Only the present moment is precious to me,
As the future may never enter my soul at all.

It is no longer in my power,
To change, correct, or add to the past;
For neither sages nor prophets could do that.
And so, what the past has embraced I must entrust to God.

O present moment, you belong to me, whole and entire.
I desire to use you as best I can.
And although I am weak and small,
You grant me the grace of your omnipotence.

And so, trusting in Your mercy,
I walk through life like a little child,
Offering You each day this heart
Burning with love for Your greater glory.   (2)

O Jesus, eternal Truth, strengthen my feeble forces; You can do all things, Lord. I know that without You all my efforts are in vain. O Jesus, do not hide from me, for I cannot live without You. Listen to the cry of my soul. Your mercy has not been exhausted, Lord, so have pity on my misery. Your mercy surpasses the understanding of all Angels and people put together; and so, although it seems to me that You do not hear me, I put my trust in the ocean of Your mercy, and I know that my hope will not be deceived.   (69)

APRIL 2

The words of Jesus during my perpetual vows: **My spouse, our hearts are joined forever. Remember to Whom you have vowed**... everything cannot be put into words.

My petition while we were lying prostrate under the pall. I begged the Lord to grant me the grace of never consciously and deliberately offending Him by even the smallest sin or imperfection.

Jesus, I trust in You! Jesus, I love You with all my heart! When times are most difficult, You are my Mother.

For love of You, O Jesus, I die completely to myself today and begin to live for the greater glory of Your Holy Name.

Love, it is for love of You, O Most Holy Trinity, that I offer myself to You as an oblation of praise, as a holocaust of total self-immolation. And through this self-immolation, I desire the exaltation of Your Name, O Lord. I cast myself as a little rosebud at Your feet, O Lord, and may the fragrance of this flower be known to You alone.   (239)

APRIL 3

Once the Lord said to me, **Act like a beggar who does not back away when he gets more alms** [than he asked for], **but offers thanks the more fervently. You too should not back away and say that you are not worthy of receiving greater graces when I give them to you. I know you are unworthy, but rejoice all the more and take as many treasures from My Heart as you can carry, for then you will please Me more. And I will tell you one** more thing: Take these graces not only for yourself, but also for others; that is, encourage the souls with whom you come in contact to trust in My infinite mercy. Oh, how I love those souls who have complete confidence in Me. I will do everything for them. (294)

Ask of my faithful servant [Father Sopocko] that, on this day, he tell the whole world of My great mercy; that whoever approaches the Fount of Life on this day will be granted complete remission of sins and punishment.

Mankind will not have peace until it turns with trust to My mercy.

Oh, how much I am hurt by a soul's distrust! Such a soul professes that I am Holy and Just, but does not believe that I am Mercy and does not trust in My Goodness. Even the devils glorify My Justice but do not believe in My Goodness.

My Heart rejoices in this title of Mercy. (300)

APRIL 4

God and Souls. An Act of Oblation.

Before heaven and earth, before all the choirs of Angels, before the Most Holy Virgin Mary, before all the powers of heaven, I declare to the One Triune God that today, in union with Jesus Christ, Redeemer of souls, I make a voluntary offering of myself for the conversion of sinners, especially for those souls who have lost hope in God's mercy. This offering consists in my accepting, with total subjection to God's will, all the sufferings, fears, and terrors with which sinners are filled. In return, I give them all the consolations which my soul receives from my communion with God. In a word, I offer everything for them: Holy Masses, Holy Communions, penances, mortifications, prayers. I do not fear the blows, blows of divine justice, because I am united with Jesus. O my God, in this way I want to make amends to You for the souls that do not trust in Your goodness. I hope against all hope in the ocean of Your mercy. My Lord and my God, my portion—my portion forever, I do not base this act of oblation on my own strength, but on the strength that flows from the merits of Jesus Christ. I will daily repeat this act of self-oblation by pronouncing the following prayer which You Yourself have taught me, Jesus:

"O Blood and Water which gushed forth from the Heart of Jesus as a Fount of Mercy for us, I trust in You!"   (309)

APRIL 5

O my God, my only hope, I have placed all my trust in You, and I know I shall not be disappointed.   (317)

Once, my confessor [Father Sopocko] asked me where the inscription should be placed, because there was not enough space in the picture for everything. I answered, "I will pray and give you an answer next week." When I left the confessional and was passing before the Blessed Sacrament, I received an inner understanding about the inscription. Jesus reminded me of what He had told me the first time; namely, that these three words must be clearly in evidence: "Jesus, I trust in You." ["Jezu, Ufam Tobie."] I understood that Jesus wanted the whole formula to be there, but He gave no direct orders to this effect as He did for these three words.

I am offering people a vessel with which they are to keep coming for graces to the fountain of mercy. That vessel is this image with the signature: "Jesus, I trust in You." (327)

Jesus, I trust in You; I trust in the ocean of your mercy. You are a Mother to me. (249)

APRIL 6

Most Holy Trinity, I trust in Your infinite mercy. God is my Father and so I, His child, have every claim to His divine Heart; and the greater the darkness, the more complete our trust should be. (357)

I do not understand how it is possible not to trust in Him who can do all things. With Him, everything; without Him, nothing. He is Lord. He will not allow those who have placed all their trust in Him to be put to shame. (358)

During one of the adorations, Jesus promised me that: **With souls that have recourse to My mercy and with those that glorify and proclaim My great mercy to others, I will deal according to My infinite mercy at the hour of their death.**

My Heart is sorrowful, Jesus said, because even chosen souls do not understand the greatness of My mercy. Their relationship [with Me] is, in certain ways, imbued with mistrust. Oh, how much that wounds My Heart! Remember My Passion, and if you do not believe My words, at least believe My wounds. (379)

APRIL 7

I feel that God will let me draw aside the veils [of heaven] so that the earth will not doubt His goodness. God is not subject to eclipse or change. He is forever one and the same; nothing can contradict His will. I feel within myself a power greater than human. I feel courage and strength thanks to the grace that dwells in me. I understand souls who are suffering against hope, for I have gone through that fire myself. But God will not give [us anything] beyond our strength. Often have I lived hoping against hope, and have advanced my hope to complete trust in God. Let that which He has ordained from all ages happen to me. (386)

On one occasion, the Lord said to me, **Why are you fearful and why do you tremble when you are united to Me? I am displeased when a soul yields to vain terrors. Who will dare to touch you when you are with Me? Most dear to Me is the soul that strongly believes in My goodness and has complete trust in Me. I heap My confidence upon it and give it all it asks.**

(453)

APRIL 8

Sunday, [April] 28, 1935. Low Sunday; that is, the Feast of the Divine Mercy, the conclusion of the Jubilee of Redemption. When we went to take part in the celebrations, my heart leapt with joy that the two solemnities were so closely united. I asked God for mercy on the souls of sinners. Toward the end of the service, when the priest took the Blessed Sacrament to bless the people, I saw the Lord Jesus as He is represented in the image. The Lord gave His blessing, and the rays extended over the whole world. Suddenly, I saw an impenetrable brightness in the form of a crystal dwelling place, woven together from waves of a brilliance unapproachable to both creatures and spirits. Three doors led to this resplendence. At that moment, Jesus, as He is represented in the image, entered this resplendence through the second door to the Unity within. It is a triple Unity, which is incomprehensible—which is infinity. I heard a voice, **This Feast emerged from the very depths of My mercy, and it is confirmed in the vast depths of My tender mercies. Every soul believing and trusting in My mercy will obtain it.** I was overjoyed at the immense goodness and greatness of my God. (420)

APRIL 9

On one occasion, I saw Jesus in a bright garment; this was in the greenhouse. [He said to me,] **Write what I say to you. My delight is to be united with you. With great desire, I wait and long for the time when I shall take up My residence sacramentally in your convent. My spirit will rest in that convent and I will bless its neighborhood in a special way. Out of love for you all, I will avert any punishments which are rightly meted out by My Father's justice. My daughter, I have inclined My heart to your requests. Your assignment and duty here on earth is to beg for mercy for the whole world. No soul will be justified until it turns with confidence to My mercy, and this is why the first Sunday after Easter is to be the Feast of Mercy. On that day, priests are to tell everyone about My great and unfathomable mercy. I am making you the administrator of My mercy. Tell the confessor that the Image is to be on view in the church and not within the enclosure in that convent. By means of this Image I shall be granting many graces to souls; so let every soul have access to it.** (570)

APRIL 10

Love casts out fear. Since I came to love God with my whole being and with all the strength of my heart, fear has left me. Even if I were to hear the most terrifying things about God's justice, I would not fear Him at all, because I have come to know Him well. God is Love, and His Spirit is Peace. I see now that my deeds which have flowed from love are more perfect than those which I have done out of fear. I have placed my trust in God and fear nothing. I have given myself over to His holy will; let Him do with me as He wishes, and I will still love Him. (589)

I have noticed many times that God tries certain people on account of those things about which He spoke to me, for mistrust displeases Jesus. Once, when I saw that God had tried a certain Archbishop [Jalbrzykowski] because he was opposed to the cause and distrustful of it, I felt sorry for him and pleaded with God for him, and God relieved his suffering. God is very displeased with lack of trust in Him, and this is why some souls lose many graces. Distrust hurts His most sweet Heart, which is full of goodness and incomprehensible love for us. A priest should sometimes be distrustful in order to better ascertain the genuineness of gifts bestowed on a given soul; and when he does so in order to direct the soul to deeper union with God, his will be a great and incomprehensible reward indeed. But there is a great difference between this and disrespect and distrust of divine graces in a soul simply because one cannot comprehend and penetrate these things with one's mind, and this latter is displeasing to the Lord. I greatly pity souls who encounter inexperienced priests. (595)

APRIL 11

March 1, 1936. Today during Holy Mass I experienced a strange force and urge to start realizing God's wishes. I had such a clear understanding of the things the Lord was asking of me that truly if I were to say that I do not understand what God is demanding from me, I would be lying, because the Lord is making His will known to me so clearly and distinctly that I do not have the least shadow of a doubt.... I realized that it would be the greatest ingratitude to delay any longer this undertaking which the Lord wishes to bring to fulfillment for His glory and the benefit of a great number of souls. And He is using me as a miserable tool through which to realize His eternal plans of mercy. Truly, how ungrateful my soul would be to resist God's will any longer. Nothing will stop me any longer, be it persecution, sufferings, sneers, threats, entreaties, hunger, cold, flattery, friendships, adversities, friends, or enemies; be it things I am experiencing now or things that will come in the future or even the hatred of hell—nothing will deter me from doing the will of God.   (615a)

APRIL 12

I am not counting on my own strength, but on His omnipotence for, as He gave me the grace of knowing His holy will, He will also grant me the grace of fulfilling it. I cannot fail to mention how much my own lower nature resists this thing, manifesting its own desires, and there results within my soul a great struggle, like that of Jesus in the Garden of Olives. And so I too cry out to God, the Eternal Father, "If it is possible, take this cup from me, but, nevertheless, not my will, but Yours be done, O Lord; may Your will be done." What I am about to go through is no secret to me, but with full knowledge I accept whatever You send me, O Lord. I trust in You, O merciful God, and I wish to be the first to manifest to You that confidence which You demand of souls. O Eternal Truth, help me and enlighten me along the roadways of life, and grant that Your will be accomplished in me.

My God, I desire nothing but the fulfillment of Your will. It does not matter whether it will be easy or difficult. I feel an extraordinary force driving me to action. One thing alone holds me back, and that is holy obedience. O my Jesus, You urge me on the one hand and hold me back and restrain me on the other. In this, too, O my Jesus, may Your holy will be done. (615b)

APRIL 13

Amid the greatest torments, I fix the gaze of my soul upon Jesus Crucified; I do not expect help from people, but place my trust in God. In His unfathomable mercy lies all my hope.
(681)

Once, as I was going down the hall to the kitchen, I heard these words in my soul: **Say unceasingly the chaplet that I have taught you. Whoever will recite it will receive great mercy at the hour of death. Priests will recommend it to sinners as their last hope of salvation. Even if there were a sinner most hardened, if he were to recite this chaplet only once, he would receive grace from My infinite mercy. I desire that the whole world know My infinite mercy. I desire to grant unimaginable graces to those souls who trust in My mercy.** (687)

Suddenly I heard these words in my soul: **My daughter, I assure you of a permanent income on which you will live. Your** duty will be to trust completely in My goodness, and My duty will be to give you all you need. I am making Myself dependent upon your trust: if your trust is great, then My generosity will be without limit. (548)

APRIL 14

On one occasion the Lord said to me, **My daughter, your confidence and love restrain My justice, and I cannot inflict punishment because you hinder Me from doing so.** Oh, how great is the power of a soul filled with confidence! (198)

Today, I heard these words: **The graces I grant you are not for you alone, but for a great number of other souls as well... And your heart is My constant dwelling place, despite the misery that you are. I unite Myself with you, take away your misery, and give you My mercy. I perform works of mercy in every soul. The greater the sinner, the greater the right he has to My mercy. My mercy is confirmed in every work of My hands. He who trusts in My mercy will not perish, for all his affairs are Mine, and his enemies will be shattered at the base of My footstool.** (723)

APRIL 15

On the initial day of the retreat, I was visited by one of the sisters who had come to make her perpetual vows. She confided to me that she had no trust in God and became discouraged at every little thing. I answered her, "It is well that you have told me this, Sister; I will pray for you." And I spoke a few words to her about how much distrust hurts the Lord Jesus, especially distrust on the part of a chosen soul. She told me that, beginning with her perpetual vows, she would practice trust. Now I know that even [some] souls that are chosen and well-advanced in the religious life or the spiritual life do not have the courage to entrust themselves completely to God. And this is so because few souls know the unfathomable mercy of God and His great goodness. (731)

APRIL 16

My daughter, if I demand through you that people revere My mercy, you should be the first to distinguish yourself by this confidence in My mercy. I demand from you deeds of mercy, which are to arise out of love for Me. You are to show mercy to your neighbors always and everywhere. You must not shrink from this or try to excuse or absolve yourself from it.

I am giving you three ways of exercising mercy toward your neighbor: the first—by deed, the second—by word, the third—by prayer. In these three degrees is contained the fullness of mercy, and it is an unquestionable proof of love for Me. By this means a soul glorifies and pays reverence to My mercy. Yes, the first Sunday after Easter is the Feast of Mercy, but there must also be acts of mercy, and I demand the worship of My mercy through the solemn celebration of the Feast and through the veneration of the Image which is painted. By means of this Image I shall grant many graces to souls. It is to be a reminder of the demands of My mercy, because even the strongest faith is of no avail without works. O my Jesus, You Yourself must help me in everything, because You see how very little I am, and so I depend solely on Your goodness, O God. (742)

APRIL 17

I have understood that at certain and most difficult moments I shall be alone, deserted by everyone, and that I must face all the storms and fight with all the strength of my soul, even with those from whom I expected to get help. But I am not alone, because Jesus is with me, and with Him I fear nothing. I am well aware of everything, and I know what God is demanding of me. Suffering, contempt, ridicule, persecution, and humiliation will be my constant lot. I know no other way. For sincere love—ingratitude; this is my path, marked out by the footprints of Jesus.

My Jesus, my strength and my only hope, in You alone is all my hope. My trust will not be frustrated.   (746)

My union with the dying is still as close as ever. Oh, how incomprehensible is God's mercy that the Lord allows me, by my unworthy prayer, to come to the aid of the dying. I try to be at the side of every dying person whenever I can. Have confidence in God, for He is good and inconceivable. His mercy surpasses our understanding.   (880)

APRIL 18

Today after Holy Communion, I heard a voice in my soul: **My daughter, stand ready, for I will come unexpectedly.** Jesus, You do not want to tell me the hour I am looking forward to with such longing: **My daughter, it is for your own good. You will learn it, but not now; keep watch.** O Jesus, do with me as You please. I know You are the merciful Savior and You will not change towards me at the hour of my death. If at this time You are showing me so much special love, and are condescending to unite Yourself with me in such an intimate way and with such great kindness, I expect even more at the hour of my death. You, my Lord God, cannot change. You are always the same. Heaven can change, as well as everything that is created; but You, Lord, are ever the same and will endure forever. So come as You like and when You like. Father of infinite mercy, I, Your child, wait longingly for Your coming. O Jesus, You said in the Holy Gospel, "Out of your mouth do I judge you." Well, Jesus, I am always speaking of Your inconceivable mercy, so I trust that You will judge me according to Your unfathomable mercy. (854)

APRIL 19

Jesus, I trust in You.

Today, at midnight, I bid good-bye to the old year 1936, and welcomed the year 1937. It was with fear and trembling that, in this first hour of the year, I faced this new period of time. Merciful Jesus, with You I go boldly and courageously into conflicts and battles. In Your Name, I will accomplish everything and overcome everything. My God, Infinite Goodness, I beg of You, let Your infinite mercy accompany me always and in all things.

As I enter this year, fear of life overwhelms me, but Jesus brings me out of this fear and lets me know what great glory this work of mercy will bring Him. (859)

There are times in life when the soul finds comfort only in profound prayer. Would that souls knew how to persevere in prayer at such times. This is very important. (860)

APRIL 20

O Jesus, how sorry I feel for poor sinners. Jesus, grant them contrition and repentance. Remember Your own sorrowful Passion. I know Your infinite mercy and cannot bear it that a soul that has cost You so much should perish. Jesus, give me the souls of sinners; let Your mercy rest upon them. Take everything away from me, but give me souls. I want to become a sacrificial host for sinners. Let the shell of my body conceal my offering, for Your Most Sacred Heart is also hidden in a Host, and certainly You are a living sacrifice.

Transform me into Yourself, O Jesus, that I may be a living sacrifice and pleasing to You. I desire to atone at each moment for poor sinners. The sacrifice of my spirit is hidden under the veil of the body; the human eye does not perceive it, and for that reason it is pure and pleasing to You. O my Creator and Father of great mercy, I trust in You, for You are Goodness Itself. Souls, do not be afraid of God, but trust in Him, for He is good, and His mercy is everlasting.   (908)

APRIL 21

Then I heard the following words spoken thus: **I want you to be My spouse.** Fear pierced my soul, but I calmly continued to reflect on what sort of an espousal this could be. However, each time fear would invade my soul, a power from on high would give it peace.

After all, I have taken perpetual vows, and I have taken them of my own completely free will. And so I continued to reflect on what this could mean. I sensed, and came to realize, that this was some special kind of grace. Whenever I think about it,

I feel faint for God, but in this swooning, my mind is clear and penetrated with light. When I am united to Him, I faint from an abundance of happiness, but my mind is bright and clear and free from all shadows. You abase Your majesty to dwell with a poor creature. Thank you, O Lord, for this great grace that makes it possible for me to commune with You. Jesus, Your Name is my delight, I have a presentiment of my Beloved from afar, and my languishing soul rests in His embrace; I don't know how to live without Him. I would rather be with Him in afflictions and suffering than without Him in the greatest heavenly delights. (912)

APRIL 22

When I began this big novena for three intentions, I saw a tiny insect on the ground and thought: How did it get here in the middle of winter? Then I heard the following words in my soul: **You see, I am thinking of it and sustaining it, and what is it compared to you? Why was your soul fearful for a moment?** I apologized to the Lord for that moment. Jesus wants me to always be a child and to leave all care to Him, and to submit blindly to His holy will. He took everything upon Himself.

(922)

O my Jesus, although I will go to You, and You will fill me with Yourself, and that will make my happiness complete, I will nevertheless not forget about humanity. I desire to draw aside the veils of heaven, so that the earth would have no doubts about the Divine Mercy. My repose is in proclaiming Your mercy. The soul gives the greatest glory to its Creator when it turns with trust to the Divine Mercy. (930)

There are moments when I mistrust myself, when I feel my own weakness and wretchedness in the most profound depths of my own being, and I have noticed that I can endure such moments only by trusting in the infinite mercy of God. Patience, prayer, and silence—these are what give strength to the soul. There are moments when one should be silent, and when it would be inappropriate to talk with creatures; these are the moments when one is dissatisfied with oneself, and when the soul feels as weak as a little child. Then the soul clings to God with all its might. At such times, I live solely by faith, and when I feel strengthened by God's grace, then I am more courageous in speaking and communicating with my neighbors. (944)

APRIL 23

I am going forward through life amidst rainbows and storms, but with my head held high with pride, for I am a royal child. I feel that the blood of Jesus is circulating in my veins, and I have put my trust in the great mercy of the Lord. (992)

Jesus is commanding me to make a novena before the Feast of Mercy, and today I am to begin it for the conversion of the whole world and for the recognition of the Divine Mercy... **so that every soul will praise My goodness. I desire trust from My creatures. Encourage souls to place great trust in My fathomless mercy. Let the weak, sinful soul have no fear to approach Me, for even if it had more sins than there are grains of sand in the world, all would be drowned in the unmeasurable depths of My mercy.** (1059)

My Jesus, support me when difficult and stormy days come, days of testing, days of ordeal, when suffering and fatigue begin to oppress my body and my soul. Sustain me, Jesus, and give me strength to bear suffering. Set a guard upon my lips that they may address no word of complaint to creatures. Your most merciful Heart is all my hope. I have nothing for my defense but only Your mercy; in it lies all my trust.   (1065)

APRIL 24

When I went for adoration, I heard these words: **My beloved daughter, write down these words, that today My Heart has rested in this convent** [the Cracow house]. **Tell the world about My mercy and My love.**

The flames of mercy are burning me. I desire to pour them out upon human souls. Oh, what pain they cause Me when they do not want to accept them!

My daughter, do whatever is within your power to spread devotion to My mercy. I will make up for what you lack. Tell aching mankind to snuggle close to My merciful Heart, and I will fill it with peace.

Tell [all people], **My daughter, that I am Love and Mercy itself. When a soul approaches Me with trust, I fill it with such an abundance of graces that it cannot contain them within itself, but radiates them to other souls.**   (1074)

Write this: Everything that exists is enclosed in the bowels of My mercy, more deeply than an infant in its mother's womb. How painfully distrust of My goodness wounds Me! Sins of distrust wound Me most painfully.   (1076)

APRIL 25

My God! In these difficult moments my spiritual director [Father Andrasz] is away, for he has gone to Rome. Jesus, since You have taken him away from me, guide me Yourself, because You alone know how much I can bear. I believe firmly that God cannot give me more than I can bear. I trust in His mercy.
(1118)

My tormented soul finds aid nowhere but in You, O Living Host. I place all my trust in Your merciful heart. I am waiting patiently for Your word, Lord. (1138)

[Let] the greatest sinners place their trust in My mercy. They have the right before others to trust in the abyss of My mercy. My daughter, write about My mercy towards tormented souls. Souls that make an appeal to My mercy delight Me. To such souls I grant even more graces than they ask. I cannot punish even the greatest sinner if he makes an appeal to My compassion, but on the contrary, I justify him in My unfathomable and inscrutable mercy. Write: Before I come as a just Judge, I first open wide the door of My mercy. He who refuses to pass through the door of My mercy must pass through the door of My justice... (1146)

APRIL 26

Today the Lord said to me, **My daughter, My pleasure and delight, nothing will stop Me from granting you graces. Your misery does not hinder My mercy. My daughter, write that the greater the misery of a soul, the greater its right to My mercy; [urge] all souls to trust in the unfathomable abyss of My mercy, because I want to save them all. On the cross, the fountain**

of My mercy was opened wide by the lance for all souls—no one have I excluded! (1182)

O my Jesus, nothing can lower my ideals; that is, the love which I have for You. Although the path is very thorny, I do not fear to go ahead. Even if a hailstorm of persecutions covers me; even if my friends forsake me; even if all things conspire against me, and the horizon grows dark; even if a raging storm breaks out, and I feel I am quite alone and must brave it all; still, fully at peace, I will trust in Your mercy, O my God, and my hope will not be disappointed. (1195)

APRIL 27

This firm resolution to become a saint is extremely pleasing to Me. I bless your efforts and will give you opportunities to sanctify yourself. Be watchful that you lose no opportunity that My providence offers you for sanctification. If you do not succeed in taking advantage of an opportunity, do not lose your peace, but humble yourself profoundly before Me and, with great trust, immerse yourself completely in My mercy. In this way, you gain more than you have lost, because more favor is granted to a humble soul than the soul itself asks for... (1361)

Jesus, do not leave me alone in suffering. You know, Lord, how weak I am. I am an abyss of wretchedness, I am nothingness itself; so what will be so strange if You leave me alone and I fall? I am an infant, Lord, so I cannot get along by myself. However, beyond all abandonment I trust, and in spite of my own feeling I trust, and I am being completely transformed into trust—often in spite of what I feel. Do not lessen any of my sufferings, only give me strength to bear them. Do with me as You please, Lord, only give me the grace to be able to love You in every event and circumstance. Lord, do not lessen my cup of bitterness, only give me strength that I may be able to drink it all.

O Lord, sometimes You lift me up to the brightness of visions, and then again You plunge me into the darkness of night and the abyss of my nothingness, and my soul feels as if it were alone in the wilderness. Yet, above all things, I trust in You, Jesus, for You are unchangeable. My moods change, but You are always the same, full of mercy. (1489)

APRIL 28

Today the Lord said to me, **I have opened My Heart as a living fountain of mercy. Let all souls draw life from it. Let them approach this sea of mercy with great trust. Sinners will attain justification, and the just will be confirmed in good. Whoever places his trust in My mercy will be filled with My divine peace at the hour of death.** (1520)

Today the Lord said to me, **My daughter, write down these words: All those souls who will glorify My mercy and spread its worship, encouraging others to trust in My mercy, will not experience terror at the hour of death. My mercy will shield them in that final battle...** (1540)

My daughter, encourage souls to say the chaplet which I have given to you. It pleases Me to grant everything they ask of Me by saying the chaplet. When hardened sinners say it, I will fill their souls with peace, and the hour of their death will be a happy one. (1541)

APRIL 29

Tell souls not to place within their own hearts obstacles to My mercy, which so greatly wants to act within them. My mercy works in all those hearts which open their doors to it. Both the sinner and the righteous person have need of My mercy. Conversion, as well as perseverance, is a grace of My mercy.

(1577)

Let souls who are striving for perfection particularly adore My mercy, because the abundance of graces which I grant them flows from My mercy. I desire that these souls distinguish themselves by boundless trust in My mercy. I myself will attend to the sanctification of such souls. I will provide them with everything they will need to attain sanctity. The graces of My mercy are drawn by means of one vessel only, and that is—trust. The more a soul trusts, the more it will receive. Souls that trust boundlessly are a great comfort to Me, because I pour all the treasures of My graces into them. I rejoice that they ask for much, because it is My desire to give much, very much. On the other hand, I am sad when souls ask for little, when they narrow their hearts. (1578)

APRIL 30

My daughter, know that My Heart is mercy itself. From this sea of mercy, graces flow out upon the whole world. No soul that has approached Me has ever gone away unconsoled. All misery gets buried in the depths of My mercy, and every saving and sanctifying grace flows from this fountain. My daughter, I desire that your heart be an abiding place of My mercy. I desire that this mercy flow out upon the whole world through your heart. Let no one who approaches you go away without that trust in My mercy which I so ardently desire for souls.

Pray as much as you can for the dying. By your entreaties, obtain for them trust in My mercy, because they have most need of trust, and have it the least. Be assured that the grace of eternal salvation for certain souls in their final moment depends on your prayer. You know the whole abyss of My mercy, so draw upon it for yourself and especially for poor sinners. Sooner would heaven and earth turn into nothingness than would My mercy not embrace a trusting soul.   (1777)

MISERY-MERCY

May

IN REFLECTING ON THIS month's theme of misery-mercy, we discover the mystery of God's use of misery: The better we know our misery, the better we come to know God's mercy. Knowledge of our misery and nothingness leads us to trust in God's mercy with greater assurance and allows us to know His mercy more deeply. Blessed Faustina records a variety of effects of her knowledge of her misery: It makes me happy; I keep one eye on my misery and the other on God's mercy; the greater the misery, the greater the trust in His mercy; I do not fear because of His mercy.

In our misery-mercy, we come to see a glimpse of the mystery of God's plan to have mercy on all (see Romans 11:32).

FOR THIS MONTH:

Practice: Rejoice in your misery!

Prayer: O Lord, Goodness beyond our understanding, Who is acquainted with our misery through and through, and knows that by our own power we cannot ascend to You, we implore You: Anticipate us with Your grace and keep on increasing Your mercy in us, that we may faithfully do Your holy will all through our life and at death's hour. Let the omnipotence of Your mercy shield us from the darts of our salvation's enemies, that we may with confidence, as Your children, await Your final coming—that day known to You alone.... Jesus is our Hope: Through His merciful Heart, as through an open gate, we pass through to heaven (1570).

Promise: The greater the misery of a soul, the greater its right to My mercy (1182).

MAY 1

Toward the end of the first year of my novitiate, darkness began to cast its shadow over my soul. I felt no consolation in prayer; I had to make a great effort to meditate; fear began to sweep over me. Going deeper into myself, I could find nothing but great misery. I could also clearly see the great holiness of God. I did not dare to raise my eyes to Him, but reduced myself to dust under His feet and begged for mercy. My soul was in this state for almost six months. Our beloved Mother Directress [Mary Joseph] encouraged me in these difficult moments. But this suffering became greater and greater.

The second year of the novitiate was approaching. Whenever I recalled that I was to make my vows, my soul shuddered. I did not understand what I was reading; I could not meditate; it seemed to me that my prayer was displeasing to God. It seemed to me that by approaching the Holy Sacraments I was offending God even more. But despite this, my confessor [Father Theodore] did not let me omit one single Holy Communion. God was working very strangely in my soul. I did not understand anything at all of what my confessor was telling me. The simple truths of the faith became incomprehensible to me. My soul was in anguish, unable to find comfort anywhere.   (23a)

MAY 2

At a certain point, there came to me the very powerful impression that I am rejected by God. This terrible thought pierced my soul right through; in the midst of the suffering my soul began to experience the agony of death. I wanted to die but could not. The thought came to me: Of what use is it to strive for virtues; why mortify oneself when all this is disagreeable to God? When I made this known to the Directress of Novices, I received this reply, "Know, dear Sister, that God has chosen you for great sanctity. This is a sign that God wants to have you very close to Himself in Heaven. Have great trust in the Lord Jesus."

That dreadful thought of being rejected by God is the actual torture suffered by the damned. I fled to Jesus' Wounds and repeated the words of trust, but these words became for me an even greater torture. I went before the Blessed Sacrament, and I began to speak to Jesus: "Jesus, You said that a mother would sooner forget her infant than God His creature, and that 'even if she would forget her infant, I, God, will never forget My creature.' O Jesus, do You hear how my soul is moaning? Deign to hear the painful whimpers of Your child. I trust in You, O God, because heaven and earth will pass, but Your word will last forever." Still I found not a moment of relief.

(23b)

MAY 3

One day, just as I had awakened, when I was putting myself in the presence of God, I was suddenly overwhelmed by despair. Complete darkness in the soul. I fought as best I could till noon. In the afternoon, truly deadly fears began to seize me; my physical strength began to leave me. I went quickly to my cell, fell on my knees before the Crucifix, and began to cry out for mercy. But Jesus did not hear my cries. I felt my physical strength leave me completely. I fell to the ground, despair flooding my whole soul. I suffered terrible tortures in no way different from the torments of hell. I was in this state for three quarters of an hour. I wanted to go and see the Directress, but was too weak; I wanted to shout, but I had no voice. Fortunately, one of the sisters [another novice, Sister Placida Putyra] came into my cell. Finding me in such a strange condition, she immediately told the Directress about it. Mother came at once. As soon as she entered the cell she said, "In the name of holy obedience get up from the ground." Immediately some force raised me up from the ground and I stood up, close to the dear Mother Directress. With kindly words she began to explain to me that this was a trial sent to me by God, saying, "Have great confidence; God is always our Father, even when He sends us trials." (24a)

MAY 4

During the night the Mother of God visited me, holding the Infant Jesus in Her arms. My soul was filled with joy, and I said, "Mary, my Mother, do You know how terribly I suffer?" And the Mother of God answered me, *I know how much you suffer, but do not be afraid. I share with you your suffering, and I shall always do so.* She smiled warmly and disappeared. At once, strength and a great courage sprang up anew in my soul; but that lasted only one day. It seemed as though hell had conspired against me. A terrible hatred began to break out in my soul, a hatred for all that is holy and divine. It seemed to me that these spiritual torments would be my lot for the rest of my life. I turned to the Blessed Sacrament and said to Jesus, "Jesus, my Spouse, do You not see that my soul is dying because of its longing for You? How can You hide Yourself from a heart that loves You so sincerely? Forgive me, Jesus; may Your holy will be done in me. I will suffer silently like a dove, without complaining. I will not allow my heart even one single cry of sorrowful complaint." (25)

MAY 5

In order to purify a soul, Jesus uses whatever instruments He likes. My soul underwent a complete abandonment on the part of creatures; often my best intentions were misinterpreted by the sisters, a type of suffering that is most painful; but God allows it, and we must accept it because in this way we become more like Jesus. There was one thing which I could not understand for a long time: Jesus ordered me to tell everything to my Superiors, but my Superiors did not believe what I said and treated me with pity as though I were being deluded or were imagining things.

Because of this, believing myself to be deluded, I resolved to avoid God interiorly for fear of these illusions. But the grace of God pursued me at every step, and God spoke to me when I least expected it. (38)

At the beginning of my religious life, suffering and adversities frightened and disheartened me. So I prayed continuously, asking Jesus to strengthen me and to grant me the power of His Holy Spirit that I might carry out His holy will in all things, because from the beginning I have been aware of my weakness. I know very well what I am of myself, because for this purpose Jesus has opened the eyes of my soul; I am an abyss of misery, and hence I understand that whatever good there is in my soul consists solely of His holy grace. The knowledge of my own misery allows me, at the same time, to know the immensity of Your mercy. In my own interior life, I am looking with one eye at the abyss of my misery and baseness, and with the other, at the abyss of Your mercy, O God. (56)

MAY 6

Today after Holy Communion, Jesus again gave me a few directives: **First, do not fight against a temptation by yourself, but disclose it to the confessor at once, and then the temptation will lose all its force. Second, during these ordeals do not lose your peace; live in My presence; ask My Mother and the Saints for help. Third, have the certitude that I am looking at you and supporting you. Fourth, do not fear either struggles of the soul or any temptations, because I am supporting you; if only you are willing to fight, know that the victory is always on your side. Fifth, know that by fighting bravely you give Me great glory and amass merits for yourself. Temptation gives you a chance to show Me your fidelity** (1560)

MAY 7

O inexhaustible treasure of purity of intention which makes all our actions perfect and so pleasing to God!

O Jesus, You know how weak I am; be then ever with me; guide my actions and my whole being, You who are my very best Teacher! Truly, Jesus, I become frightened when I look at my own misery, but at the same time I am reassured by Your unfathomable mercy, which exceeds my misery by the measure of all eternity. This disposition of soul clothes me in Your power. O joy that flows from the knowledge of one's self! O unchanging Truth, Your constancy is everlasting!...(66)

O my Jesus, despite the deep night that is all around me and the dark clouds which hide the horizon, I know that the sun never goes out. O Lord, though I cannot comprehend You and do not understand Your ways, I nonetheless trust in Your mercy. If it is Your will, Lord, that I live always in such darkness, may You be blessed. I ask You only one thing, Jesus: Do not allow me to offend You in any way. O my Jesus, You alone know the longings and the sufferings of my heart. I am glad I can suffer for You, however little. When I feel that the suffering is more than I can bear, I take refuge in the Lord in the Blessed Sacrament, and I speak to Him with profound silence. (73)

MAY 8

Once when I was being crushed by these dreadful sufferings, I went into the chapel and said from the bottom of my soul, "Do what You will with me, O Jesus; I will adore You in everything. May Your will be done in me, O my Lord and my God, and I will praise Your infinite mercy." Through this act of submission, these terrible torments left me. Suddenly I saw Jesus, who said to me, **I am always in your heart.** An inconceivable joy entered my soul, and a great love of God set my heart aflame. I see that God never tries us beyond what we are able to suffer. Oh, I fear nothing; if God sends such great suffering to a soul, He upholds it with an even greater grace, although we are not aware of it. One act of trust at such moments gives greater glory to God than whole hours passed in prayer filled with consolations. Now I see that if God wants to keep a soul in darkness, no book, no confessor can bring it light. (78)

MAY 9

Suddenly I saw the Lord interiorly, and He said to me, **Fear not, My daughter; I am with you.** In that single moment, all the darkness and torments vanished, my senses were inundated with unspeakable joy, [and] the faculties of my soul filled with light. (103)

Once, one of the older Mothers [probably Mother Jane] summoned me, and it was as if fiery bolts from the blue were coming down upon my head, so much so that I could not even discover what it was all about. But after a while I understood that it was about a matter over which I had no control whatsoever. She said to me, "Get it out of your head, Sister, that the Lord Jesus might be communing in such an intimate way with such a miserable bundle of imperfections as you! Bear in mind that it is only with holy souls that the Lord Jesus communes in this way!" I acknowledged that she was right, because I am indeed a wretched person, but still I trust in God's mercy. When I met the Lord I humbled myself and said, "Jesus, it seems that You do not associate intimately with such wretched people as I." **Be at peace, My daughter, it is precisely through such misery that I want to show the power of My mercy....** (133)

MAY 10

Once as I was talking with my spiritual director, I had an interior vision—quicker than lightning—of his soul in great suffering, in such agony that God touches very few souls with such fire. The suffering arises from this work. There will come a time when this work, which God is demanding so very much, will be as though utterly undone. And then God will act with great power, which will give evidence of its authenticity. It will be a new splendor for the Church, although it has been dormant in it from long ago. That God is infinitely merciful, no one can deny. He desires everyone to know this before He comes again as Judge. He wants souls to come to know Him first as King of Mercy. When this triumph comes, we shall already have entered the new life in which there is no suffering. But before this, your soul [of the spiritual director] will be surfeited with bitterness at the sight of the destruction of your efforts. However, this will only appear to be so, because what God has once decided upon, He does not change. But although this destruction will be such only in outward appearance, the suffering will be real. When will this happen? I do not know. How long will it last? I do not know. But God has promised a great grace especially to you and to all those... **who will proclaim My great mercy. I shall protect them Myself at the hour of death, as My own glory. And even if the sins of soul are as dark as night, when the sinner turns to My mercy he gives Me the greatest praise and is the glory of My Passion. When a soul praises My goodness, Satan trembles before it and flees to the very bottom of hell.** (378)

MAY 11

I know that I live, not for myself, but for a great number of souls. I know that graces granted me are not for me alone, but for souls. O Jesus, the abyss of Your mercy has been poured into my soul, which is an abyss of misery itself. Thank You, Jesus, for the graces and the pieces of the Cross which You give me at each moment of my life. (382)

Jesus made known to me how very pleasing to Him were prayers of atonement. He said to me, **The prayer of a humble and loving soul disarms the anger of My Father and draws down an ocean of blessings.** After the adoration, half way to my cell, I was surrounded by a pack of huge black dogs who were jumping and howling and trying to tear me to pieces. I realized that they were not dogs, but demons. One of them spoke up in a rage, "Because you have snatched so many souls away from us this night, we will tear you to pieces." I answered, "If that is the will of the most merciful God, tear me to pieces, for I have justly deserved it, because I am the most miserable of all sinners, and God is ever holy, just, and infinitely merciful." To these words all the demons answered as one, "Let us flee for she is not alone; the Almighty is with her!" And they vanished like dust, like the noise of the road, while I continued on my way to my cell undisturbed, finishing my *Te Deum* and pondering the infinite and unfathomable mercy of God.

(320)

MAY 12

O Holy Trinity, Eternal God, I thank You for allowing me to know the greatness and the various degrees of glory to which souls attain. Oh, what a great difference of depth in the knowledge of God there is between one degree and another! Oh, if people could only know this! O my God, if I were thereby able to attain one more degree, I would gladly suffer all the torments of the martyrs put together. Truly, all those torments seem as nothing to me compared with the glory that is awaiting us for all eternity. O Lord, immerse my soul in the ocean of Your divinity and grant me the grace of knowing You; for the better I know You, the more I desire You, and the more my love for You grows. I feel in my soul an unfathomable abyss which only God can fill. I lose myself in Him as a drop does in the ocean. The Lord has inclined Himself to my misery like a ray of the sun upon a barren and rocky desert. And yet, under the influence of His rays, my soul has become covered with verdure, flowers, and fruit, and has become a beautiful garden for His repose.

(605)

MAY 13

My Jesus, despite Your graces, I see and feel all my misery. I begin my day with battle and end it with battle. As soon as I conquer one obstacle, ten more appear to take its place. But I am not worried, because I know that this is the time of struggle, not peace. When the burden of the battle becomes too much for me, I throw myself like a child into the arms of the heavenly Father and trust I will not perish. O my Jesus, how prone I am to evil, and this forces me to be constantly vigilant. But I do not lose heart. I trust God's grace, which abounds in the worst misery.   (606)

MAY 14

Inner torment for more than two hours. Agony.... Suddenly, God's presence pervades me and I feel as though I am coming under the power of the just God. His justice pervades me to the marrow; outwardly I lose strength and consciousness. With this, I come to know the great holiness of God and my own great misery. A great torment afflicts my soul; the soul perceives its deeds to be not without blemish. Then the strength of trust is awakened in the soul, which longs for God with all its might. Yet it sees how miserable it is and what utter vanity everything that surrounds it. And face to face with such holiness, Oh, poor soul....   (672)

Tonight God's presence is pervading me, and in an instant I come to know the great holiness of God. Oh, how the greatness of God overwhelms me! I then come to know the whole depth of my nothingness. This is a great torment, for this knowledge is followed by love. The soul bounds forward vehemently toward God, and the two loves come face to face: the Creator and the creature; one little drop seeks to measure itself with the ocean. At first, the little drop wants to enclose the infinite ocean within itself; but at the same moment, it knows itself to be just one small drop, and thus it is vanquished, and it passes completely into God like a drop into the ocean. At first, this moment is a torment, but so sweet that, on experiencing it, the soul is happy. (702)

MAY 15

There were two occasions when my soul was plunged into despair, once for half an hour, and the second time for three quarters of an hour. Just as I cannot describe the greatness of the graces, so too with these ordeals sent by the Lord; whatever words I might use, they are only a pale shadow [of the reality]. However, just as the Lord plunged me into these torments, so too He brought me out of them. Only this lasted for a few years, after which I again received this extraordinary grace of union which has continued to this day. Still, during this second period of union, there also have been short interruptions. But for some time now, I have not experienced any interruption at all; on the contrary, I am more and more deeply steeped in God. The great light which illumines the mind gives me a knowledge of the greatness of God; but it is not as if I were getting to know the individual attributes, as before—no, it is different now: In one moment, I come to know the entire essence of God. (770)

MAY 16

In that same moment, the soul drowns entirely in Him and experiences a happiness as great as that of the chosen ones in heaven. Although the chosen ones in heaven see God face to face and are completely and absolutely happy, still their knowledge of God is not the same. God has given me to understand this. This deeper knowledge begins here on earth, depending on the grace [given], but to a great extent it also depends on our faithfulness to that grace.

However, the soul receiving this unprecedented grace of union with God cannot say that it sees God face to face, because even here there is a very thin veil of faith, but so very thin that the soul can say that it sees God and talks with Him. It is "divinized." God allows the soul to know how much He loves it, and the soul sees that better and holier souls than itself have not received this grace. Therefore, it is filled with holy amazement, which maintains it in deep humility, and it steeps itself in its own nothingness and holy astonishment; and the more it humbles itself, the more closely God unites Himself with it and descends to it.

The soul, at this moment is, as it were, hidden; its senses are inactive; in one moment, it knows God and drowns in Him. It knows the whole depth of the Unfathomable One, and the deeper this knowledge, the more ardently the soul desires Him.   (771)

MAY 17

I am reliving these moments with Our Lady. With great longing, I am waiting for the Lord's coming. Great are my desires. I desire that all humankind come to know the Lord. I would like to prepare all nations for the coming of the Word Incarnate. O Jesus, make the fount of Your mercy gush forth more abundantly, for humankind is seriously ill and thus has more need than ever of Your compassion. You are a bottomless sea of mercy for us sinners; and the greater the misery, the more right we have to Your mercy. You are a fount which makes all creatures happy by Your infinite mercy.   (793)

O inexhaustible spring of Divine Mercy, pour yourself out upon us! Your Goodness knows no limits. Confirm, O Lord, the power of Your mercy over the abyss of my misery, for You have no limit to Your mercies. Wonderful and matchless is Your mercy, astonishing the human and angelic mind.   (819)

MAY 18

Today during Holy Mass, I was unwittingly absorbed in the infinite majesty of God. The whole immensity of God's love flooded my soul. At that particular moment, I became aware of how much God abases Himself for my sake. He, the Lord of Lords—and what am I, miserable being that I am, that You would commune thus with me? The wonder that took hold of me after this special grace continued very vividly throughout the entire day. Taking advantage of the intimacy to which the Lord was admitting me, I interceded before Him for the whole world. At such moments I have the feeling that the whole world is depending on me.   (870)

My Master, cause my heart never to expect help from anyone, but I will always strive to bring assistance, consolation, and all manner of relief to others. My heart is always open to the sufferings of others; and I will not close my heart to the sufferings of others, even though because of this I have been scornfully nicknamed "dump"; that is, [because] everyone dumps his pain into my heart. [To this] I answered that everyone has a place in my heart and I, in return, have a place in the Heart of Jesus. Taunts regarding the law of love will not narrow my heart. My soul is always sensitive on this point, and Jesus alone is the motive for my love of neighbor.   (871)

MAY 19

Today, Jesus entered my room wearing a bright robe girded with a golden belt, His whole figure resplendent with great majesty. He said, **My daughter, why are you giving in to thoughts of fear?** I answered, "O Lord, You know why." And He said, **Why?** "This work frightens me. You know that I am incapable of carrying it out." And He said, **Why?** "You see very well that I am not in good health, that I have no education, that I have no money, that I am an abyss of misery, that I fear contacts with people. Jesus, I desire only You. You can release me from this." And the Lord said to me, **My daughter, what you have said is true. You are very miserable, and it pleased Me to carry out this work of mercy precisely through you who are nothing but misery itself. Do not fear; I will not leave you alone. Do whatever you can in this matter; I will accomplish everything that is lacking in you. You know what is within your power to do; do that.** The Lord looked into the depth of my being with great kindness; I thought I would die for joy under that gaze. The Lord disappeared, and joy, strength, and power to act remained in my soul. But I was surprised that the Lord did not want to release me and that He is not changing anything He has once said. And despite all these joys, there is always a shadow of sorrow. I see that love and sorrow go hand in hand. (881)

MAY 20

My Jesus, support me when difficult and stormy days come, days of testing, days of ordeal, when suffering and fatigue begin to oppress my body and my soul. Sustain me, Jesus, and give me strength to bear suffering. Set a guard upon my lips that they may address no word of complaint to creatures. Your most merciful Heart is all my hope. I have nothing for my defense but only Your mercy; in it lies all my trust.   (1065)

Although the temptations are strong, a whole wave of doubts beats against my soul, and discouragement stands by, ready to enter into the act, the Lord, however, strengthens my will, against which all the attempts of the enemy are shattered as if against a rock. I see how many actual graces God grants me; these support me ceaselessly. I am very weak, and I attribute everything solely to the grace of God.   (1086)

MAY 21

Jesus: **My daughter, do you think you have written enough about My mercy? What you have written is but a drop compared to the ocean. I am Love and Mercy itself. There is no misery that could be a match for My mercy, neither will misery exhaust it, because as it is being granted—it increases. The soul that trusts in My mercy is most fortunate, because I myself take care of it.**   (1273)

MAY 22

I experience great torments of soul when I see God offended. Today I recognized that mortal sins were being committed not far from our door. It was evening. I prayed earnestly in the chapel, and then I went to scourge myself. When I knelt down to pray, however, the Lord allowed me to experience how a soul rejected by God suffers. It seems to me that my heart was torn to pieces, and at the same time I understood how much such a soul wounds the most merciful Heart of Jesus. The poor creature does not want to accept God's mercy. The more

God has pursued a soul with His mercy, the more just will He be towards it. (1274)

My Secretary, write that I am more generous toward sinners than toward the just. It was for their sake that I came down from heaven; it was for their sake that My Blood was spilled. Let them not fear to approach Me; they are most in need of My mercy. (1275)

In times of interior desolation I do not lose my peace, because I know that God never abandons a soul, except perhaps only when the soul itself breaks the bond of love by its unfaithfulness. However, all creatures without exception depend on the Lord and are maintained by His omnipotence. Some are under the rule of love, others under the rule of justice. It depends on us under which rule we want to live, because no one is refused the aid of sufficient grace. I am not frightened at all by my apparent abandonment. I examine myself more profoundly to discover whether this is due to my fault. If this is not the case—then may [the Lord] be blessed! (1315)

MAY 23

O my Jesus, in thanksgiving for Your many graces, I offer You my body and soul, intellect and will, and all the sentiments of my heart. Through the vows, I have given myself entirely to You; I have then nothing more that I can offer You. Jesus said to me, **My daughter, you have not offered Me that which is really yours.** I probed deeply into myself and found that I love God with all the faculties of my soul and, unable to see what it was that I had not yet given to the Lord, I asked, "Jesus, tell me what it is, and I will give it to You at once with a generous heart." Jesus said to me with kindness, **Daughter, give Me your**

misery, because it is your exclusive property. At that moment, a ray of light illumined my soul, and I saw the whole abyss of my misery. In that same moment I nestled close to the Most Sacred Heart of Jesus with so much trust that even if I had the sins of all the damned weighing on my conscience, I would not have doubted God's mercy but, with a heart crushed to dust, I would have thrown myself into the abyss of Your mercy. I believe, O Jesus, that You would not reject me, but would absolve me through the hand of Your representative. (1318)

MAY 24

Fourth day. O Jesus, I have been feeling extraordinarily well, close to Your Heart, during this retreat. Nothing disturbs the depths of my peace. With one eye, I gaze on the abyss of my misery and with the other, on the abyss of Your mercy. (1345)

Today, the Lord gave me to know interiorly that He would never abandon me. He gave me to know His majesty and His holiness as well as His love and mercy towards me; and He gave me a deeper knowledge of my own wretchedness. However, this great misery of mine does not deprive me of trust. On the contrary, the better I have come to know my own misery, the stronger has become my trust in God's mercy. I have come to understand how all this depends on the Lord. I know that no one will touch a single hair of my head without His willing it.
(1406)

Lord, although You often make known to me the thunders of Your anger, Your anger vanishes before lowly souls. Although You are great, Lord, You allow yourself to be overcome by a lowly and deeply humble soul. O humility, the most precious of virtues, how few souls possess you! I see only a semblance of this virtue everywhere, but not the virtue itself. Lord, reduce me to nothingness in my own eyes that I may find grace in Yours.   (1436)

MAY 25

O my Jesus, in terrible bitterness and pain,
I yet feel the caress of Your Divine Heart.
Like a good mother, You press me to Your bosom,
And even now You give me to experience what the veil hides.

> O my Jesus, in this wilderness and terror which
>   surround me,
> My heart still feels the warmth of Your gaze,
> Which no storm can blot out from me,
> As You give me the assurance of Your great love, O God.

O my Jesus, midst the great miseries of this life,
You shine like a star, O Jesus, protecting me from shipwreck.
And though my miseries be great,
I have great trust in the power of Your mercy.

> O hidden Jesus, in the many struggles of my last hour,
> May the omnipotence of Your grace be poured out
>   upon my soul,
> That at death's moment I may gaze upon You
> And see You face to face, as do the chosen in heaven.

O my Jesus, midst the dangers which surround me,
I go through life with a cry of joy, my head raised proudly,
Because against Your Heart so filled with love, O Jesus,
All enemies will be crushed, all darkness dispelled.   (1479)

MAY 26

February 2, [1938]. Darkness of the soul. Today is the Feast of the Mother of God, and in my soul it is so dark. The Lord has hidden Himself, and I am alone, all alone. My mind has become so dimmed that I see only fantasies about me. Not a single ray of light penetrates my soul. I do not understand myself or those who speak to me. Frightful temptations regarding the holy faith assail me. O my Jesus, save me. I cannot say anything more. I cannot describe these things in detail, for I fear lest someone be scandalized on reading this. I am astounded that such torments could befall a soul. O hurricane, what are you doing to the boat of my heart? This storm has lasted the whole day and night.

When Mother Superior [Irene] came in to see me and asked, "Would you like to take advantage of this occasion, Sister, since Father An. [Andrasz] is coming to hear confessions?" I answered, no. It seemed to me that Father would not understand me, nor would I be able to make a confession.

I spent the whole night with Jesus in Gethsemane. From my breast there escaped one continuous moan. A natural dying will be much easier, because then one is in agony and will die; while here, one is in agony, but cannot die. O Jesus, I never thought such suffering could exist. Nothingness: that is the reality. O Jesus, save me! I believe in You with all my heart. So many times have I seen the radiance of Your face, and now, where are You, Lord?... I believe, I believe, and again I believe in You, Triune God, Father, Son, and Holy Spirit, and in all the truths which Your holy Church gives me to believe... But the darkness does not recede, and my spirit plunges into even greater agony. And at that moment, such terrible torment overwhelmed me that now I am amazed at myself that I did not breathe my last, but this was for only a brief instant. (1558)

MAY 27

At that moment I saw Jesus, and from His Heart there issued those same two rays, which enveloped me, whole and entire. At the same moment, all my torments vanished. **My daughter, the Lord said, know that of yourself you are just what you have gone through, and it is only by My grace that you are a participant of eternal life and all the gifts I lavish on you.** And with these words of the Lord, there came to me a true knowledge of myself. Jesus is giving me a lesson in deep humility and, at the same time, one of total trust in Him. My heart is reduced to dust and ashes, and even if all people were to trample me under their feet, I would still consider that a favor.

I feel and am, in fact, very deeply permeated with the knowledge that I am nothing, so that real humiliations will be a refreshment for me.   (1559)

And at that very moment I saw myself in some kind of a palace; and Jesus gave me His hand, sat me at His side, and said with kindness, **My bride, you always please Me by your humility. The greatest misery does not stop Me from uniting Myself to a soul, but where there is pride, I am not there.**

When I came to myself, I reflected on what had happened in my heart, thanking God for His love and for the mercy that He had shown me.   (1563)

MAY 28

O Greatly Merciful God, Infinite Goodness, today all mankind calls out from the abyss of its misery to Your mercy—to Your compassion, O God; and it is with its mighty voice of misery that it cries out. Gracious God, do not reject the prayer of this earth's exiles! O Lord, Goodness beyond our understanding, Who is acquainted with our misery through and through, and knows that by our own power we cannot ascend to You, we implore You: Anticipate us with Your grace and keep on increasing Your mercy in us, that we may faithfully do Your holy will all through our life and at death's hour. Let the omnipotence of Your mercy shield us from the darts of our salvation's enemies, that we may with confidence, as Your children, await Your final coming—that day known to You alone. And we expect to obtain everything promised us by Jesus in spite of all our wretchedness. For Jesus is our Hope: Through His merciful Heart, as through an open gate, we pass through to heaven. (1570)

Know, My daughter, that between Me and you there is a bottomless abyss, an abyss which separates the Creator from the creature. But this abyss is filled with My mercy. I raise you up to Myself, not that I have need of you, but it is solely out of mercy that I grant you the grace of union with Myself. (1576)

MAY 29

Today the Lord said to me, **Daughter, when you go to confession, to this fountain of My mercy, the Blood and Water which came forth from My Heart always flows down upon your soul and ennobles it. Every time you go to confession, immerse yourself entirely in My mercy, with great trust, so that I may**

pour the bounty of My grace upon your soul. When you approach the confessional, know this, that I Myself am waiting there for you. I am only hidden by the priest, but I Myself act in your soul. Here the misery of the soul meets the God of mercy. Tell souls that from this fount of mercy souls draw graces solely with the vessel of trust. If their trust is great, there is no limit to My generosity. The torrents of grace inundate humble souls. The proud remain always in poverty and misery, because My grace turns away from them to humble souls. (1602)

O Christ, suffering for You is the delight of my heart and my soul. Prolong my sufferings to infinity, that I may give You a proof of my love. I accept everything that Your hand will hold out to me. Your love, Jesus, is enough for me. I will glorify You in abandonment and darkness, in agony and fear, in pain and bitterness, in anguish of spirit and grief of heart. In all things may You be blessed. My heart is so detached from the earth, that You Yourself are enough for me. There is no longer any moment in my life for self concern. (1662)

MAY 30

May You be adored, O merciful God of ours,
O All-powerful Lord and Creator.
In deepest humility, we give You praise,
Plunging ourselves into the ocean of Your Godhead.

But man did not persevere in the hour of trial.
At the instigation of the evil one, he became unfaithful to You.
He lost Your grace and gifts; only misery was left him,
And tears, suffering, sorrow, and bitterness, until he would rest in the grave.

But you, O merciful God, did not let humanity perish,
And gave it the promise of a Redeemer.
You did not let us despair, despite our grave offenses,
And You sent Your prophets to Israel.

> Still, day and night, mankind cries out to You,
> From the abyss of misery, sin, and all pain.
> Hear the moaning and the tears, You who reign in heaven,
> God of great mercy, God of compassion....

Humanity calls out to You unceasingly, O Lord of lords,
Calls out to Your unfathomable mercy, to Your compassion.
O great Yahweh, grant that we may make atonement,
Remember Your goodness, and forgive us our sins.   (1744)

MAY 31

One day during Holy Mass, the Lord gave me a deeper knowledge of His holiness and His majesty, and at the same time I saw my own misery. This knowledge made me happy, and my soul drowned itself completely in His mercy. I felt enormously happy.   (1801)

One day, when I was preparing for Holy Communion and noticed that I had nothing to offer Him, I fell at His feet, calling down all His mercy upon my poor soul: "May Your grace, which flows down upon me from Your Compassionate Heart, strengthen me for the struggle and sufferings, that I may remain faithful to You. And, although I am such misery, I do not fear You, because I know Your mercy well. Nothing will frighten me away from You, O God, because everything is so much less than what I know [Your mercy to be]—I see that clearly.   (1803)

Today, I am not forcing myself to make any special preparation. I cannot think of anything, though I feel many things. I long for the time when God will come to my heart. I throw myself in His arms and tell Him about my inability and my misery. I pour out all the pain of my heart, for not being able to love Him as much as I want. I arouse within myself acts of faith, hope, and charity and live on that throughout the day.

(1813)

THANKS

June

IN THE FIRST PART of this month's readings of the Diary of Blessed Faustina, we focus on giving thanks to God as a way of glorifying the Lord. Glorifying God will be the focus of the rest of the month.

In giving thanks we acknowledge that God is the source of all gifts, and we turn to Him with praise and gratitude to return something of the gift given to us, like the one leper out of ten; who seeing that he was cured, returned to give thanks and praise to Jesus.

It was the desire of Blessed Faustina to thank and glorify the Lord "always and everywhere." It was her desire that her whole life would be one act of thanksgiving—one act of Eucharist. In her great desire to give thanks, she plunged herself into thanksgiving, becoming a flame of gratitude, a fire consuming her soul. Her desire was to live in a spirit of faith, accepting everything God sent her with gratitude.

FOR THE FIRST PART
OF THIS MONTH, JUNE 1-10:

Practice: Dedicate yourself to thankfulness (see Colossians 3:15). Give thanks always and everywhere.

Prayer: Thank You, Jesus.
Thank You, Abba.
Thank You, Spirit.

Promise: Be grateful for the smallest of My graces, because your gratitude compels Me to grant you new graces (1701).

FOR THE SECOND PART
OF THIS MONTH, JUNE 11-30:

Practice: Each day glorify God's mercy in one of the many ways described by Blessed Faustina.

Prayer: Pray the *Gloria* of the Mass:
Glory to God in the highest, and peace to His people on earth. Lord God, heavenly King, almighty God and Father, we worship You, we give You thanks, we praise You for Your glory. Lord Jesus Christ, only Son of the Father, Lord God, Lamb of God, You take away the sin of the world: Have mercy on us. You are seated at the right hand of the Father: Receive our prayer. For You alone are the Holy One, You alone are the Lord, You alone are the Most High, Jesus Christ, with the Holy Spirit, in the glory of God the Father. Amen.

Promise: Souls who especially venerate and glorify My mercy... will shine with a special brightness in the next life (1224).

JUNE 1

Thank You, O God, for all the graces
Which unceasingly You lavish upon me,
Graces which enlighten me with the brilliance of the sun,
For by them You show me the sure way.

Thank You, O Lord, for creating me,
For calling me into being from nothingness,
For imprinting Your divinity on my soul,
The work of sheer merciful love.

Thank You, O God, for Holy Baptism
Which engrafted me into Your family,
A gift great beyond all thought or expression
Which transforms my soul.

Thank You, O Lord, for Holy Confession,
For that inexhaustible spring of great mercy,
For that inconceivable fountain of graces
In which sin-tainted souls become purified.

Thank You, O Jesus, for Holy Communion
In which You give us Yourself.
I feel Your Heart beating within my breast
As You cause Your divine life to unfold within me.

Thank You, O Holy Spirit, for the Sacrament of Confirmation,
Which dubs me Your knight
And gives strength to my soul at each moment,
Protecting me from evil.   (1286a)

JUNE 2

Thank You, O God, for the grace of a vocation,
For being called to serve You alone,
Leading me to make You my sole love,
An unequal honor for my soul.

Thank You, O Lord, for perpetual vows,
For that union of pure love,
For having deigned to unite Your pure heart with mine
And uniting my heart to Yours in the purest of bonds.

Thank You, O Lord, for the Sacrament of Anointing
Which, in my final moments, will give me strength;
My help in battle, my guide to salvation,
Fortifying my soul till we rejoice forever.

Thank You, O God, for all the inspirations
That Your goodness lavishes upon me,
For the interior lights given my soul,
Which the heart senses, but words cannot express.

Thank You, O Holy Trinity, for the vastness of the graces
Which You have lavished on me unceasingly through life.
My gratitude will intensify as the eternal dawn rises,
When, for the first time, I sing to Your glory.   (1286b)

JUNE 3

I thank God for this illness and these physical discomforts,
because I have time to converse with the Lord Jesus. It is my
delight to spend long hours at the feet of the hidden God,

and the hours pass like minutes as I lose track of time. I feel that a fire is burning within me, and I understand no other life but that of sacrifice, which flows from pure love.   (784)

Oh, how drab and full of misunderstandings is this life! My patience is exercised, and after it comes experience. I understand and learn many things each day and see that I know very little, and I am constantly discovering faults in my conduct. Still, I am not discouraged by this, but thank God that He deigns to grant me His light that I may know myself.   (900)

JUNE 4

O Uncreated Beauty, whoever comes to know You once cannot love anything else. I can feel the bottomless abyss of my soul, and nothing will fill it but God Himself. I feel that I am drowned in Him like a single grain of sand in a bottomless ocean....   (343)

You have surrounded my life with Your tender and loving care, more than I can comprehend, for I will understand Your goodness in its entirety only when the veil is lifted. I desire that my whole life be but one act of thanksgiving to You, O God....
(1285)

Having awakened several times during the night, I thanked God briefly, but with all my heart, for all the graces He has given to me and to our Congregation, [and] I reflected on His great goodness.   (1291)

JUNE 5

I made an hour of adoration in thanksgiving for the graces which had been granted me and for my illness. Illness also is a great grace. I have been ill for four months, but I do not recall having wasted so much as a minute of it. All has been for God and souls; I want to be faithful to Him everywhere.

During this adoration, I realized the utter care and goodness that Jesus has been lavishing upon me and the protection He has given me against all evil. I thank You especially, Jesus, for visiting me in my solitude, and I thank You also for inspiring my superiors to send me for this treatment. Give them, Jesus, the omnipotence of Your blessing and compensate them for all the losses incurred because of me. (1062)

JUNE 6

God of great mercy, who deigned to send us Your only-begotten Son as the greatest proof of Your fathomless love and mercy, You do not reject sinners; but in Your boundless mercy You have opened for them also Your treasures, treasures from which they can draw abundantly, not only justification, but also all the sanctity that a soul can attain. Father of great mercy, I desire that all hearts turn with confidence to Your infinite mercy. No one will be justified before You if he is not accompanied by Your unfathomable mercy. When You reveal the mystery of Your mercy to us, there will not be enough of eternity to properly thank You for it. (1122)

JUNE 7

The Lord gave me knowledge of the graces which He has been constantly lavishing on me. This light pierced me through and through, and I came to understand the inconceivable favors that God has been bestowing on me. I stayed in my cell for a long act of thanksgiving, lying face down on the ground and shedding tears of gratitude. I could not rise from the ground because, whenever I tried to do so, God's light gave me new knowledge of His grace. It was only at the third attempt that I was able to get up. As His child, I felt that everything the heavenly Father possessed was equally mine. He Himself lifted me from the ground up to His Heart. I felt that everything that existed was exclusively mine, but I had no desire for it all, because God alone is enough for me. (1279)

JUNE 8

O my Lord, while calling to mind all Your blessings, in the presence of Your Most Sacred Heart, I have felt the need to be particularly grateful for so many graces and blessings from God. I want to plunge myself in thanksgiving before the Majesty of God and to continue in this prayer of thanksgiving for seven days and seven nights; and although I will outwardly carry out all my duties, my spirit will nonetheless stand continually before the Lord, and all my exercises will be imbued with the spirit of thanksgiving. Each evening, I will kneel for a half hour in my cell, alone with the Lord. As often as I shall awake at night, I shall steep myself in a prayer of thanksgiving. In this way I want to repay, at least in some small way, for the immensity of God's blessings. (1367)

However, in order to make all this more pleasing in the eyes of God and to remove the least shadow of doubt from my mind, I went to my spiritual director [Father Andrasz] and revealed these desires of my soul to him; that is to say, the desire to be steeped in such thanksgiving. I received permission for everything, except that I should not force myself to pray at night should I awaken. (1368)

With what great joy I returned to the convent! And on the next day I began this great act of thanksgiving by renewing my vows. My soul became thoroughly immersed in God, and there issued from my whole being but one single flame of gratitude and thanksgiving to God. There were not many words because God's blessings, like a fierce fire, consumed my soul, and all sufferings and sorrows were like wood thrown into the flames, without which the fire would go out. I called upon all heaven and earth to join me in my act of thanksgiving. (1369)

JUNE 9

This has been a great day for me. During this day I remained as though in unceasing contemplation; the very thought of this grace drew me into further contemplation; and throughout the whole day I continued in thanksgiving which I never stopped, because each recollection of this grace [of the Immaculate Conception of Mary] caused my soul ever anew to lose itself in God... (1416)

I want to live in the spirit of faith. I accept everything that comes my way as given me by the loving will of God, who sincerely desires my happiness. And so I will accept with submission and gratitude everything that God sends me. I will pay no attention to the voice of nature and to the promptings of self-love. Before each important action, I will stop to consider for a moment what relationship it has to eternal life and what may be the main reason for my undertaking it: is it for the glory of God, or for the good of my own soul, or for the good of the souls of others? If my heart says yes, then I will not swerve from carrying out the given action, unmindful of either obstacles or sacrifices. I will not be frightened into abandoning my intention. It is enough for me to know that it is pleasing to God. On the other hand, if I learn that the action has nothing in common with what I have just mentioned, I will try to elevate it to a loftier sphere by means of a good intention. And if I learn that something flows from my self-love, I will cancel it out right from the start. (1549)

JUNE 10

I spent the whole day in thanksgiving, and gratitude kept flooding my soul. O my God, how good You are, how great is Your mercy! You visit me with so many graces, me who am a most wretched speck of dust. Prostrating myself at Your feet, O Lord, I confess with a sincere heart that I have done nothing to deserve even the least of Your graces. It is in Your infinite goodness that You give Yourself to me so generously. Therefore, the greater the graces which my heart receives, the deeper it plunges itself in humility. (1661)

O Jesus, eternal God, thank You for Your countless graces and blessings. Let every beat of my heart be a new hymn of thanksgiving to You, O God. Let every drop of my blood circulate for You, Lord. My soul is one hymn in adoration of Your mercy. I love You, God, for Yourself alone. (1794)

JUNE 11

Praise the Lord, my soul, for everything, and glorify His mercy, for His goodness is without end. Everything will pass, but His mercy is without limit or end. And although evil will attain its measure, in mercy there is no measure.

O my God, even in the punishments You send down upon the earth I see the abyss of Your mercy, for by punishing us here on earth You free us from eternal punishment. Rejoice, all you creatures, for you are closer to God in His infinite mercy than a baby to its mother's heart. O God, You are compassion itself for the greatest sinners who sincerely repent. The greater the sinner, the greater his right to God's mercy.   (423)

JUNE 12

After Communion, I heard the voice saying, **My daughter, look into the abyss of My mercy and give praise and glory to this mercy of Mine. Do it in this way: Gather all sinners from the entire world and immerse them in the abyss of My mercy. I want to give Myself to souls; I yearn for souls, My daughter. On the day of My feast, the Feast of Mercy, you will go through the whole world and bring fainting souls to the spring of my mercy. I shall heal and strengthen them.**   (206)

God, One in the Holy Trinity, I want to love You as no human soul has ever loved You before; and although I am utterly miserable and small, I have nevertheless cast the anchor of my trust deep down into the abyss of Your mercy, O my God and Creator! In spite of my great misery I fear nothing, but hope to sing You a hymn of glory forever. Let no soul, even the most miserable, fall prey to doubt; for, as long as one is alive, each one can become a great saint, so great is the power of God's grace. It remains only for us not to oppose God's action. (283)

JUNE 13

Oh, how ardently I desire that every soul would praise Your mercy. Happy is the soul that calls upon the mercy of the Lord. It will see that the Lord will defend it as His glory, as He said. And who would dare fight against God? All you souls, praise the Lord's mercy by trusting in His mercy all your life and especially at the hour of your death. And fear nothing, dear soul, whoever you are; the greater the sinner, the greater his right to Your mercy, O Lord. O incomprehensible goodness! God is the first to stoop to the sinner. O Jesus, I wish to glorify Your mercy on behalf of thousands of souls. I know very well, O my Jesus, that I am to keep telling souls about Your goodness, about Your incomprehensible mercy.   (598)

Jesus, You know that I love suffering and want to drain the cup of suffering to the last drop; and yet, my nature experienced a slight shudder and fear. Quickly, however, my trust in the infinite mercy of God was awakened in all its force, and everything else had to give way before it, like a shadow retreating before the sun's rays. O Jesus, how great is Your goodness! Your infinite goodness, so well known to me, enables me to bravely look death itself in the eye. I know that nothing will happen to me without God's permission. I desire to glorify Your infinite mercy during my life, at the hour of death, in the resurrection, and throughout eternity.   (697)

JUNE 14

Eternal Truth, give me a ray of Your light that I may come to know You, O Lord, and worthily glorify Your infinite mercy. And at the same time, grant me to know myself, the whole abyss of misery that I am. (727)

During the meditation on creation... at a certain point, my soul became closely united to its Lord and Creator. In this union, I recognized the purpose and destiny of my life. My purpose is to become closely united to God through love, and my destiny is to praise and glorify God's mercy. The Lord has allowed me to know and experience this in a distinct and even physical way. I become lost in admiration when I recognize and experience this incomprehensible love of God with which God loves me. Who is God—and what am I? I cannot meditate on this any further. Only love can understand this meeting of two spirits, namely, God-who-is-Spirit and the soul-who-is-creature. The more I know Him, the more completely with all the strength of my being I drown in Him. (729)

JUNE 15

During Holy Mass, I was so enveloped in the great interior fire of God's love and the desire to save souls that I do not know how to express it. I feel I am all aflame. I shall fight all evil with the weapon of mercy. I am being burned up by the desire to save souls. I traverse the world's length and breadth and venture as far as its ultimate limits and its wildest lands to save souls. I do this through prayer and sacrifice. I want every soul to glorify the mercy of God, for each one experiences the effects of that mercy on himself. The Saints in heaven worship the mercy of the Lord. I want to worship it even now, here on earth, and to spread devotion to it in the way that God demands of me.... (745)

The mercy of the Lord is praised by the holy souls in heaven who have themselves experienced that infinite mercy. What these souls do in heaven, I already will begin to do here on earth. I will praise God for His infinite goodness, and I will strive to bring other souls to know and glorify the inexpressible and incomprehensible mercy of God. (753)

JUNE 16

O God of fathomless mercy, who allows me to give relief and help to the dying by my unworthy prayer, be blessed as many thousand times as there are stars in the sky and drops of water in all the oceans! Let Your mercy resound throughout the orb of the earth, and let it rise to the foot of Your throne, giving praise to the greatest of Your attributes; that is, Your incomprehensible mercy. O God, this unfathomable mercy enthralls anew all the holy souls and all the spirits of heaven. These pure spirits are immersed in holy amazement as they glorify this inconceivable mercy of God, which in turn arouses even greater admiration in them, and their praise is carried out in a perfect manner. O eternal God, how ardently I desire to glorify this greatest of Your attributes; namely, Your unfathomable mercy. I see all my littleness, and cannot compare myself to the heavenly beings who praise the Lord's mercy with holy admiration. But I, too, have found a way to give perfect glory to the incomprehensible mercy of God. (835b)

JUNE 17

O most sweet Jesus, who has deigned to allow miserable me to gain a knowledge of Your unfathomable mercy; O most sweet Jesus, who has graciously demanded that I tell the whole world of Your incomprehensible mercy, this day I take into my hands the two rays that spring from Your merciful Heart; that is, the Blood and the Water; and I scatter them all over the globe so that each soul may receive Your mercy and, having received it, may glorify it for endless ages. O most sweet Jesus who, in Your incomprehensible kindness, has deigned to unite my wretched heart to Your most merciful Heart, it is with Your own Heart that I glorify God, our Father, as no soul has ever glorified Him before. (836)

JUNE 18

Today the doctor decided that I am not to go to Mass, but only to Holy Communion. I wanted very much to assist at Mass, but my confessor, in agreement with the doctor, told me to obey. "It is God's will, Sister, that you should get well, and you must not undertake mortifications of any kind. Be obedient, Sister, and God will reward you for it." I felt that the confessor's words were Jesus' words, and although it made me sad to miss Holy Mass, during which God had been granting me the grace of seeing the Infant Jesus; nevertheless, I placed obedience above everything else.

I became absorbed in prayer and said my penance. Then I suddenly saw the Lord, who said to me, **My daughter, know that you give Me greater glory by a single act of obedience than by long prayers and mortifications.** Oh, how good it is to live under obedience, to live conscious of the fact that every-thing I do is pleasing to God! (894)

During my meditation, I heard these words: **My daughter, you give Me most glory by patiently submitting to My will, and you win for yourself greater merit than that which any fast or mor-tification could ever gain for you. Know, My daughter, that if you submit your will to Mine, you draw upon yourself My spe-cial delight. This sacrifice is pleasing to Me and full of sweet-ness. I take great pleasure in it; there is power in it.** (904)

JUNE 19

Today, I took part in a one-day retreat. When I was at the last conference, the priest was speaking of how much the world needs God's mercy, and that this seems to be a special time when people have great need of prayer and God's mercy. Then I heard a voice in my soul: **These words are for you. Do all you possibly can for this work of My mercy. I desire that My mercy be worshiped, and I am giving mankind the last hope of salvation; that is, recourse to My mercy. My Heart rejoices in this feast.** After these words, I understood that nothing can dispense me from the obligation which the Lord demands from me. (998)

Let the glory and praise to the Divine Mercy rise from every creature throughout all ages and times. (1005)

Praise and glory be to You, O Holy Trinity, Eternal God. May the mercy springing from Your very bowels protect us from Your just anger. Let the praise of Your incomprehensible mercy resound everywhere. All Your works bear the seal of Your unfathomable mercy, O God. (1007)

JUNE 20

Then, in an instant, I was caught up to stand near Jesus, and I stood on the altar next to the Lord Jesus, and my spirit was filled with a happiness so great that I am unable to comprehend it or write about it. A profound peace as well as repose filled my soul. Jesus bent toward me and said with great kindness, **What is it you desire, My daughter?** And I answered, "I desire worship and glory be given to Your mercy." **I already am receiving worship by the institution and celebration of this Feast; what else do you desire?** I then looked at the immense crowd worshiping the Divine Mercy and I said to the Lord, "Jesus, bless all those who are gathered to give glory to You and to venerate Your infinite mercy." Jesus made a sign of the cross with His hand, and this blessing was reflected in the souls like a flash of light. My spirit was engulfed in His love. I felt as if I had dissolved and disappeared completely in God. When I came to myself, a profound peace was flooding my soul, and an extraordinary understanding of many things was communicated to my intellect, an understanding that had not been granted me previously.   (1048)

On several occasions, I have learned how some religious defend their own glory under the pretext of being concerned for the glory of God, whereas it is not a question of the glory of God, but of glory of self. O Jesus, how painful this has been for me! What secrets the day of Your judgment will bring to light! How can one steal God's gifts?   (1149)

JUNE 21

O my most sweet Master, good Jesus, I give You my heart. You shape and mold it after Your liking. O fathomless Love, I open the calyx of my heart to You, like a rosebud to the freshness of dew. To You alone, my Betrothed, is known the fragrance of the flower of my heart. Let the fragrance of my sacrifice be pleasing to You. O Immortal God, my everlasting delight, already here on earth You are my heaven. May every beat of my heart be a new hymn of praise to You, O Holy Trinity! Had I as many hearts as there are drops of water in the ocean or grains of sand in the whole world, I would offer them all to You, O my Love, O Treasure of my heart! Whomever I shall meet in my life, no matter who they may be, I want to draw them all to love You, O my Jesus, my Beauty, my Repose, my sole Master, Judge, Savior, and Spouse, all in one; I know that one title will modify the other—I have entrusted everything to Your mercy. (1064)

JUNE 22

When once I asked the Lord Jesus how He could tolerate so many sins and crimes and not punish them, the Lord answered me, **I have eternity for punishing** [these], **and so I am prolonging the time of mercy for the sake of** [sinners]. **But woe to them if they do not recognize this time of My visitation. My daughter, secretary of My mercy, your duty is not only to write about and proclaim My mercy, but also to beg for this grace for them, so that they too may glorify My mercy.** (1160)

O Jesus, I want to live in the present moment, to live as if this were the last day of my life. I want to use every moment scrupulously for the greater glory of God, to use every circumstance for the benefit of my soul. I want to look upon everything, from the point of view that nothing happens without the will of God.

God of unfathomable mercy, embrace the whole world and pour Yourself out upon us through the merciful Heart of Jesus. (1183)

JUNE 23

All for You, Jesus. I desire to adore Your mercy with every beat of my heart and, to the extent that I am able, to encourage souls to trust in that mercy, as You Yourself have commanded me, O Lord. (1234)

On passing through Cracow, Father Sopocko paid me a short visit today. I had wanted to see him, and God fulfilled my desire. This priest is a great soul, entirely filled with God. My joy was very great, and I thanked God for this great grace, because it was for the greater glory of God that I wanted to see him. (1238)

My Jesus, penetrate me through and through so that I might be able to reflect You in my whole life. Divinize me so that my deeds may have supernatural value. Grant that I may have love, compassion, and mercy for every soul without exception. O my Jesus, each of Your Saints reflects one of Your virtues; I desire to reflect Your compassionate heart, full of mercy; I want to glorify it. Let Your mercy, O Jesus, be impressed upon my heart and soul like a seal, and this will be my badge in this and the future life. Glorifying Your mercy is the exclusive task of my life. (1242)

JUNE 24

Reverend Father Sopocko left this morning. When I was steeped in a prayer of thanksgiving for the great grace that I had received from God; namely, that of seeing Father, I became united in a special way with the Lord who said to me, **He is a priest after My own Heart; his efforts are pleasing to Me. You see, My daughter, that My will must be done and that which I had promised you, I shall do. Through him I spread comfort to suffering and careworn souls. Through him it pleased Me to proclaim the worship of My mercy. And through this work of mercy more souls will come close to Me than otherwise would have, even if he had kept giving absolution day and night for the rest of his life, because by so doing, he would have labored only for as long as he lived; whereas, thanks to this work of mercy, he will be laboring till the end of the world.** (1256)

JUNE 25

O my God, let everything that is in me praise You, my Lord and Creator; and with every beat of my heart I want to praise Your unfathomable mercy. I want to tell souls of Your goodness and encourage them to trust in Your mercy. That is my mission, which You Yourself have entrusted to me, O Lord, in this life and in the life to come. (1325)

After Communion today, Jesus told me how much He desires to come to human hearts. **I desire to unite Myself with human souls; My great delight is to unite Myself with souls. Know, My daughter, that when I come to a human heart in Holy Communion, My hands are full of all kinds of graces which I want to give to the soul. But souls do not even pay any atten-**

tion to Me; they leave Me to Myself and busy themselves with other things. Oh, how sad I am that souls do not recognize Love! They treat Me as a dead object. I answered Jesus, "O Treasure of my heart, the only object of my love and entire delight of my soul, I want to adore You in my heart as You are adored on the throne of Your eternal glory. My love wants to make up to You at least in part for the coldness of so great a number of souls. Jesus, behold my heart which is for You a dwelling place to which no one else has entry. You alone repose in it as in a beautiful garden. (1385)

JUNE 26

At that moment, I saw Jesus, who said, **I am pleased with what you are doing. And you can continue to be at peace if you always do the best you can in respect to this work of mercy. Be absolutely as frank as possible with your confessor.**

Satan gained nothing by tempting you, because you did not enter into conversation with him. Continue to act in this way. You gave Me great glory today by fighting so faithfully. Let it be confirmed and engraved on your heart that I am always with you, even if you don't feel My presence at the time of battle.

(1499)

My health has improved somewhat. I went down to the refectory and the chapel today. I still cannot resume my duties, and so I stay in my cell at the hand-loom [making borders for altar linens]. I enjoy this work very much, but still, even with such light work, I tire easily. I see how feeble I am. There are no indifferent moments in my life, since every moment of my life is filled with prayer, suffering, and work. If not in one way, then in another, I glorify God; and if God were to give me a second life, I do not know whether I would make better use of it...

(1545)

JUNE 27

January 30, 1938. One-day retreat. The Lord gave me to know, during meditation, that as long as my heart beats in my breast, I must always strive to spread the Kingdom of God on earth. I am to fight for the glory of my Creator.

I know that I will give God the glory He expects of me if I try faithfully to cooperate with God's grace. (1548)

O my Jesus, Life of my soul, my Life, my Savior, my sweetest Bridegroom, and at the same time my Judge, You know that in this last hour of mine I do not count on any merits of my own, but only on Your mercy. Even as of today, I immerse myself totally in the abyss of Your mercy, which is always open to every soul.

O my Jesus, I have only one task to carry out in my lifetime, in death, and throughout eternity, and that is to adore Your incomprehensible mercy. No mind, either of Angel or of man, will ever fathom the mysteries of Your mercy, O God. The Angels are lost in amazement before the mystery of divine mercy, but cannot comprehend it. Everything that has come from the Creator's hand is contained in this inconceivable mystery; that is to say, in the very depths of His tender mercy. When I meditate on this, my spirit swoons, and my heart dissolves in joy. O Jesus, it is through Your most compassionate Heart, as through a crystal, that the rays of divine mercy have come to us. (1553)

JUNE 28

As I took the pen in hand, I addressed a short prayer to the Holy Spirit and said, "Jesus, bless this pen so that everything You order me to write may be for the glory of God." Then I heard a voice: **Yes, I bless** [it], **because this writing bears the seal of obedience to your superior and confessor, and by that very fact I am already given glory, and many souls will be drawing profit from it. My daughter, I demand that you devote all your free moments to writing about My goodness and mercy. It is your office and your assignment throughout your life to continue to make known to souls the great mercy I have for them and to exhort them to trust in My bottomless mercy.**

(1567)

JUNE 29

When, during adoration, I repeated the prayer, "Holy God" several times, a vivid presence of God suddenly swept over me, and I was caught up in spirit before the majesty of God. I saw how the Angels and the Saints of the Lord give glory to God. The glory of God is so great that I dare not try to describe it, because I would not be able to do so, and souls might think that what I have written is all there is. Saint Paul, I understand now why you did not want to describe heaven, but only said that eye has not seen, nor ear heard, nor has it entered into the heart of man what God has prepared for those who love Him [cf. 1 Corinthians 2:9; 2 Corinthians 12:1-7]. Yes, that is indeed so. And all that has come forth from God returns to Him in the same way and gives Him perfect glory. Now I have seen the way in which I adore God; oh, how miserable it is! And what a tiny drop it is in comparison to that perfect heavenly glory. O my God, how good You are to accept my praise as well, and to turn Your Face to me with kindness and let us know that our prayer is pleasing to You.   (1604)

Oh, how greatly I desire the glory of Your mercy—for me, bitterness and suffering! When I see the glory of Your mercy, I am immeasurably happy. Let all disgrace, humiliation, and abasement come down upon me, as long as the glory and praise of Your mercy resounds everywhere—that's all that matters.

(1691)

JUNE 30

On my way to the veranda, I went into the chapel for a moment. My heart was plunged in profound adoration, praising God's incomprehensible goodness and His mercy. Then I heard these words in my soul: **I am and will be for you such as you praise Me for being. You shall experience My goodness, already in this life and then, to the full, in the life to come.**

(1707)

O Christ, I am most delighted when I see that You are loved, and that Your praise and glory resound, especially the praise of Your mercy. O Christ, to the last moment of my life, I will not stop glorifying Your goodness and mercy. With every drop of my blood, with every beat of my heart, I glorify Your mercy. I long to be entirely transformed into a hymn of Your glory. When I find myself on my deathbed, may the last beat of my heart be a loving hymn in praise of Your unfathomable mercy.

(1708)

Today I saw the glory of God which flows from the Image. Many souls are receiving graces, although they do not speak of it openly. Even though it has met up with all sorts of vicissitudes, God is receiving glory because of it; and the efforts of Satan and of evil men are shattered and come to naught. In spite of Satan's anger, the Divine Mercy will triumph over the whole world and will be worshiped by all souls.   (1789)

DESIRE

July

OUR DESIRES ARE a fascinating part of our human make-up. We want and desire various things; some for the needs of life, others for pleasure or to possess, and still others for our grandisement. Yet at the root of all our various desires, there is one deep tap root that is the basic desire of our life. Most of us do not express that desire because it is so deep and pervasive. The psalmist expresses this desire of our soul:

> Like the deer that yearns for running streams,
> so my soul is yearning for you, my God.
> My soul is thirsting for God, the God of my life;
> When can I enter and see the face of God? (Psalm 42)

St. Augustine in his *Confessions* writes:

> You inspire us, O Lord, to delight in praising you, because you made us for yourself; our hearts are restless until they rest in you. (Morning Prayer, Aug. 28)

If your one great desire is for God, then He will give you the grace and fulfill your desire. Blessed Faustina tells us that what is needed is "a bit of good will":

> O my Jesus, how very easy it is to become holy; all that is needed is a bit of good will. If Jesus sees this little bit of good will in the soul, He hurries to give himself to the soul,

and nothing can stop Him, neither shortcomings nor falls—absolutely nothing. Jesus is anxious to help that soul, and if it is faithful to this grace from God, it can very soon attain the highest holiness possible for a creature here on earth. God is very generous and does not deny His grace to anyone. Indeed He gives more than what we ask of Him. Faithfulness to the inspirations of the Holy Spirit — that is the shortest route. (291)

FOR THIS MONTH:

Practice, Prayer and **Promise** are combined:

The world needs millions of saints. And it is the Lord's one great desire that we, you and I, be saints! We can begin now by exercising our desire and asking the intercession of Blessed Faustina to be faithful to the inspirations of the Holy Spirit and to be a saint:

Pray Daily:
Blessed Faustina, you told us that your mission would continue after your death and that you would not forget us (281, 1582).

Our Lord also granted you a great privilege, telling you to "distribute graces as you will, to whom you will, and when you will" (31).

Relying on this, I ask your intercession for the graces I need, especially to be faithful to the inspirations of the Holy Spirit and *to be a Saint.*

Help me, above all, to trust in Jesus as you did and thus to glorify His mercy every moment of my life.

JULY 1

To stay at Your feet, O hidden God,
Is the delight and paradise of my soul.
Here, You give me to know You, O incomprehensible One,
And You speak to me sweetly: **Give Me, Give Me your heart.**

Silent conversation, alone with You,
Is to experience what heavenly beings enjoy,
And to say to God, "I will, I will give You my heart, O Lord,"
While You, O great and incomprehensible One,
    accept it graciously.

Love and sweetness are my soul's life,
And Your unceasing presence in my soul.
I live on earth in constant rapture,
And like a Seraph I repeat, "Hosanna!"

O You Who are hidden, body, soul, and divinity,
Under the fragile form of bread,
You are my life from Whom springs an abundance of graces;
And, for me, You surpass the delights of heaven.

When You unite Yourself with me in Communion, O God,
I then feel my unspeakable greatness,
A greatness which flows from You, O Lord, I humbly confess,
And despite my misery, with Your help, I can become a saint.

(1718)

JULY 2

O God, how much I desire to be a small child. You are my Father, and You know how little and weak I am. So I beg You, keep me close by Your side all my life and especially at the hour of my death. Jesus, I know that Your goodness surpasses the goodness of a most tender mother. (242)

O my Jesus, delight of my heart, You know my desires. I should like to hide from people's sight so as to be like one alive and yet not living. I want to live pure as a wild flower; I want my love always to be turned to You, just as a flower that is always turning to the sun. I want the fragrance and the freshness of the flower of my heart to be always preserved for You alone. I want to live beneath Your divine gaze, for You alone are enough for me. When I am with You, Jesus, I fear nothing, for nothing can do me harm. (306b)

Jesus, You know how ardently I desire to hide so that no one may know me but Your sweetest Heart. I want to be a tiny violet, hidden in the grass, unknown in a magnificent enclosed garden in which beautiful lilies and roses grow. The beautiful rose and the lovely lily can be seen from afar, but in order to see a little violet, one has to bend low; only its scent gives it away. Oh, how happy I am to be able to hide myself in this way! O my divine Bridegroom, the flower of my heart and the scent of my pure love are for You. My soul has drowned itself in You, Eternal God. From the moment when You Yourself drew me to Yourself, O my Jesus, the more ardently I have desired You. (591)

JULY 3

O my Jesus, You are the life of my life. You know only too well that I long for nothing but the glory of Your Name and that souls come to know Your goodness. Why do souls avoid You, Jesus?—I don't understand that. Oh, if I could only cut my heart into tiny pieces and in this way offer to You, O Jesus, each piece as a heart whole and entire, to make up in part for the hearts that do not love You! I love You, Jesus, with every drop of my blood, and I would gladly shed my blood for You to give You a proof of the sincerity of my love. O God, the more I know You the less I can comprehend You, but this "non-comprehension" lets me realize how great You are! And it is this impossibility of comprehending You which enflames my heart anew for you, O Lord. From the moment when You let me fix the eyes of my soul on You, O Jesus, I have been at peace and desired nothing else. I found my destiny at the moment when my soul lost itself in You, the only object of my love. In comparison with You, everything is nothing. Sufferings, adversities, humiliations, failures, and suspicions that have come my way are splinters that keep alive the fire of my love for You, O Jesus.   (57)

JULY 4

O my Creator, I long for You! You understand me, O Lord of mine! All that is on earth seems to be like a pale shadow. It is You I long for and desire. Although You do so inconceivably much for me, for You Yourself visit me in a special way, yet those visits do not soothe the wound of the heart, but make me long all the more for You, O Lord. Oh, take me to Yourself, Lord, if such is Your will! You know that I am dying, and I am dying of longing for You; and yet, I cannot die.

Death, where are you? You draw me into the abyss of Your divinity, and You veil yourself with darkness. My whole being is immersed in You, yet I desire to see You face to face. When will this come about for me? (841)

JULY 5

My Lord and Creator, Your goodness encourages me to converse with You. Your mercy abolishes the chasm which separates the Creator from the creature. To converse with You, O Lord, is the delight of my heart. In You I find everything that my heart could desire. Here Your light illumines my mind, enabling it to know You more and more deeply. Here streams of graces glow down upon my heart. Here my soul draws eternal life. O my Lord and Creator, You alone, beyond all these gifts, give Your own self to me and unite Yourself intimately with Your miserable creature. Here, without searching for words, our hearts understand each other. Here, no one is able to interrupt our conversation. What I talk to You about is our secret, which creatures shall not know and Angels dare not ask about. These are secret acts of forgiveness, known only to Jesus and me; this is the mystery of His mercy, which embraces each soul separately. For this incomprehensible goodness of Yours, I adore You, O Lord and Creator, with all my heart and all my soul. And, although my worship is so little and poor, I am at peace because I know that You know it is sincere, however inadequate... (1692)

JULY 6

O day of eternity, O day so long desired,
With thirst and longing, my eyes search You out.
Soon love will tear the veil asunder,
    and You will be my salvation.

    O day most solemn, O day of brightness,
    When the soul will know God in His omnipotence
    And drown totally in His love.
    Knowing the miseries of exile are o'er.

O happy day, O blessed day,
When my heat will burn for You with fire eternal,
For even now I feel Your presence, though through the veil.
Through life and death, O Jesus,
    You are my rapture and delight.

    O day, of which I dreamed through all my life,
    Waiting long for You, O God,
    For it is You alone whom I desire.
    You are the one and only of my heart; all else is naught.

O day of delight, day of eternal bliss,
God of great majesty, my beloved Spouse,
You know that nothing will satisfy a virgin heart.
On Your tender Heart I rest my brow.   (1230)

JULY 7

O Jesus, eternal Truth, strengthen my feeble forces; You can
do all things, Lord. I know that without You all my efforts are
in vain. O Jesus, do not hide from me, for I cannot live without

You. Listen to the cry of my soul. Your mercy has not been exhausted, Lord, so have pity on my misery. Your mercy surpasses the understanding of all Angels and people put together; and so, although it seems to me that You do not hear me, I put my trust in the ocean of Your mercy, and I know that my hope will not be deceived. (69)

JULY 8

January 10, 1937. I asked the Lord today to give me strength in the morning so that I could go to receive Holy Communion. My Master, I ask You with all my thirsting heart to give me, if this is according to Your holy will, any suffering and weakness that You like—I want to suffer all day and all night—but please, I fervently beg You, strengthen me for the one moment when I am to receive Holy Communion. You see very well, Jesus, that here they do not bring Holy Communion to the sick; so, if You do not strengthen me for that moment so that I can go down to the chapel, how can I receive You in the Mystery of Love? And You know how much my heart longs for You. O my sweet Spouse, what's the good of all these reasonings? You know how ardently I desire You, and if You so choose You can do this for me.

On the following morning, I felt as if I were perfectly well; the faintings and the weaknesses ceased. But as soon as I returned from the chapel, all the sufferings and weaknesses immediately returned, as if they had been waiting for me. But I had no fear of them at all, because I had been nourished by the Bread of the Strong. I boldly look at everything; even death itself I look straight in the eye. (876)

JULY 9

O Lord, I feel Your grace and Your peace filling my poor soul. I feel overwhelmed by Your mercy, O Lord. You forgive me, which is more than I dared to hope for or could imagine. Your goodness surpasses all my desires. And now, filled with gratitude for so many graces, I invite You to my heart. I wandered, like a prodigal child gone astray; but you did not cease to be my Father. Increase Your mercy toward me, for You see how weak I am.

Jesus: **Child, speak no more of your misery; it is already forgotten. Listen, My child, to what I desire to tell you. Come close to My wounds and draw from the Fountain of Life whatever your heart desires. Drink copiously from the Fountain of Life and you will not weary on your journey. Look at the splendors of My mercy and do not fear the enemies of your salvation. Glorify My mercy.** (1485b)

JULY 10

O Wound of Mercy, Heart of Jesus, hide me in Your depths as a drop of Your own blood, and do not let me out forever! Lock me in Your depths, and You Yourself teach me to love You! Eternal Love, do You Yourself form my soul that it be made capable of returning Your love. O Christ, a single gaze from You is dearer to me than a thousand worlds, than all heaven itself. Lord, You can make my soul capable of understanding completely who You are. I know and I believe that You can do all things; if You have deigned to give Yourself to me so generously, then I know that You can be even more generous. Bring me into an intimacy with You so far as it is possible for human nature to be brought... (1631)

JULY 11

Today, I went to meditate before the Blessed Sacrament [in the sanatorium chapel]. When I approached the altar, God's presence pervaded my soul, I was plunged into the ocean of His divinity, and Jesus said to me, **My daughter, all that exists is yours.** I answered the Lord, "My heart wants nothing but You alone, O Treasure of my heart. For all the gifts You give me, thank you, O Lord, but I desire only Your Heart. Though the heavens are immense, they are nothing to me without You. You know very well, O Jesus, that I am constantly swooning because of my longing for You." **Know this, My daughter, that you are already tasting now what other souls will obtain only in eternity.**   (969)

And all of a sudden, my soul was flooded with the light of the knowledge of God. Oh, would that I could express even a little of what my soul experiences when resting near the Heart of the incomprehensible Majesty! I cannot put it into words. Only a soul who has experienced such a grace at least once in his life, will recognize it. When I returned to my room, it seemed to me that I was coming from real life to death. When the doctor came to take my pulse, he was surprised: "Sister, what happened? You have never had a pulse like this! I would like to know what has speeded it up so much." What could I tell him, when I myself did not know that my pulse was so rapid. I only know that I am dying of yearning for God, but this I did not tell him, for how can medicine help in this instance?   (970)

JULY 12

Holy Thursday, April 18. This morning I heard these words: **From today until the** [celebration of the] **Resurrection, you will not feel My presence, but your soul will be filled with great longing.** And immediately a great longing filled my soul; I felt a separation from my beloved Jesus, and when the moment for Holy Communion came, I saw the suffering Face of Jesus in every Host [contained] in the chalice. From that moment, I felt a more intense yearning in my heart.   (413)

On the evening of that same day, I felt in my soul a great yearning for God. I do not see Him at this moment with my bodily eyes as I have on other occasions, but I sense His presence and yet do not grasp Him [with my mind]. This causes me great yearning and torment beyond words. I am dying from the desire to possess Him, to be drowned in Him forever. My spirit pursues Him with all its might; there is nothing in the world that could comfort me. O Love Eternal, now I understand in what close intimacy my heart was with You! For what else can satisfy me in heaven or on earth except You, O my God, in Whom my soul is drowned.   (469)

JULY 13

One day, when I was at adoration, my spirit seemed to be dying for Him, and I could no longer hold back my tears. I saw a spirit of great beauty who spoke these words to me: "Don't cry—says the Lord." After a moment I asked, "Who are you?" He answered me, "I am one of the seven spirits who stand before the throne of God day and night and give Him ceaseless praise." Yet this spirit did not soothe my yearning, but roused me to even greater longing for God. This spirit is very beautiful, and his beauty comes from close union with God. This spirit does not leave me for a single moment, but accompanies me everywhere.

JULY 14

On the following day during Holy Mass, before the Elevation, this spirit began to sing these words: "Holy, Holy, Holy." His voice was like that of a thousand voices; it is impossible to put it into words. Suddenly my spirit was united with God, and in that instant I saw the grandeur and the inconceivable holiness of God and, at the same time, I realized the nothingness I am of myself.   (471)

JULY 15

Jesus, there is one more secret in my life, the deepest and dearest to my heart; it is You Yourself when You come to my heart under the appearance of bread. Herein lies the whole secret of my sanctity. Here my heart is so united with Yours as to be but one. There are no more secrets, because all that is Yours is mine, and all that is mine is Yours. Such is the omnipotence and the miracle of Your mercy. All the tongues of men and of Angels united could not find words adequate to this mystery of Your love and mercy.

When I contemplate this mystery, my heart falls into a new ecstasy. In silence I tell You everything, Lord, because the language of love is without words; not a single stirring of my heart escapes You. O Lord, the extent of Your great condescension has awakened in my soul an even greater love for You, the sole object of my love. The life of union manifests itself in perfect purity, deep humility, gentle silence, and great zeal for the salvation of souls. (1489)

JULY 16

I go, Lord, at Your command. I go to conquer souls. Sustained by Your grace, I am ready to follow You, Lord, not only to Tabor, but also to Calvary. I desire to lead souls to the fount of Your mercy so that the splendor of Your mercy may be reflected in all souls, and the home of our Father be filled to overflowing. And when the enemy begins to attack me, I shall take refuge behind the shield of Your mercy. (1488b)

JULY 17

The desires of my heart are so great and incomprehensible
That nothing can fill the abyss of my heart.
Even the most beautiful things,
    gathered from all over the world,
Would not for a moment fill Your place for me, O God.

    With one glance, I penetrated the whole world,
    And I found no other love like the love of my heart.
    Therefore I looked into the world of eternity—
    Because this one is too small for me.
    My heart has desired the love of the Immortal One.

My heart has sensed that I am a royal child,
That I have found myself in exile, in a foreign land.
I see that the heavenly palace is my home;
Only there will I feel as in my own fatherland.

You Yourself have drawn my soul to You, O Lord;
O Eternal Word, You Yourself have stooped to me,
Giving my soul a deeper knowledge of Yourself.
Behold, the mystery of love for which You have created me!

Pure love has made me strong and brave.
I fear neither the Seraphim nor the Cherubim, standing with
    sword in hand,
And I pass over with ease where others tremble,
Because there is nothing to fear, there where love is the guide.

And suddenly the eye of my soul came to rest upon You,
O Lord Jesus Christ, stretched upon the Cross.
Here is my Love, with whom I will rest in my grave.
This is my Bridegroom, my incomprehensible
    Lord and God.   (1632)

JULY 18

February 5, 1937. My Jesus, in spite of everything, I desire very much to unite myself to You. Jesus, if this be possible, take me to Yourself, for it seems to me that my heart will burst of longing for You!

Oh, how very much I feel that I am in exile! When will I find myself in the house of our Father, delighting in the happiness that streams from the Most Holy Trinity? But, if it is Your will that I still go on living and suffering, then I desire what You have destined for me. Keep me here on earth for as long as You wish, even though this be until the end of the world. O will of my Lord, be my delight and the rapture of my soul. Although the earth is so filled with people, I feel all alone, and the earth is a terrible desert to me. O Jesus, Jesus, You know and understand the fervors of my heart; You, O Lord, alone can fill me. (918)

JULY 19

With longing I gaze into the starlit sky,
Into the sapphire of fathomless firmaments.
There the pure heart leaps out to find You, O God,
And yearns to be freed of the bonds of the flesh.

With great longing, I gaze upon you, my homeland,
When will this, my exile, come to an end?
O Jesus, such is the call of Your bride
Who suffers agony in her thirst for You.

With longing, I gaze at the footprints of the saints
Who crossed this wilderness on their way to the fatherland.
They left me the example of their virtue and their counsels,
And they say to me, "Patience, Sister, soon the fetters will
break."

But my longing soul hears not these words.
Ardently it yearns for its Lord and its God,
And it understands not human language,
Because it is enamored of Him alone.

My longing soul, wounded with love,
Forces its way through all created things
And unites itself with infinite eternity,
With the Lord whom my heart has espoused.

Allow my longing soul, O God,
To be drowned in Your Divine Three-fold Essence.
Fulfill my desires, for which I humbly beg You,
With a heart brimming with love's fire.   (1304)

JULY 20

O Jesus, I want to bring souls to the fount of Your mercy to draw the reviving water of life with the vessel of trust. The soul desirous of more of God's mercy should approach God with greater trust; and if her trust in God is unlimited, then the mercy of God toward it will be likewise limitless. O my God, Who know every beat of my heart, You know how eagerly I desire that all hearts would beat for You alone, that every soul glorify the greatness of Your mercy.

Jesus: **My beloved child, delight of My Heart, your words are dearer and more pleasing to me than the angelic chorus. All the treasures of My Heart are open to you. Take from this Heart all that you need for yourself and for the whole world. For the sake of your love, I withhold the just chastisements, which mankind has deserved. A single act of pure love pleases Me more than a thousand imperfect prayers. One of your sighs of love atones for many offenses with which the godless overwhelm Me. The smallest act of virtue has unlimited value in My eyes because of your great love for Me. In a soul that lives on My love alone, I reign as in heaven. I watch over it day and night. In it I find My happiness; My ear is attentive to each request of its heart; often I anticipate its requests. O child, especially beloved by Me, apple of My eye, rest a moment near My Heart and taste of the love in which you will delight for all eternity. But child, you are not yet in your homeland; so go, fortified by My grace, and fight for My kingdom in human** souls; fight as a king's child would; and remember that the days of your exile will pass quickly, and with them the possibility of earning merit for heaven. I expect from You, My child, a great number of souls who will glorify My mercy for all eternity. My child, that you may answer My call worthily, receive Me daily in Holy Communion. It will give you strength...

(1489b)

JULY 21

Eight-day Retreat. Eternal God, Goodness itself, whose mercy is incomprehensible to every intellect, whether human or angelic, help me, Your feeble child, to do Your holy will as You make it known to me. I desire nothing but to fulfill God's desires. Lord, here are my soul and my body, my mind and my will, my heart and all my love. Rule me according to Your eternal plans.   (492)

All my nothingness is drowned in the sea of Your mercy. With the confidence of a child, I throw myself into Your arms, O Father of Mercy, to make up for the unbelief of so many souls who are afraid to trust in You. Oh, how very few souls really know You! How ardently I desire that the Feast of Mercy be known by souls! Mercy is the crown of Your works; You provide for all with the love of a most tender mother.   (505)

JULY 22

I am reliving these moments with Our Lady. With great longing, I am waiting for the Lord's coming. Great are my desires. I desire that all humankind come to know the Lord. I would like to prepare all nations for the coming of the Word

Incarnate. O Jesus, make the fount of Your mercy gush forth more abundantly, for humankind is seriously ill and thus has more need than ever of Your compassion. You are a bottomless sea of mercy for us sinners; and the greater the misery, the more right we have to Your mercy. You are a fount which makes all creatures happy by Your infinite mercy.   (793)

JULY 23

You have surrounded my life with Your tender and loving care, more than I can comprehend, for I will understand Your goodness in its entirety only when the veil is lifted. I desire that my whole life be but one act of thanksgiving to You, O God.

(1285)

Most sweet Jesus, set on fire my love for You and transform me into Yourself. Divinize me that my deeds may be pleasing to You. May this be accomplished by the power of the Holy Communion which I receive daily. Oh, how greatly I desire to be wholly transformed into You, O Lord!   (1289)

My God, despite all the graces, I long cease to be eternally united with my God; and the better I know Him, the more ardently I desire Him.   (1303)

JULY 24

Today I heard the words: **In the Old Covenant I sent prophets wielding thunderbolts to My people. Today I am sending you with My mercy to the people of the whole world. I do not want to punish aching mankind, but I desire to heal it, pressing it to My Merciful Heart. I use punishment when they themselves**

force Me to do so; My hand is reluctant to take hold of the sword of justice. Before the Day of Justice I am sending the Day of Mercy. I replied, "O my Jesus, speak to souls Yourself, because my words are insignificant."   (1588)

JULY 25

I do not know, O Lord, at what hour You will come.
And so I keep constant watch and listen
As Your chosen bride,
Knowing that You like to come unexpected.
Yet, a pure heart will sense You from afar, O Lord.

    I wait for You, Lord, in calm and silence,
    With great longing in my heart
    And with invincible desire.
    I feel that my love for You is changing into fire,
    And that it will rise up to heaven like a flame at life's end,
    And then all my wishes will be fulfilled.

Come then, at last my most sweet Lord
And take my thirsting heart
There, to Your home in the lofty regions of heaven,
Where Your eternal life perdures.

    Life on this earth is but an agony,
    As my heart feels it is created for the heights.
    For it the lowlands of this life hold no interest,
    For my homeland is in heaven—this I firmly believe. (1589)

JULY 26

My Jesus, You see that Your holy will is everything to me. It makes no difference to me what You do with me. You command me to set to work—and I begin calmly, although I know that I am incapable of it; through Your representatives, You order me to wait—so I wait patiently; You fill my soul with enthusiasm—but You do not make it possible for me to act; You attract me to Yourself in heaven—and You leave me in this world; You pour into my soul a great yearning for Yourself—and You hide Yourself from me. I am dying of the desire to be united with You forever, and You do not let death come near me. O will of God, You are the nourishment and delight of my soul. When I submit to the holy will of my God, a deep peace floods my soul.

O my Jesus, You do not give a reward for the successful performance of a work, but for the good will and the labor undertaken. Therefore, I am completely at peace, even if all my undertakings and efforts should be thwarted or should come to naught. If I do all that is in my power, the rest is not my business. And therefore the greatest storms do not disturb the depths of my peace; the will of God dwells in my conscience. (952)

JULY 27

My heart is drawn there where my God is hidden,
Where He dwells with us day and night,
Clothed in the White Host;
He governs the whole word, He communes with souls.

My heart is drawn there where my God is hiding,
Where His love is immolated.
But my heart senses that the living water is here;
It is my living God, though a veil hides Him.   (1591)

JULY 28

During meditation, the Lord gave me knowledge of the joy of heaven and of the saints on our arrival there; they love God as the sole object of their love, but they also have a tender and heartfelt love for us. It is from the face of God that this joy flows out upon all, because we see Him face to face. His face is so sweet that the soul falls anew into ecstasy.   (1592)

The Lord Himself moves me to write prayers and hymns about His mercy, and these hymns of praise force themselves upon my lips. I have noticed that ready-formulated words of praise of God's mercy enter my mind, and so I have resolved to write them down in so far as is within my power, I can feel God urging me to do so.   (1593)

JULY 29

Today I said to the Lord, "When will You take me to Yourself? I've been feeling so ill, and I've been waiting for Your coming with such longing!" Jesus answered me, **Be always ready; I will not leave you in this exile for long. My holy will must be fulfilled in you.** O Lord, if Your holy will has not yet been entirely fulfilled in me, here I am, ready for everything that You want, O Lord! O my Jesus, there is only one thing which surprises me; namely, that You make so many secrets known to me; but that one secret—the hour of my death—You do not want to tell me. And the Lord answered me, **Be at peace; I will let you know, but not just now.** Ah, my Lord, I beg Your pardon for wanting to know this. You know very well why, because You know my yearning heart, which is eagerly going out to You. You know that I would not want to die even a minute before the time which You have appointed for me before the ages. Jesus listened with wondrous kindness to the outpourings of my heart.   (1539)

O my God, I am overcome with great longing for You today. Oh, nothing else any longer occupies my heart. The earth no longer contains anything for me. O Jesus, how strongly I feel this exile, how very prolonged it is for me! O death, messenger of God, when will you announce to me that longed-for moment, through which I will be united to my God forever?
                                                      (1573)

JULY 30

My day is drawing to a close,
Even now I glimpse the refulgence of Your light, O my God.
No one shall learn of what my heart is feeling;
My lips shall fall silent in great humility.

Even now, I draw night to the eternal nuptials,
To heaven unending, to spaces without limit.
I long for no repose or reward;
The pure love of God draws me to heaven.

Even now, I go to meet You, eternal Love,
With a heart languishing in its desire for You.
I feel that Your pure love, Lord, dwells in my heart,
And I sense my eternal destiny in heaven.

Even now, I go to my Father, in heaven eternal,
From the land of exile, from this vale of tears,
The earth can no longer hold back my pure heart,
And the heights of heaven have drawn me close.

I go, O my Bridegroom, I go to see Your glory,
Which even now fills my soul with joy
There where all heaven is plunged in Your adoration.
I feel that my worship is pleasing to You,
    nothingness though I am.

In eternal happiness, I will not forget those on earth,
I will obtain God's mercy for all,
And I will remember especially those who
    were dear to my heart,
And the deepest absorption in God
    will not allow me to forget them.

In these last moments I know not how to converse with others.
In silence I await only You, O Lord.
I know the time will come when all will understand the work
    of God in my soul.
I know that such is Your will. So be it.   (1653b)

JULY 31

Good night, my Jesus; the bell is calling me to sleep. My Jesus,
You see that I am dying from the desire to save souls. Good
night, my Beloved; I rejoice at being one day closer to eternity.
And if You let me wake up tomorrow, Jesus, I shall begin a new
hymn to Your praise.   (679)

Jesus, You know that I love suffering and want to drain the cup of suffering to the last drop; and yet, my nature experienced a slight shudder and fear. Quickly, however, my trust in the infinite mercy of God was awakened in all its force, and everything else had to give way before it, like a shadow retreating before the sun's rays. O Jesus, how great is Your goodness! Your infinite goodness, so well known to me, enables me to bravely look death itself in the eye. I know that nothing will happen to me without God's permission. I desire to glorify Your infinite mercy during my life, at the hour of death, in the resurrection and throughout eternity.

My Jesus, my strength, my peace, my repose; my soul bathes daily in the rays of Your mercy. There is not a moment in my life when I do not experience Your mercy, O God. I could do nothing in my whole life, but only on Your infinite mercy. It is the guiding thread of my life, O Lord. My soul is filled with God's mercy.   (697)

UNION

August

THE TEXTS OF THE Diary of Blessed Faustina on union with God reveal an extraordinary *call* to her by Christ to a rare and intimate spiritual union with Him. Christ called her to constantly unite herself with Him in an intimate and unique union, like no other person was united with Him. This is truly a "Mystery of Mercy" as Blessed Faustina called it—that the almighty God should so humble Himself out of love for her.

In a simple, humble, and beautiful way, Blessed Faustina described her union with God as an intimate and continuous presence, penetrating and permeating her whole being. Had she not been sustained by the Lord's strength, especially by Holy Communion, she could not have endured this union. However, it was through this union that Blessed Faustina experienced mysteries and special graces. United with Jesus, she was enabled to plead for the salvation of souls. From this union, her mission of mercy was powerful on earth, and now continues in heaven.

FOR THIS MONTH:

Practice: Live in the presence of God dwelling in your heart.

Prayer: Draw me Lord, that I may be drawn.
    Love me that I may love.

Promise: Live on in me, as I do in you.... As the Father has loved me, so I have loved you. Live on in my love (Jn 15:4-9).

AUGUST 1

When a soul has come out of these tribulations, it is deeply humble. Its purity of soul is great. It knows better without need of reflecting, as it were, what it ought to do at a given moment and what to forbear. It feels the lightest touch of grace and is very faithful to God. It recognizes God from afar and continuously rejoices in Him. It discovers God very quickly in other souls and in its environment in general. The soul has been purified by God Himself. God, as Pure Spirit, introduces the soul to a life which is purely spiritual. God Himself has first prepared and purified the soul; that is, He has made it capable of close communion with Himself. The soul, in a state of loving repose, communes spiritually with the Lord. It speaks to God without the need of expressing itself through the senses. God fills it with His light.

The enlightened mind sees clearly and distinguishes the various degrees of the spiritual life. It recognizes [that state] when its union with God was imperfect: where the senses were involved, and the spirit was linked with the senses in a manner—exalted and special, to be sure—but not yet perfect. There is a higher and more perfect union with God; namely, intellectual union. Here, the soul is safer from illusions; its spirituality is purer and more profound. In a life where the senses are involved, there is more danger of illusion. Both for the soul and for its confessor, prudence must play a greater part. There are moments when God introduces the soul to a purely spiritual state. The senses dim and are seemingly dead. The soul is most closely united to God; it is immersed in the Deity; its knowledge is complete and perfect, not sporadic as before, but total and absolute. It rejoices in this. But I want to say more about those moments of trial; at those times the confessor must have patience with such a soul. But the soul must have even greater patience with itself.   (115)

AUGUST 2

There is a series of graces which God pours into the soul after these trials by fire. The soul enjoys intimate union with God. It has many visions, both corporeal and intellectual. It hears many supernatural words, and sometimes distinct orders. But despite these graces, it is not self-sufficient. In fact it is even less so as a result of God's graces, because it is now open to many dangers and can easily fall prey to illusions. It ought to ask God for a spiritual director; but not only must it pray for one, it must also make every effort to find a leader who is an expert in these things, just as a military leader must know the ways along which he will lead [his followers] into battle. A soul that is united with God must be prepared for great and hard-fought battles.

After these purifications and tears, God abides in the soul in a special way, but the soul does not always cooperate with these graces. Not that the soul itself is not willing to work, but it encounters so many interior and exterior difficulties that it really takes a miracle to sustain the soul on these summits. In this, it absolutely needs a director. People have often sown doubt in my soul, and I myself have sometimes become frightened at the thought that I was, after all, an ignorant person and did not have knowledge of many things, above all, spiritual things. But when my doubts increased, I sought light from my confessor or my superiors. Yet I did not obtain what I desired.   (121)

AUGUST 3

Suddenly, when I had consented to the sacrifice with all my heart and all my will, God's presence pervaded me. My soul became immersed in God and was inundated with such happiness that I cannot put in writing even the smallest part of it. I felt that His Majesty was enveloping me. I was extraordinarily fused with God. I saw that God was well pleased with me and, reciprocally, my spirit drowned itself in Him. Aware of this union with God, I felt I was especially loved and, in turn, I loved with all my soul. A great mystery took place during that adoration, a mystery between the Lord and myself. It seemed to me that I would die of love [at the sight of] His glance. I spoke much with the Lord, without uttering a single word. And the Lord said to me, **You are the delight of My Heart; from today on, every one of your acts, even the very smallest, will be a delight to My eyes, whatever you do.** At that moment I felt transconsecrated. My earthly body was the same, but my soul was different; God was now living in it with the totality of His delight. This is not a feeling, but a conscious reality that nothing can obscure. (137)

AUGUST 4

A great mystery has been accomplished between God and me. Courage and strength have remained in my soul. When the time of adoration came to an end, I came out and calmly faced everything I had feared so much before. When I came out into the corridor, a great suffering and humiliation, at the hands of a certain person, was awaiting me. I accepted it with submission to a higher will and snuggled closely to the Most Sacred Heart of Jesus, letting Him know that I was ready for that which I had offered myself.

Suffering seemed to spring out of the ground. Even Mother Margaret herself was surprised. For others, many things passed unnoticed, for indeed it wasn't worth paying any attention to them; but in my case, nothing passed unnoticed; each word was analyzed, each step watched. One sister said to me, "Get ready, Sister, to receive a small cross at the hands of Mother Superior. I feel sorry for you." But as for me, I rejoiced at this in the depths of my soul and had been ready for it for a long time. When she saw my courage, she was surprised. I see now that a soul cannot do much itself, but with God it can do all things. Behold what God's grace can do. Few are the souls that are always watchful for divine graces, and even fewer of such souls who follow those inspirations faithfully.   (138)

AUGUST 5

When I was set at peace and taught how to follow God's paths, my spirit rejoiced in the Lord, and it seemed to me that I was running, not walking. My wings were spread for flight; I soared into the very heat of the sun, and I will not descend until I rest in Him, in whom my soul has lost itself forever. And I subjected myself totally to the action of grace. God stoops very low to my soul. I do not draw back, nor do I resist Him, but I lose myself in Him as my only treasure. I am one with the Lord. It is as if the gulf between us, Creator and creature, disappears. For a few days, my soul was in a state of continuous ecstasy. God's presence did not leave me for a single moment. And my soul remained in a continuous loving union with the Lord. But this in no way interfered with the performance of my duties. I felt I was transformed into love; I was all afire, but without being burned up. I lost myself in God unceasingly; God drew me to Himself so strongly and powerfully that sometimes I was not aware of being on earth. I had impeded and feared God's grace for so long, and now God himself, through Father Andrasz, has removed all difficulties. My spirit has been turned towards the Sun and has blossomed in His rays for Him alone; I understand no more... [The sentence breaks off here and begins a completely new thought in the next line.]

(142)

AUGUST 6

Union with Jesus on the day of perpetual vows. Jesus, from now on Your Heart is mine, and mine is Yours alone. The very thought of Your Name, Jesus, is the delight of my heart. I truly would not be able to live without You, even for a moment, Jesus. Today my soul has lost itself in You, my only treasure. My love knows no obstacles in giving proof of itself to its Beloved.

The words of Jesus during my perpetual vows: **My spouse, our hearts are joined forever. Remember to Whom you have vowed**... everything cannot be put into words.

My petition while we were lying prostrate under the pall. I begged the Lord to grant me the grace of never consciously and deliberately offending Him by even the smallest sin or imperfection.

Jesus, I trust in You! Jesus, I love You with all my heart! When times are most difficult, You are my Mother.

For love of You, O Jesus, I die completely to myself today and begin to live for the greater glory of Your Holy Name.

Love, it is for love of You, O Most Holy Trinity, that I offer myself to You as an oblation of praise, as a holocaust of total self-immolation. And through this self-immolation, I desire the exaltation of Your Name, O Lord. I cast myself as a little rosebud at Your feet, O Lord, and may the fragrance of this flower be known to You alone. (239)

AUGUST 7

I often feel God's presence after Holy Communion in a special and tangible way. I know God is in my heart. And the fact that I feel Him in my heart does not interfere with my duties. Even when I am dealing with very important matters which require attention, I do not lose the presence of God in my soul, and I am closely united with Him. With Him I go to work, with Him I go for recreation, with Him I suffer, with Him I rejoice; I live in Him and He in me. I am never alone, because He is my constant companion. He is present to me at every moment. Our intimacy is very close, through a union of blood and of life. (318)

December 24, 1934. The Vigil of Christmas. During the morning Mass, I felt the closeness of God. Though I was hardly aware of it, my spirit was drowned in God. Suddenly, I heard these words: **You are My delightful dwelling place; My Spirit rests in you.** After these words, I felt the Lord looking into the depths of my heart; and seeing my misery, I humbled myself in spirit and admired the immense mercy of God, that the Most High Lord would approach such misery.

During Holy Communion, joy filled my soul. I felt that I am closely united to the Godhead. His omnipotence enveloped my whole being. Throughout the whole day I felt the closeness of God in a special manner; and although my duties prevented me throughout the whole day from going to chapel even for a moment, there was not a moment when I was not united with God. I felt Him within me more distinctly than ever. Unceasingly greeting the Mother of God and entering into her spirit, I begged her to teach me true love of God. And then I heard these words: *I will share with you the secret of my happiness this night during Holy Mass.* (346)

AUGUST 8

Oh, how astonished I was, for everything the Father said about union with God and the obstacles to this union I had experienced literally in my soul and heard from Jesus, who speaks to me in the depths of my soul. Perfection consists in this close union with God. (457)

Throughout the whole retreat, I was in uninterrupted communion with Jesus and entered into an intimate relationship with Him with all the might of my heart. (467)

AUGUST 9

September 29. The Feast of St. Michael the Archangel. I have become interiorly united with God. His presence penetrates me to my very depths and fills me with peace, joy, and amazement. After such moments of prayer, I am filled with strength and an extraordinary courage to suffer and struggle. Nothing terrifies me, even if the whole world should turn against me. All adversities touch only the surface, but they have no entry to the depths, because God, Who strengthens me, Who fills me, dwells there. All the snares of the enemy are crushed at His footstool. During these moments of union, God sustains me with His might. His might passes on to me and makes me capable of loving Him. A soul never reaches this state by its own efforts. At the beginning of this interior grace, I was filled with fright, and I started to give in to it; but very quickly, the Lord let me know how much this displeases Him. But it is also He, Himself, who set my fears at rest. (480)

O my God, I am conscious of my mission in the Holy Church. It is my constant endeavor to plead for mercy for the world. I unite myself closely with Jesus and stand before Him as an atoning sacrifice on behalf of the world. God will refuse me nothing when I entreat Him with the voice of His Son. My sacrifice is nothing in itself, but when I join it to the sacrifice of Jesus Christ, it becomes all-powerful and has the power to appease divine wrath. God loves us in His Son; the painful Passion of the Son of God constantly turns aside the wrath of God. (482)

AUGUST 10

Jesus, when You come to me in Holy Communion, You Who together with the Father and the Holy Spirit have deigned to dwell in the little heaven of my heart, I try to keep You company throughout the day, I do not leave You alone for even a moment. Although I am in the company of other people or with our wards, my heart is always united to Him. When I am asleep I offer Him every beat of my heart; when I awaken I immerse myself in Him without saying a word. When I awaken I adore the Holy Trinity for a short while and thank God for having deigned to give me yet another day, that the mystery of the incarnation of His Son may once more be repeated in me, and that once again His sorrowful Passion may unfold before my eyes. I then try to make it easier for Jesus to pass through me to other souls. I go everywhere with Jesus; His presence accompanies me everywhere. (486)

When I entered the chapel, once again the majesty of God overwhelmed me. I felt that I was immersed in God, totally immersed in Him and penetrated by Him, being aware of how much the heavenly Father loves us. Oh, what great happiness fills my heart from knowing God and the divine life! It is my desire to share this happiness with all people. I cannot keep this happiness locked in my own heart alone, for His flames burn me and cause my bosom and my entrails to burst asunder. I desire to go throughout the whole world and speak to souls about the great mercy of God. Priests, help me in this; use the strongest words [at your disposal] to proclaim His mercy, for every word falls short of how merciful He really is. (491)

AUGUST 11

O Holy Trinity, Eternal God, my spirit is drowned in Your beauty. The ages are as nothing in Your sight. You are always the same. Oh, how great is Your Majesty. Jesus, why do You conceal Your Majesty, why have You left Your heavenly throne and dwelt among us? The Lord answered me, **My daughter, love has brought Me here, and love keeps Me here. My daughter, if you knew what great merit and reward is earned by one act of pure love for Me, you would die of joy. I am saying this that you may constantly unite yourself with Me through love, for this is the goal of the life of your soul. This act is an act of the will. Know that a pure soul is humble. When you lower and empty yourself before My Majesty, I then pursue you with My graces and make use of My omnipotence to exalt you.** (576)

AUGUST 12

Once, when my confessor told me to say "Glory be to the Father" as my penance, it took me a very long time; and I began many times, but did not finish, because my spirit became united with God, and I could not stick to the prayer. Quite frequently, I am unwittingly enveloped by God's omnipotence and become entirely plunged in Him through love, and then I do not know what is going on around me. When I told my confessor that this short prayer often takes very much of my time and that sometimes I cannot even finish it, he told me to say it right away, there, at the confessional. However, my spirit became immersed in God and, in spite of my efforts, I could not think as I wished. And so the confessor said, "Please repeat after me." I repeated every word, but while I was pronouncing each word, my spirit would be steeped in the Person I was naming. (577)

AUGUST 13

October 2, 1936, the First Friday of the month. After Holy Communion, I suddenly saw the Lord Jesus, who spoke these words to me: **Now I know that it is not for the graces or gifts that you love me, but because My will is dearer to you than life. That is why I am uniting Myself with you so intimately as with no other creature.** (707)

At that moment, Jesus disappeared. My soul was filled with the presence of God. I know that the gaze of the Mighty One rests upon me. I plunged myself completely in the joy that flows from God. I continued throughout the whole day without interruption, thus immersed in God. In the evening, I fell as if into a faint and a strange sort of agony. My love wants to equal the love of the Mighty One. It is drawn to Him so vehemently that it is impossible, without some special grace from God, to bear the vastness of such a grace in this life. But I see clearly that Jesus Himself is sustaining me and strengthening me and making me capable of communing with Him. In all this, the soul is particularly active. (708)

It sometimes happens, while I am listening to the meditation, that one word puts me in very close union with the Lord, and I no longer know what Father is saying. I know that I am close to the most merciful Heart of Jesus; my whole spirit is entirely plunged in Him, and in one moment I learn more than during long hours of intellectual inquiry and meditation. These are sudden lights which permit me to know things as God sees them, regarding matters of both the interior and the exterior world. (733)

AUGUST 14

Union with the merciful Christ. With my heart I encompass the whole world, especially countries which are uncivilized or where there is persecution. I am praying for mercy upon them. (742)

Jesus, my spirit yearns for You, and I desire very much to be united with You, but Your works hold me back. The number of souls that I am to bring to You is not yet complete. I desire toil and suffering; let everything You have planned before the ages be fulfilled in me, O my Creator and Lord! It is only Your word that I understand; it alone gives me strength. Your Spirit, O Lord, is the Spirit of Peace; and nothing troubles my depths because You dwell there, O Lord.

I know that I am under Your special gaze, O Lord. I do not examine with fear Your plans regarding me; my task is to accept everything from Your hand. I do not fear anything, although the storm is raging, and frightful bolts strike all around me, and I then feel quite alone. Yet, my heart senses You, and my trust grows, and I see all Your omnipotence which upholds me. With You, Jesus, I go through life, amid storms and rainbows, with a cry of joy, singing the song of Your mercy. I will not stop singing my song of love until the choir of Angels picks it up. There is no power that can stop me in my flight toward God. I see that even the superiors do not always understand the road along which God is leading me, and I am not surprised at this.   (761)

AUGUST 15

My communion with the Lord is now purely spiritual. My soul is touched by God and wholly absorbs itself in Him, even to the complete forgetfulness of self. Permeated by God to its very depths, it drowns in His beauty; it completely dissolves in Him—I am at a loss to describe this, because in writing I am making use of the senses; but there, in that union, the senses are not active; there is a merging of God and the soul; and the life of God to which the soul is admitted is so great that the human tongue cannot express it.

When the soul returns to its habitual form of life, it then sees that this life is all darkness and mist and dreamlike confusion, an infant's swaddling clothes. In such moments the soul only receives from God, for of itself it does nothing; it does not make even the slightest effort; all is wrought by God. But when the soul returns to its ordinary state, it sees that it is not within its power to continue in this union.

These moments are short, but their effects are lasting. The soul cannot remain long in this state; or else it would be forcibly freed of the bonds of the body forever. Even as it is, it is sustained by a miracle of God. God allows the soul to know in a clear way how much He loves it, as though it were the only object of His delight. The soul recognizes this clearly and without a veil, so to speak. It reaches out for God with all its might, but it feels like a baby; it knows that this is not within its power. Therefore, God descends to the soul and unites it to himself in a way that... here, I must be silent, for I cannot describe what the soul experiences. (767)

AUGUST 16

It is a strange thing that although the soul which experiences this union with God cannot find words and expressions to describe it, nevertheless, when it meets a similar soul, the two understand each other extraordinarily well in regard to these matters, even though they speak but little with each other. A soul united with God in this way easily recognizes a similar soul, even if the latter has not revealed its interior [life] to it, but merely speaks in an ordinary way. It is a kind of spiritual kinship. Souls united with God in this way are few, fewer than we think. (768)

I have noticed that the Lord grants this grace to souls for two purposes. The first is when the soul is to do some great work which is, humanly speaking, absolutely beyond its power. In the second case, I have noticed that the Lord grants it in order that kindred souls might be guided and set at peace, although the Lord can grant this grace as He pleases and to whomever He pleases. However, I have noticed this grace in three priests, one of whom is a secular priest [probably Father Sopocko] and the other two, religious priests [probably Father Elter and Father Andrasz], and also in two religious sisters [probably Mother Michael and Sister Mary Joseph], but not in the same degree. (769)

AUGUST 17

Great is the mutual exchange between the soul and God. When the soul leaves its concealment, the senses get a taste of what the soul has delighted in. Although this also is a great grace from God, it is not a purely spiritual one, for in the first moments the senses do not take part. Every grace gives the soul power and strength to act, and courage to suffer. The soul knows very well what God is asking of it, and it carries out His holy will despite adversities. (772)

Today I was in heaven, in spirit, and I saw its inconceivable beauties and the happiness that awaits us after death. I saw how all creatures give ceaseless praise and glory to God. I saw how great is happiness in God, which spreads to all creatures, making them happy; and then all the glory and praise which springs from this happiness returns to its source; and they enter into the depths of God, contemplating the inner life of God, the Father, the Son, and the Holy Spirit, Whom they will never comprehend or fathom.

This source of happiness is unchanging in its essence, but it is always new, gushing forth happiness for all creatures. Now I understand Saint Paul, who said, "Eye has not seen, nor has ear heard, nor has it entered into the heart of man what God has prepared for those who love Him." (777)

AUGUST 18

The sight of this great majesty of God, which I came to understand more profoundly and which is worshiped by the heavenly spirits according to their degree of grace and the hierarchies into which they are divided, did not cause my soul to be stricken with terror or fear; no, no, not at all! My soul was filled with peace and love, and the more I come to know the greatness of God, the more joyful I become that He is as He is. And I rejoice immensely in His greatness and am delighted that I am so little because, since I am little, He carries me in His arms and holds me close to His Heart.   (779)

O my God, how I pity those people who do not believe in eternal life; how I pray for them that a ray of mercy would envelop them too, and that God would clasp them to His fatherly bosom.   (780)

In this seclusion, Jesus Himself is my Master. He Himself educates and instructs me. I feel that I am the object of His special action. For His inscrutable purposes and unfathomable decrees, He unites me to Himself in a special way and allows me to penetrate His incomprehensible mysteries. There is one mystery which unites me with the Lord, of which no one—not even Angels—may know. And even if I wanted to tell of it, I would not know how to express it. And yet, I live by it and will live by it forever. This mystery distinguishes me from every other soul here on earth or in eternity.   (824)

AUGUST 19

January 8. On Friday morning, as I was going to the chapel to attend Holy Mass, I suddenly saw a huge juniper tree on the pavement and in it a horrible cat who, looking angrily at me, blocked my way to the chapel. One whisper of the name of Jesus dissipated all that. I offered the whole day for dying sinners. During Holy Mass, I felt the closeness of the Lord in a special way. After Holy Communion, I turned my gaze with trust toward the Lord and told him, "Jesus, I so much desire to tell You something." And the Lord looked at me with love and said, **And what is it that you desire to tell Me?**

"Jesus, I beg You, by the inconceivable power of Your mercy, that all the souls who will die today escape the fire of hell, even if they have been the greatest sinners. Today is Friday, the memorial of Your bitter agony on the Cross; because Your mercy is inconceivable, the Angels will not be surprised at this." Jesus pressed me to His Heart and said, **My beloved daughter, you have come to know well the depths of My mercy. I will do what you ask, but unite yourself continually with My agonizing Heart and make reparation to My justice. Know that you have asked Me for a great thing, but I see that this was dictated by your pure love for Me; that is why I am complying with your requests.** (873)

AUGUST 20

Nothing disturbs my union with the Lord, neither conversation with others nor any duties; even if I am to go about settling very important matters, this does not disturb me. My spirit is with God, and my interior being is filled with God, so I do not look for Him outside myself. He, the Lord, penetrates my soul just as a ray from the sun penetrates clear glass. When I was enclosed in my mother's womb, I was not so closely united with her as I am with my God. There, it was an unawareness; but here, it is the fullness of reality and the consciousness of

union. My visions are purely interior, but the more I understand them, the less I am able to express them in words. (883)

Jesus, give me the strength and wisdom to get through this terrible wilderness, that my heart may bear patiently this longing
for You, O my Lord! I always remain in holy amazement when
I sense that You are approaching me, You, the Lord of the
awesome throne; that You descend to this miserable exile and
visit this poor beggar who has nothing but misery! I do not
know how to entertain You, my Royal Prince, but You know
that I love You with every beat of my heart. I see how You
lower yourself, but nevertheless Your majesty does not diminish in my eyes. I know that You love me with the love of a
bridegroom, and that is enough for me. Although we are separated by a great chasm, for You are the Creator and I am Your
creature, nevertheless, love alone explains our union. Without
it, all is incomprehensible. Only love makes it possible to
understand these incomprehensible intimacies with which
You visit me. O Jesus, Your greatness terrifies me, and I would
be in constant astonishment and fear, if You Yourself did not
set me at peace. You make me capable of communing with
You before each approach.   (885)

AUGUST 21

January 21, 1937. Since early morning today, I have been won-
drously united with the Lord. In the evening, the hospital
chaplain visited me. After we had talked for a while, I felt my
spirit beginning to immerse itself in God, and I began to lose
all sense of what was happening around me. I ardently
implored Jesus, "Give me the ability to talk." And the Lord
granted that I could talk freely with him. But there was a
moment when I could not understand what the priest was say-

ing. I heard his voice, but it was impossible for me to understand him, and I apologized for not understanding him although I could hear his voice. This is a moment of the grace of union with God, but imperfect, because exteriorly the senses are acting imperfectly too. There is no total immersion in God; that is, suspension of the senses, as often happens when one neither sees nor hears anything exteriorly, the whole soul being freely absorbed in God. When such a grace visits me, I want to be alone, and I ask Jesus to protect me from the eyes of creatures. I was really very embarrassed before the priest, but I was reassured, because he got to know a little of my soul in confession.   (891)

AUGUST 22

Then I heard the following words spoken thus: **I want you to be My spouse.** Fear pierced my soul, but I calmly continued to reflect on what sort of an espousal this could be. However, each time fear would invade my soul, a power from on high would give it peace.

After all, I have taken perpetual vows, and I have taken them of my own completely free will. And so I continued to reflect on what this could mean. I sensed, and came to realize, that this was some special kind of grace. Whenever I think about it, I feel faint for God, but in this swooning, my mind is clear and penetrated with light. When I am united to Him, I faint from an abundance of happiness, but my mind is bright and clear and free from all shadows. You abase Your majesty to dwell with a poor creature. Thank you, O Lord, for this great grace that makes it possible for me to commune with You. Jesus, Your Name is my delight, I have a presentiment of my Beloved from afar, and my languishing soul rests in His embrace; I don't know how to live without Him. I would rather be with Him in afflictions and suffering than without Him in the greatest heavenly delights. (912)

February 19, 1937. Contact with the dying. They ask me for prayer, and I can pray, as the Lord grants me an extraordinary spirit of prayer. I am constantly united with Him, and I am fully aware that I live for souls in order to bring them to Your mercy, O Lord. In this matter, no sacrifice is too insignificant. (971)

AUGUST 23

Today, the Majesty of God enveloped and transpierced my soul to its very depths. The greatness of God is pervading my being and flooding me so that I am completely drowning in His greatness. I am dissolving and disappearing entirely in Him as in my life-source, as in perfect life. (983)

My Lord and my God, You know that it is You alone whom my soul has come to love. My soul is entirely drowned in You, O Lord. Even if I did not accomplish any of the things that You have made known to me, O Lord, I would be completely at peace because I would have done what I could. (989)

This evening, when I heard the hymn, "Good night, Holy Head of my Jesus," on the radio, my spirit was suddenly swept away to God's mysterious bosom, and I knew in what the greatness of a soul consists and what matters to God: love, love, and once again, love. And I understood how all that exists is saturated with God, and such a love of God inundated my soul that I am at a loss to describe it. Happy the soul that knows how to love unreservedly, for in this lies its greatness. (997)

AUGUST 24

At eleven o'clock Jesus said to me, **My host, you are refresh-ment for My tormented Heart.** I thought, after these words, that my heart would burn up. And He brought me into such close intimacy with Himself that my heart was espoused to His Heart in a loving union, and I could feel the faintest stir of His Heart and He, of mine. The fire of my created love was joined to the ardor of His eternal love. This one grace surpasses all others in its immensity. His Trinitarian Being enveloped me entirely, and I am totally immersed in Him. My littleness is, as it were, wrestling with this Immortal Mighty One. I am immersed in incomprehensible love and incomprehensible torture because of His Passion. All that concerns His Being is imparted to me also.   (1056)

Up to now, Jesus has been bringing me to know about, and to have a presentiment of, this grace, but today He granted it to me. I would not even dare to dream about it. My heart is in ceaseless ecstasy, as it were, although outwardly nothing dis-turbs my contacts with my neighbor or my attending to various matters. Nothing is capable of interrupting my ecstasy, nor can anyone suspect it, because I have asked God to protect me from detection by people. And, together with this grace, there entered my soul a whole ocean of light, enabling me to under-stand God and myself. Amazement overwhelms me entirely and leads me as if into a new ecstasy [aroused by the fact] that God has deigned to descend to me, who am so little.   (1057)

AUGUST 25

This deeper knowledge of God gives me full liberty and spiri-tual freedom, and nothing can disturb my close union with

Him, not even the angelic powers. I feel that I am great when I am united to God. What happiness it is to have the consciousness of God in one's heart and to live in close intimacy with Him. (1135)

In the evening, He gave me to understand how fleeting all earthly things are, and [how] everything that appears great disappears like smoke, and does not give the soul freedom, but weariness. Happy the soul that understands these things and with only one foot touches the earth. My repose is to be united with You; everything else tires me. Oh, how much I feel I am in exile! I see that no one understands my interior life. You alone understand me, You who are hidden in my heart and yet are eternally alive. (1141)

Today, my soul entered into close union with the Lord. He made known to me how I should always abandon myself to His holy will: **In one moment, I can give you more than you are able to desire.** (1169)

AUGUST 26

August 1937. After Holy Communion, I saw the Lord Jesus in all His majesty, and He said to me, **My daughter, during the weeks when you neither saw Me nor felt My presence, I was more profoundly united to you than at times** [when you experienced] **ecstasy. And the faithfulness and fragrance of your prayer have reached Me.** After these words, my soul became flooded with God's consolation. I did not see Jesus, and there was only one word I could utter and that was: "Jesus." And after pronouncing that Name, my soul was again filled with light and deeper recollection, which lasted uninterruptedly for three days. However, outwardly I could still carry out my usual duties.

My whole being was stirred to its most secret depths. God's greatness does not frighten me, but makes me happy. By giving Him glory, I myself am lifted up. On seeing His happiness, I myself am made happy, because all that is in Him flows back upon me. (1246)

AUGUST 27

I receive Holy Communion in the manner of the Angels, so to speak. My soul is filled with God's light and nourishes itself from Him. My feelings are as if dead. This is a purely spiritual union with God; it is a great predominance of spirit over nature. (1278)

The Lord gave me knowledge of the graces which He has been constantly lavishing on me. This light pierced me through and through, and I came to understand the inconceivable favors that God has been bestowing on me. I stayed in my cell for a long act of thanksgiving, lying face down on the ground and shedding tears of gratitude. I could not rise from the ground because, whenever I tried to do so, God's light gave me new knowledge of His grace. It was only at the third attempt that I was able to get up. As His child, I felt that everything the heavenly Father possessed was equally mine. He Himself lifted me from the ground up to His Heart. I felt that everything that existed was exclusively mine, but I had no desire for it all, because God alone is enough for me. (1279)

Today, I have come to understand many of God's mysteries. I have come to know that Holy Communion remains in me until the next Holy Communion. A vivid and clearly felt presence of God continues in my soul. The awareness of this plunges me into deep recollection, without the slightest effort on my part. My heart is a living tabernacle in which the living Host is reserved. I have never sought God in some far-off place, but within myself. It is in the depths of my own being that I commune with my God. (1302)

AUGUST 28

Unity with the merciful Christ. Because I am united to Jesus, I must be faithful always and everywhere, and I must be interiorly united with the Lord, while exteriorly observing fidelity to the rule, particularly that of silence. (1352)

At that moment, the Lord gave me to know how jealous He is of my heart.

Even among the sisters you will feel lonely. Know then that I want you to unite yourself more closely to Me. I am concerned about every beat of your heart. Every stirring of your love is reflected in My Heart. I thirst for your love. "Yes, O Jesus, but my heart would not be able to live without You, either; for even if the hearts of all creatures were offered to me, they would not satisfy the depths of my heart." (1542)

AUGUST 29

When I had gone to the chapel for a moment, the Lord gave me to know that, among His chosen ones, there are some who are especially chosen, and whom He calls to a higher form of holiness, to exceptional union with Him. These are seraphic souls, from whom God demands greater love than He does from others. Although all live in the same convent, yet He sometimes demands of a particular soul a greater degree of love. Such a soul understands this call, because God makes this known to it interiorly, but the soul may either follow this call or not. It depends on the soul itself whether it is faithful to these touches of the Holy Spirit, or whether it resists them. I have learned that there is a place in purgatory where souls will pay their debt to God for such transgressions; this kind of torment is the most difficult of all. The soul which is specially marked by God will be distinguished everywhere, whether in heaven or in purgatory or in hell. In heaven, it will be distinguished from other souls by greater glory and radiance and deeper knowledge of God. In purgatory, by greater pain, because it knows God more profoundly and desires Him more vehemently. In hell, it will suffer more profoundly than other souls, because it knows more fully Whom it has lost. This indelible mark of God's exclusive love, in the [soul], will not be obliterated.   (1556)

At that moment, the light of God penetrated my being, and I felt that I was God's exclusive property; and I experienced the greatest spiritual freedom, of which I had had no previous idea. And at the same time, I saw the glory of the Divine Mercy and an infinite multitude of souls who were praising His goodness. My soul was completely drowned in God, and I heard the words, **You are My well-beloved daughter.** The vivid presence of God continued throughout the whole day.   (1681)

AUGUST 30

Today, my preparation for the coming of Jesus is brief, but imprinted deeply with vehement love. The presence of God penetrates me and sets aflame my love for Him. There are no words; there is only interior understanding. I drown completely in God through love. The Lord approaches the dwelling of my heart. After receiving Communion, I have just enough presence of mind to return to my kneeler. At the same time, my soul is completely lost in God, and I no longer know what is going on about me. God gives me an interior knowledge of His Divine Being. These moments are short, but penetrating. The soul leaves the chapel in profound recollection, and it is not easy to distract it. At such times, I touch the ground with only one foot, as it were. No sacrifice throughout such a day is either difficult or burdensome. Every situation evokes a new act of love. (1807)

Today, I invite Jesus to my heart, as Love. You are Love itself. All heaven catches the flame from You and is filled with love. And so my soul covets You as a flower yearns for the sun. Jesus, hasten to my heart, for You see that, as the flower is eager for the sun, so my heart is for You. I open the calyx of my heart to receive Your love. (1808)

AUGUST 31

What am I, and who are You, O Lord, King of eternal glory? O my heart, are you aware of who is coming to you today? Yes, I know, but—strangely—I am not able to grasp it. Oh, if He were just a king, but He is the King of kings, the Lord of lords. Before Him, all power and dominion tremble. He is coming to my heart today. But I hear Him approaching. I go out to meet Him and invite Him. When He entered the dwelling of my heart, it was filled with such reverence that it fainted with fear, falling at His feet. Jesus gives her His hand and graciously permits her to take her place beside Him. He reassures her, saying, **See, I have left My heavenly throne to become united with you. What you see is just a tiny part and already your soul swoons with love. How amazed will your heart be when you see Me in all My glory.** (1810)

But I want to tell you that eternal life must begin already here on earth through Holy Communion. Each Holy Communion makes you more capable of communing with God throughout eternity.

And so, my King, I do not ask You for anything, although I know that You can give me everything. I ask You for one thing only: Remain forever the King of my heart; that is enough for me. (1811)

GOD'S WILL

September

"HUMBLE OBEDIENCE to the will of God," stands out as a very special characteristic of the life of Sister Faustina, as she offered herself as a victim of love for sinners. In this "humble obedience to the will of God," she not only imitated and identified with Jesus (see Philippians 2:7-8), but also with Mary, the Mother of God. In her humble obedience to the will of God, Blessed Faustina was instructed by both Jesus and Mary in order to be fully identified with them.

We learn from Blessed Faustina that (our) seeking and desiring to do God's will is a giant step in fulfilling His will. Each time we pray the Our Father we express our desire for His will to be done, that He reign among us and His kingdom come.

FOR THIS MONTH:

Practice: Be humbly obedient to the will of God in your state of life.

Prayer: Pray the Our Father slowly, especially: "Thy will be done." Repeat it often.

Promise: It is when you submit yourself to My will that you give me the greatest glory and draw down upon yourself a sea of blessings (954).

SEPTEMBER 1

I am to write down the encounters of my soul with You, O God, at the moments of Your special visitations. I am to write about You, O Incomprehensible in mercy towards my poor soul. Your holy will is the life of my soul. I have received this order through him who is for me Your representative here on earth, who interprets Your holy will to me. Jesus, You see how difficult it is for me to write, how unable I am to put down clearly what I experience in my soul. O God, can a pen write down that for which many a time there are no words? But You give the order to write, O God; that is enough for me.   (6)

O my Jesus, You have tested me so many times in this short life of mine! I have come to understand so many things, and even such that now amaze me. Oh, how good it is to abandon oneself totally to God and to give Him full freedom to act in one's soul!   (134)

SEPTEMBER 2

O Jesus, today my soul is as though darkened by suffering. Not a single ray of light. The storm is raging, and Jesus is asleep. O my Master, I will not wake You; I will not interrupt Your sweet sleep. I believe that You fortify me without my knowing it. Throughout the long hours I adore You, O living Bread, amidst the great drought in my soul. O Jesus, pure Love, I do not need consolations; I am nourished by Your will, O Mighty One! Your will is the goal of my existence. It seems to me that the whole world serves me and depends on me. You, O Lord, understand my soul with all its aspirations. Jesus, when I myself cannot sing You the hymn of love, I admire the singing of the Seraphim, they who are so dearly loved by You. I desire to drown myself in You as they do. Nothing will stem such love, for no might has power over it. It is like lightning that illuminates the darkness, but does not remain in it. O my Master, shape my soul according to Your will and Your eternal designs! (195)

After perpetual vows, I stayed in Cracow throughout the month of May, because it was undecided whether I was to go to Rabka or to Vilnius. Once Mother General [Michael] asked me, "Why are you sitting here so quietly and not getting ready to go somewhere, Sister?" I answered, "I want to do God's pure will; wherever you bid me to go, dear Mother, I will know God's pure will for me will be there, without any admixture on my part." (251)

SEPTEMBER 3

Jesus, King of Mercy, again the time has come when I am alone with You. Therefore I beg You, by all the love with which Your Heart burns, to destroy completely within me my self-love and, on the other hand, to enkindle in my heart the fire of Your purest love. (371)

In the evening, after the conference, I heard these words: **I am with you. During this retreat, I will strengthen you in peace and in courage so that your strength will not fail in carrying out My designs. Therefore you will cancel out your will absolutely in this retreat and, instead, My complete will shall be accomplished in you. Know that it will cost you much, so write these words on a clean sheet of paper: "From today on, my own will does not exist," and then cross out the page. And on the other side write these words: "From today on, I do the will of God everywhere, always, and in everything." Be afraid**

of nothing; love will give you strength and make the realization of this easy. (372)

The moment I knelt down to cross out my own will, as the Lord had bid me to do, I heard this voice in my soul: **From today on, do not fear God's judgment, for you will not be judged.** (374)

SEPTEMBER 4

On one occasion I heard these words, **I desire that you live according to My will, in the most secret depths of your soul.** I reflected on these words, which spoke very much to my heart. This was on the day of confessions for the community. When I went to confession and had accused myself of my sins, the priest [Father Sopocko] repeated to me the same words that the Lord had previously spoken. (443)

The priest spoke these profound words to me, "There are three degrees in the accomplishment of God's will: in the first, the soul carries out all rules and statutes pertaining to external observance; in the second degree, the soul accepts interior inspirations and carries them out faithfully; in the third degree, the soul, abandoned to the will of God, allows Him to dispose of it freely, and God does with it as He pleases, and it is a docile tool in His hands." And the priest said that I was at the second degree in the accomplishment of God's will and that I had not yet reached the third degree, but that I should strive to attain it. These words pierced my soul. I see clearly that God often gives the priest knowledge of what is going on in the depths of my soul. This does not surprise me at all; indeed, I thank God that He has such chosen persons. (444)

SEPTEMBER 5

Now I understand well that what unites our soul most closely to God is self-denial; that is, joining our will to the will of God. This is what makes the soul truly free, contributes to profound recollection of the spirit, and makes all life's burdens light, and death sweet. (462)

After Holy Communion, my soul was again flooded with God's love. I rejoiced in His greatness. Here I see distinctly His will, which I am to carry out, and at the same time my own weakness and misery; I see how I can do nothing without His help. (493)

O Eternal Truth, Word Incarnate, who most faithfully fulfilled Your Father's will, today I am becoming a martyr of Your inspirations, since I cannot carry them out because I have no will of my own, though interiorly I see Your will clearly. I submit in everything to the will of my superiors and my confessor. I will follow Your will insofar as You will permit me to do so through Your representative. O my Jesus, it cannot be helped, but I give priority to the voice of the Church over the voice with which You speak to me. (497)

SEPTEMBER 6

January 29, 1936. In the evening, when I was in my cell, I suddenly saw a great light and a dark gray cross high up within the light. Suddenly, I found myself caught up close to the cross. I gazed at it intently, but could not understand anything, and so I prayed, asking what it could mean. At that moment I saw the Lord Jesus, and the cross disappeared. The Lord Jesus was sitting in a great light, and His legs, up to the knees, were drowned in the light so that I could not see them. Jesus bent toward me, looked at me kindly, and spoke to me about the will of the Heavenly Father. He told me that the most perfect and holy soul is the one that does the will of the Father, but there are not many such, and that He looks with special love upon the soul who lives His will. And Jesus told me that I was doing the will of God perfectly... **and for this reason I am uniting Myself with you and communing with you in a special and intimate way.**

SEPTEMBER 7

God embraces with His incomprehensible love the soul who lives by His will. I understood how much God loves us, how simple He is, though incomprehensible, and how easy it is to commune with Him, despite His great majesty. With no one do I feel as free and as much at ease as with Him. Even a mother and her truly loving child do not understand each other so well as God and I do. When I was in that state of communion with God, I saw two particular persons, and their sad interior condition was revealed to me. They were in a sorrowful state, but I trust that they, too, will glorify the mercy of God.   (603)

SEPTEMBER 8

My physical strength declined, and though I did not speak to anyone about it, nevertheless Mother Superior [Borgia] noticed my pain and remarked that I had changed in appearance and was very pale. She told me to go to bed earlier and to sleep longer, and she had a cup of hot milk brought to me in the evening. She had a motherly heart, full of care, and tried to help me. But in the case of spiritual sufferings, external things have no influence, and they do not bring much relief. It was from the confessional that I drew my strength and the consolation of knowing that it would not be long before I could begin to act. (615)

On Thursday, when I went to my cell, I saw over me the Sacred Host in great brightness. Then I heard a voice that seemed to be coming from above the Host: **In the Host is your power; it will defend you.** After these words, the vision disappeared, but a strange power entered my soul, and a strange light as to what our love for God consists in; namely, in doing His will. (616)

SEPTEMBER 9

Jesus, drive away from me the thoughts that are not in accord with Your will. I know that nothing now binds me to this earth but this work of mercy. (638)

Thursday. During the evening adoration, I saw Jesus scourged and tortured. He said to me, **My daughter, I desire that even in the smallest things, you rely on your confessor. Your greatest sacrifices do not please Me if you practice them without the confessor's permission; on the other hand, the smallest sacrifice finds great value in My eyes, if it is done with his permission. The greatest works are worthless in My eyes if they are done out of self-will, and often they are not in accord with My will and merit punishment rather than reward. And on the other hand, even the smallest of your acts, done with the confessor's permission, is pleasing in My eyes and very dear to Me. Hold firmly to this always. Be constantly on the watch, for many souls will turn back from the gates of hell and worship My mercy. But fear nothing, as I am with you. Know that of yourself you can do nothing.** (639)

There is one word I heed and continually ponder; it alone is everything to me; I live by it and die by it, and it is the holy will of God. It is my daily food. My whole soul listens intently to God's wishes. I do always what God asks of me, although my nature often quakes and I feel that the magnitude of these things is beyond my strength. I know well what I am of myself, but I also know what the grace of God is, which supports me.

(652)

SEPTEMBER 10

O my Jesus, my Master and Director, strengthen and enlighten me in these difficult moments of my life. I expect no help from people; all my hope is in You. I feel alone in the face of Your demands, O Lord. Despite the fears and qualms of my nature, I am fulfilling Your holy will and desire to fulfill it as faithfully as possible throughout my life and in my death. Jesus, with You I can do all things. Do with me as You please; only give me Your merciful Heart and that is enough for me.

O Jesus my Lord, help me. Let what You have planned before all ages happen to me. I am ready at each beckoning of Your holy will. Enlighten my mind that I may know Your will. O God, You who pervade my soul, You know that I desire nothing but Your glory.

O Divine Will, You are the delight of my heart, the food of my soul, the light of my intellect, the omnipotent strength of my will; for when I unite myself with Your will, O Lord, Your power works through me and takes the place of my feeble will. Each day, I seek to carry out God's wishes. (650)

SEPTEMBER 11

O my Jesus, I know that a person's greatness is evidenced by his deeds and not by his words or feelings. It is the works that have come from us that will speak about us. My Jesus, do not allow me to daydream, but give me the courage and strength to fulfill Your holy will.

Jesus, if You wish to leave me in uncertainty, even to the end of my life, may Your Holy Name be blessed. (663)

I understood that all striving for perfection and all sanctity consist in doing God's will. Perfect fulfillment of God's will is maturity in sanctity; there is no room for doubt here. To receive God's light and recognize what God wants of us and yet not do it is a great offense against the majesty of God. Such a soul deserves to be completely forsaken by God. It resembles Lucifer, who had great light, but did not do God's will. An extraordinary peace entered my soul when I reflected on the fact that, despite great difficulties, I had always faithfully followed God's will as I knew it. O Jesus, grant me the grace to put Your will into practice as I have come to know it, O God.
(666)

SEPTEMBER 12

On the eve of the retreat, I started to pray that the Lord Jesus might give me just a little health so that I could take part in the retreat, because I was feeling so ill that I thought perhaps it might be my last. However, as soon as I had started praying I felt a strange dissatisfaction. I interrupted the prayer of supplication and began to thank the Lord for everything He sends me, submitting myself completely to His holy will. Then I felt profound peace of soul.

Faithful submission to the will of God, always and everywhere, in all events and circumstances of life, gives great glory to God. Such submission to the will of God carries more weight with Him than long fasts, mortifications, and the most severe penances. Oh, how great is the reward for one act of loving submission to the will of God! As I write, my soul is enraptured at the thought of how much God loves it and of the peace that my soul already enjoys, here on earth. (724)

SEPTEMBER 13

And so You see, Jesus, that everything is now up to You. I am perfectly at peace, despite these great urgings. For my part, I have done everything, and it is now Your turn, my Jesus, and in this way Your cause will be made apparent. I am totally in accord with Your will; do with me as You please, O Lord, but only grant me the grace of loving You more and more ardently. This is what is most precious to me. I desire nothing but You, O Love Eternal! It matters not along what paths You will lead me, paths of pain or paths of joy. I want to love You at every moment of my life. If You tell me to leave, O Jesus, in order to carry out Your will, I will leave. If You tell me to stay, I will stay. It matters not what I will suffer, in the one instance or the other. O my Jesus, if I leave, I know what I shall have to suffer and endure. I agreed to this with full awareness, and I have already accepted it by an act of the will. It does not matter what the chalice holds for me. It is enough for me to know that it has been given to me by the loving hand of God. If you tell me to turn back and stay, I will stay in spite of all interior urgings. If You still keep them in my soul and leave me in this inner agony even to the end of my life, I accept this in the full consciousness of my will and in loving submission to You, O my God. If I stay, I shall hide myself in Your mercy, my God, so deeply that no human eye will see me. Throughout my life, I want to be a thurible filled with hidden fire, and may the smoke rising up to You, O Living Host, be pleasing to You. I feel in my own heart that every little sacrifice arouses the fire of my love for You, but in such a silent and secret way that no one will detect it.   (751)

SEPTEMBER 14

Today, during the morning meditation, the Lord gave me to see and understand clearly that His demands are unchangeable. I see clearly that no one can release me from the duty of doing the known will of God. A great lack of health and physical strength is not a sufficient reason and does not release me from this work that the Lord Himself is carrying out through me. I am to be just a tool in His hands. And so, O Lord, here I am to carry out Your will. Command me according to Your eternal plans and desires. Only give me the grace that I may always be faithful to You.   (787)

I have accepted the favor of this treatment, but I am fully resigned to the will of God. Let God do with me as He pleases. I desire nothing but the fulfillment of His holy will. I am uniting myself with the Mother of God, and I am leaving Nazareth and going to Bethlehem. I will spend Christmas there among strangers, but with Jesus, Mary, and Joseph, because such is the will of God. I am striving to do the will of God in all things. I do not desire a return to health more than death. I entrust myself completely to His infinite mercy and, as a little child, I am living in the greatest peace. I am trying only to make my love for Him deeper and purer, to be a delight to His divine glance...   (795)

SEPTEMBER 15

The Lord Jesus gave me to know how very pleasing to Him is a soul who lives in accordance with the will of God. It thereby gives very great glory to God... (821)

O Light Eternal, who came to this earth, enlighten my mind and strengthen my will that I may not give up in times of great affliction. May Your light dissipate all the shadows of doubt. May Your omnipotence act through me. I trust in You, O uncreated Light! You, O Infant Jesus, are a model for me in accomplishing Your Father's will, You, who said, "Behold, I come to do Your will." Grant that I also may do God's will faithfully in all things. O Divine Infant, grant me this grace!
(830)

SEPTEMBER 16

Sorrow will not establish itself in a heart which loves the will of God. My heart, longing for God, feels the whole misery of exile. I keep going forward bravely—though my feet become wounded—to my homeland and, on the way, I nourish myself on the will of God. It is my food. Help me, happy inhabitants of the heavenly homeland, so that your sister may not falter on the way. Although the desert is fearful, I walk with lifted head and eyes fixed on the sun; that is to say, on the merciful Heart of Jesus. (886)

SEPTEMBER 17

I feel considerable improvement in my health. Jesus is bringing me from the gates of death to life, because there was so little left but for me to die, and lo, the Lord grants me the fullness of life. Although I am still to remain in the sanatorium, I am almost completely well. I see that the will of God has not yet been fulfilled in me, and that is why I must live, for I know that if I fulfill everything the Lord has planned for me in this world, He will not leave me in exile any longer, for heaven is my home. But before we go to our Homeland, we must fulfill the will of God on earth; that is, trials and struggles must run their full course in us. (897)

SEPTEMBER 18

I have desired death so much! I do not know whether I shall ever again in my life experience such great longing for God. There have been times when I fell into a swoon for Him. Oh, how ugly the earth when one knows heaven! I must do violence to myself in order to live. O will of God, You are my nourishment. (899)

Today, the Lord said to me, **I demand of you a perfect and whole-burnt offering; an offering of the will. No other sacrifice can compare with this one. I Myself am directing your life and arranging things in such a way that you will be for Me a continual sacrifice and will always do My will. And for the accomplishment of this offering, you will unite yourself with Me on the Cross. I know what you can do. I Myself will give you many orders directly, but I will delay the possibility of their being carried out and make it depend on others. But what the superiors will not manage to do, I Myself will accom-**

plish directly in your soul. And in the most hidden depths of your soul, a perfect holocaust will be carried out, not just for a while, but know, My daughter, that this offering will last until your death. But there is time, so that I the Lord will fulfill all your wishes. I delight in you as in a living host; let nothing terrify you; I am with you. (923)

SEPTEMBER 19

February 15, 1937. Today, I heard these words in my soul: **Host pleasing to My Father, know, My daughter, that the entire Holy Trinity finds Its special delight in you, because you live exclusively by the will of God. No sacrifice can compare with this.** (955)

After these words, the knowledge of God's will came to me; that is to say, I now see everything from a higher point of view and accept all events and things, pleasant and unpleasant, with love, as tokens of the heavenly Father's special affection. (956)

The pure offering of my will will burn on the altar of love. That my sacrifice may be perfect, I unite myself closely with the sacrifice of Jesus on the cross. When great sufferings will cause my nature to tremble, and my physical and spiritual strength will diminish, then will I hide myself deep in the open wound of the Heart of Jesus, silent as a dove, without complaint. Let all my desires, even the holiest, noblest, and most beautiful, take always the last place and Your holy will, the very first. The least of Your desires, O Lord, is more precious to me than heaven, with all its treasures. I know very well that people will not understand me; that is why my sacrifice will be purer in Your eyes. (957)

SEPTEMBER 20

Today, the doctor decided that I am to stay here until April. It is God's will, even though I did want to be back in the company of my sisters. (972)

I understood that these two years of interior suffering which I have undergone in submission to God's will in order to know it better have advanced me further in perfection than the previous ten years. For two years now, I have been on the cross between heaven and earth. That is to say, I am bound by the vow of obedience and must obey the superior as God Himself. And on the other hand, God makes His will known to me directly, and so my inner torture is so great that no one will either understand or imagine these spiritual sufferings. It seems to me that it would be easier to give up my life than to go again and again through one hour of such pain. I am not even going to write much about this matter, because one cannot describe what it is like to know God's will directly and at the same time to be perfectly obedient to the divine will as expressed indirectly through the superiors. Thanks be to God that He has given me a director; otherwise, I would not have advanced one single step. (981)

SEPTEMBER 21

Today during meditation, God gave me inner light and the understanding as to what sanctity is and of what it consists. Although I have heard these things many times in conferences, the soul understands them in a different way when it comes to know of them through the light of God which illumines it.

Neither graces, nor revelations, nor raptures, nor gifts granted to a soul make it perfect, but rather the intimate union of the soul with God. These gifts are merely ornaments of the soul, but constitute neither its essence nor its perfection. My sanctity and perfection consist in the close union of my will with the will of God. God never violates our free will. It is up to us whether we want to receive God's grace or not. It is up to us whether we will cooperate with it or waste it.   (1107)

In spite of the profound peace my soul is enjoying, I am struggling continuously, and it is often a hard-fought battle for me to walk faithfully along my path; that is, the path which the Lord Jesus wants me to follow. And my path is to be faithful to the will of God in all things and at all times, especially by being faithful to inner inspirations in order to be a receptive instrument in God's hands for the carrying out of the work of His fathomless mercy.   (1173)

SEPTEMBER 22

Act of total abandonment to the will of God, which is for me love and mercy itself.

Act of Oblation

Jesus-Host, whom I have this very moment received into my heart, through this union with You I offer myself to the heavenly Father as a sacrificial host, abandoning myself totally and completely to the most merciful and holy will of my God. From today onward, Your will, Lord, is my food. Take my whole being; dispose of me as You please. Whatever Your fatherly hand gives me, I will accept with submission, peace, and joy. I fear nothing, no matter in what direction You lead me; helped by Your grace I will carry out everything You demand of me. I no longer fear any of Your inspirations nor do I probe anxiously to see where they will lead me. Lead me, O God, along whatever roads You please; I have placed all my trust in Your will which is, for me, love and mercy itself.

Bid me to stay in this convent, I will stay; bid me to undertake the work, I will undertake it; leave me in uncertainty about the work until I die, be blessed; give me death when, humanly speaking, my life seems particularly necessary, be blessed. Should You take me in my youth, be blessed; should You let me live to a ripe old age, be blessed. Should You give me health and strength, be blessed; should You confine me to a bed of pain for my whole life, be blessed. Should You give only failures and disappointments in life, be blessed. Should You allow my purest intentions to be condemned, be blessed. Should You enlighten my mind, be blessed. Should You leave me in darkness and with all kinds of torments, be blessed.

From this moment on, I live in the deepest peace, because the Lord Himself is carrying me in the hollow of His hand. He, Lord of unfathomable mercy, knows that I desire Him alone in all things, always and everywhere. (1264)

SEPTEMBER 23

Prayer. O Jesus, stretched out upon the cross, I implore You, give me the grace of doing faithfully the most holy will of Your Father, in all things, always and everywhere. And when this will of God will seem to me very harsh and difficult to fulfill, it is then I beg You, Jesus, may power and strength flow upon me from Your wounds, and may my lips keep repeating, "Your will be done, O Lord." O Savior of the world, Lover of man's salvation, who in such terrible torment and pain forget Yourself to think only of the salvation of souls, O most compassionate Jesus, grant me the grace to forget myself that I may live totally for souls, helping You in the work of salvation, according to the most holy will of Your Father...   (1265)

Jesus, my most perfect model, with my eyes fixed on You, I will go through life in Your footsteps, adapting nature to grace, according to Your most holy will and Your light which illumines my soul, trusting completely in Your help.   (1351)

Sixth day. O my God, I am ready to accept Your will in every detail, whatever it may be. However You may direct me, I will bless You. Whatever You ask of me I will do with the help of Your grace. Whatever Your holy will regarding me might be, I accept it with my whole heart and soul, taking no account of what my corrupt nature tells me.   (1356)

SEPTEMBER 24

November, 1937, monthly one-day retreat. In the course of this retreat, the Lord has given me the light to know His will more profoundly and to abandon myself completely to the holy will of God. This light has confirmed me in profound peace, making me understand that I should fear nothing except sin. Whatever God sends me, I accept with complete submission to His holy will. Wherever He puts me, I will try faithfully to do His holy will, as well as His wishes, to the extent of my power to do so, even if the will of God were to be as hard and difficult for me as was the will of the Heavenly Father for His Son, as He prayed in the Garden of Olives. I have come to see that if the will of the Heavenly Father was fulfilled in this way in His well-beloved Son, it will be fulfilled in us in exactly the same way: by suffering, persecution, abuse, disgrace. It is through all this that my soul becomes like unto Jesus. And the greater the sufferings, the more I see that I am becoming like Jesus. This is the surest way. If some other way were better, Jesus would have shown it to me. Sufferings in no way take away my peace. On the other hand, although I enjoy profound peace, that peace does not lessen my experience of suffering. Although my face is often bowed to the ground, and my tears flow profusely, at the same time my soul is filled with profound peace and happiness... (1394)

SEPTEMBER 25

O my Jesus, although I have such very strong impulsions, I am to act on them slowly, and this only in order not to spoil Your work with my haste. O my Jesus, You give me to know Your mysteries, and You want me to transmit them to other souls. Soon now it will be possible for me to act. At the moment of apparent absolute destruction, my mission, now no longer hindered by anything, will begin. Such is the will of God in this, and it will not change; although many persons will oppose it, nothing will change God's will. (1389)

Today the Lord Jesus is giving me an awareness of Himself and of His most tender love and care for me. He is bringing me to understand deeply how everything depends on His will, and how He allows certain difficulties precisely for our merit, so that our fidelity might be clearly manifest. And through this, I have been given strength for suffering and self-denial. (1409)

So today I submit myself completely and with loving consent to Your holy will, O Lord, and to Your most wise decrees, which are always full of clemency and mercy for me, though at times I can neither understand nor fathom them. O my

Master, I surrender myself completely to You, who are the rudder of my soul; steer it Yourself according to Your divine wishes. I enclose myself in Your most compassionate Heart, which is a sea of unfathomable mercy. (1450)

SEPTEMBER 26

O my Jesus, from the moment I gave myself completely to You, I have given no thought whatsoever for myself. You may do with me whatever You like. There is only one thing I think about; that is, what do You prefer; what can I do, O Lord, to please You. I listen and watch for each opportunity. It matters not if I am outwardly judged otherwise in this matter... (1493)

Today, since early in the morning, my soul has been in darkness. I cannot ascend to Jesus, and I feel as though I have been forsaken by Him. I will not turn to creatures for light because I know that they will not enlighten me if Jesus wills to keep me in darkness. I submit myself to His holy will and suffer. Still, the struggle is becoming more and more desperate. During Vespers, I wanted to unite myself with the sisters through prayer. (1496)

Lord, You know that since my youth I have always sought Your will and, recognizing it, have always tried to carry it out. My heart has been accustomed to the inspirations of the Holy Spirit, to whom I am faithful. In the midst of the greatest din I have heard the voice of God. I always know what is going on in my interior... (1504)

SEPTEMBER 27

Then I heard the words: **As you are united with Me in life, so will you be united at the moment of death.** After these words, such great trust in God's great mercy was awakened in my soul that, even if I had had the sins of the whole world, as well as the sins of all the condemned souls weighing on my conscience, I would not have doubted God's goodness but, without hesitation, would have thrown myself into the abyss of the divine mercy, which is always open to us; and, with a heart crushed to dust, I would have cast myself at His feet, abandoning myself totally to His holy will, which is mercy itself.   (1552)

This month I will practice the three virtues recommended to me by the Mother of God: humility, purity, and love of God, accepting with profound submission to the will of God everything that He will send me.   (1624)

I began Holy Lent in the way that Jesus wanted me to, making myself totally dependent upon His holy will and accepting with love everything that He sends me. I cannot practice any greater mortifications, because I am so very weak. This long illness has sapped my strength completely. I am uniting myself with Jesus through suffering. When I meditate on His Painful Passion, my physical sufferings are lessened.   (1625)

SEPTEMBER 28

I do not know how to describe all that I suffer, and what I have written thus far is merely a drop. There are moments of suffering about which I really cannot write. But there are also moments in my life when my lips are silent, and there are no words for my defense, and I submit myself completely to the will of God; then the Lord Himself defends me and makes claims on my behalf, and His demands are such that they can be noticed exteriorly. Nevertheless, when I perceive His major interventions, which manifest themselves by way of punishment, then I beg Him earnestly for mercy and forgiveness. Yet I am not always heard. The Lord acts toward me in a mysterious manner. There are times when He Himself allows terrible sufferings, and then again there are times when He does not let me suffer and removes everything that might afflict my soul. These are His ways, unfathomable and incomprehensible to us. It is for us to submit ourselves completely to His holy will. There are mysteries that the human mind will never fathom here on earth; eternity will reveal them.   (1656)

April 16, 1938, Holy Saturday. During adoration, the Lord said to me, **Be at peace, My daughter. This Work of Mercy is Mine; there is nothing of you in it. It pleases Me that you are carrying out faithfully what I have commanded you to do, not adding or taking away a single word.** And He gave me an interior light by which I learned that not a single word was mine; despite difficulties and adversities, I have always, always, fulfilled His will, as He has made it known to me.   (1667)

SEPTEMBER 29

After the first examination, the doctor [Silberg] found that my condition was grave. "We suspect, Sister, that you do have the illness about which you spoke to me. But Almighty God can do all things."

When I entered my room, I steeped myself in prayer of thanksgiving for everything the Lord had been sending me throughout my whole life, surrendering myself totally to His most holy will. A deep joy and peace flooded my soul. I felt a peace so great that, if death had come at that moment, I would not have said to it, "Wait, for I still have some matters to attend to." No, I would have welcomed it with joy, because I am ready for the meeting with the Lord, not only today, but ever since the moment when I placed my complete trust in the Divine Mercy, resigning myself totally to His most holy will, full of mercy and compassion. I know what I am of myself...

(1679)

O my Jesus, You alone know of my efforts. I seem to be a bit better, but better only to the point that I can go out on the veranda instead of lying in bed. I see and am fully aware of what is happening to me. Despite the diligent care of my superiors and the efforts of the doctors, my health is fading and running out. But I rejoice greatly at Your call, my God, my Love, because I know that my mission will begin at the moment of my death. Oh, how much I desire to be set free from the bonds of this body. O my Jesus, You know that, in all my desires, I always want to see Your will. Of myself, I would not want to die one minute sooner, or to live one minute longer, or to suffer less, or to suffer more, but I only want to do Your holy will. Although I have great enthusiasm, and the desires burning in my heart are immense, they are never above Your will. (1729)

SEPTEMBER 30

O my Jesus, give me strength to endure suffering so that I may not make a wry face when I drink the cup of bitterness. Help me Yourself to make my sacrifice pleasing to You. May it not be tainted by my self-love, even though it extend over many years. May purity of intention make it pleasing to You, fresh and full of life. This life of mine is a ceaseless struggle, a constant effort to do Your holy will; but may everything that is in me, both my misery and my strength, give praise to You, O Lord. (1740)

When I met with the Lord, I said to Him, "You are fooling me, Jesus; You show me the open gate of heaven, and again You leave me on earth." The Lord said to me, **When, in heaven, you see these present days, you will rejoice and will want to see as many of them as possible. I am not surprised, My daughter, that you cannot understand this now, because your heart is overflowing with pain and longing for Me. Your vigilance pleases Me. Let My word be enough for you; it will not be long now.**

And my soul found itself once again in exile. I lovingly united myself to the will of God, submitting myself to His gracious decrees. (1787)

EUCHARIST

October

THE SPECIAL PLACE of the Holy Eucharist in the life of Sister Faustina can be summed up in her full official name, Sister Maria Faustina of the Most Blessed Sacrament. Her greatest desire was to *be* Eucharist, hidden, like Jesus, blessed by her union with the Lord, broken like Jesus in the Passion and totally given for the salvation of souls.

A special gift given to Sister Faustina was the *continuous presence* of the Eucharist from one Holy Communion until the next. Blessed Faustina regularly experienced a *vision* of the Lord during Holy Mass. Over sixty such visions are recorded in her diary (see 420, 441, 1046).

The Eucharist is closely tied to the vessels of mercy that are a part of the Divine Mercy devotion. Reception of Holy Communion is integral to the celebration of the Feast of Divine Mercy. On a number of occasions, Sister saw the Eucharist radiate with rays, as in the Image of the Merciful Savior. The Chaplet of Divine Mercy is an offering of the Body and Blood, Soul and Divinity of the Lord Jesus Christ, to the Father, in atonement for the sins of the world. The vessels the Lord gave us through Sister Faustina are eucharistic.

FOR THIS MONTH:

Practice: Attend daily Mass and receive Holy Communion or, if possible, make a visit to the Blessed Sacrament or other frequent "spiritual communion."

Prayer: O Sacrament most Holy,
O Sacrament Divine,
All praise and all thanksgiving
Be every moment Thine.

Promise: He who eats my flesh and drinks my blood has eternal life, and I raise him up on the last day (Jn 6:54).

OCTOBER 1

O my Jesus, You alone know what persecutions I suffer, and this only because I am being faithful to You and following Your orders. You are my strength; sustain me that I may always carry out what You ask of me. Of myself I can do nothing, but when You sustain me, all difficulties are nothing for me. O my Lord, I can see very well that from the time when my soul first received the capacity to know You, my life has been a continual struggle which has become increasingly intense.

Every morning during meditation, I prepare myself for the whole day's struggle. Holy Communion assures me that I will win the victory; and so it is. I fear the day when I do not receive Holy Communion. This Bread of the Strong gives me all the strength I need to carry on my mission and the courage to do whatever the Lord asks of me. The courage and strength that are in me are not of me, but of Him who lives in me—it is the Eucharist.

O my Jesus, the misunderstandings are so great; sometimes, were it not for the Eucharist, I would not have the courage to go any further along the way You have marked out for me.

(91)

OCTOBER 2

Once, I desired very much to receive Holy Communion, but I had a certain doubt, and I did not go. I suffered greatly because of this. It seemed to me that my heart would burst from the pain. When I set about my work, my heart full of bitterness, Jesus suddenly stood by me and said, **My daughter, do not omit Holy Communion unless you know well that your fall**

was serious; apart from this, no doubt must stop you from uniting yourself with Me in the mystery of My love. Your minor faults will disappear in My love like a piece of straw thrown into a great furnace. Know that you grieve Me much when you fail to receive Me in Holy Communion. (156)

One morning after Holy Communion, I heard this voice, **I desire that you accompany Me when I go to the sick.** I answered that I was quite willing, but after a moment of reflection I started wondering how I was going to do so; the sisters of the second choir* do not accompany the Blessed Sacrament. It is always the sister-directresses who go. I thought to myself: Jesus will find a way. Shortly afterwards, Mother Raphael sent for me and said, "Sister, you will accompany the Lord Jesus when the priest goes to visit the sick." And all through the time of my probation I carried the light, accompanying the Lord and, as a knight of Jesus, I always tried to gird myself with an iron belt, for it would not be proper to accompany the King in everyday dress. And I offered this mortification for the sick. (183)

---

*At that time the Congregation was divided into two choirs, the so-called director sisters and coadjutor sisters. The membership to one or the other was decided by the Congregation's governing body on the basis of the candidate's intellectual level, age, and abilities. The director sisters' task was to manage the Congregation and the penitents' home. The coadjutor sisters did the manual work and served as helpers to the director sisters, especially in the area of physical labor.

OCTOBER 3

O living Host, my one and only Strength, Fountain of love and mercy, embrace the whole world, fortify faint souls. Oh, blessed be the instant and the moment when Jesus left us His most merciful Heart! (223)

To suffer without complaining, to bring comfort to others, and to drown my own sufferings in the most Sacred Heart of Jesus!

I will spend all my free moments at the feet of [Our Lord in] the Blessed Sacrament. At the feet of Jesus, I will seek light, comfort, and strength. I will show my gratitude unceasingly to God for His great mercy towards me, never forgetting the favors He has bestowed on me, especially the grace of a vocation.

I will hide myself among the sisters like a little violet among lilies. I want to blossom for my Lord and Maker, to forget about myself, to empty myself totally for the sake of immortal souls—this is my delight. (224)

Prayer during the Mass on the day of the perpetual vows. Today I place my heart on the paten where Your Heart has been placed, O Jesus, and today I offer myself together with You to God, Your Father and mine, as a sacrifice of love and praise. Father of Mercy, look upon the sacrifice of my heart, but through the wound in the Heart of Jesus. (239)

OCTOBER 4

I often feel God's presence after Holy Communion in a special and tangible way. I know God is in my heart. And the fact that I feel Him in my heart does not interfere with my duties. Even when I am dealing with very important matters which require attention, I do not lose the presence of God in my soul, and I am closely united with Him. With Him I go to work, with Him I go for recreation, with Him I suffer, with Him I rejoice; I live in Him and He in me. I am never alone, because He is my constant companion. He is present to me at every moment. Our intimacy is very close, through a union of blood and of life. (318)

OCTOBER 5

The next day, I felt very weak, but experienced no further suffering. After Holy Communion, I saw the Lord Jesus just as I had seen Him during one adoration. The Lord's gaze pierced my soul through and through, and not even the least speck of dust escaped His notice. And I said to Jesus, "Jesus, I thought You were going to take me." And Jesus answered, **My will has not yet been fully accomplished in you; you will still remain on earth, but not for long. I am well pleased with your trust, but your love should be more ardent. Pure love gives the soul strength at the very moment of dying. When I was dying on the cross, I was not thinking about Myself, but about poor sinners, and I prayed for them to My Father. I want your last moments to be completely similar to Mine on the cross. There is but one price at which souls are bought, and that is suffering united to My suffering on the cross. Pure love understands these words; carnal love will never understand them.** (324)

OCTOBER 6

One evening as I entered my cell, I saw the Lord Jesus exposed in the monstrance under the open sky, as it seemed. At the feet of Jesus I saw my confessor, and behind him a great number of the highest ranking ecclesiastics, clothed in vestments the like of which I had never seen except in this vision; and behind them, groups of religious from various orders; and further still I saw enormous crowds of people, which extended far beyond my vision. I saw the two rays coming out from the Host, as in the image, closely united but not intermingled; and they passed through the hands of my confessor, and then through the hands of the clergy and from their hands to the people, and then they returned to the Host... and at that moment I saw myself once again in the cell which I had just entered.   (344)

That same day, when I was in church waiting for confession, I saw the same rays issuing from the monstrance and spreading throughout the church. This lasted all through the service. After the Benediction, [the rays shone out] to both sides and returned again to the monstrance. Their appearance was bright and transparent like crystal. I asked Jesus that He deign to light the fire of His love in all souls that were cold. Beneath these rays a heart will grow warm even if it were like a block of ice; even if it were hard as a rock, it will crumble into dust.

                                                                            (370)

OCTOBER 7

Jesus likes to intervene in the smallest details of our life, and He often fulfills secret wishes of mine that I sometimes hide from Him, although I know that from Him nothing can be hidden.

There is a custom among us of drawing by lot, on New Year's Day, special Patrons for ourselves for the whole year. In the morning during meditation, there arose within me a secret desire that the Eucharistic Jesus be my special Patron for this year also, as in the past. But, hiding this desire from my Beloved, I spoke to Him about everything else but that. When we came to refectory for breakfast, we blessed ourselves and began drawing our patrons. When I approached the holy cards on which the names of the patrons were written, without hesitation I took one, but I didn't read the name immediately as I wanted to mortify myself for a few minutes. Suddenly, I heard a voice in my soul: **I am your patron. Read.** I looked at once at the inscription and read, "Patron for the year 1935— the Most Blessed Eucharist." My heart leapt with joy, and I slipped quietly away from the sisters and went for a short visit before the Blessed Sacrament, where I poured out my heart. But Jesus sweetly admonished me that I should be at that moment together with the sisters. I went immediately in obedience to the rule.   (360)

OCTOBER 8

Often during Mass, I see the Lord in my soul; I feel His presence which pervades my being. I sense His divine gaze; I have long talks with Him without saying a word; I know what His divine Heart desires, and I always do what will please Him the most. I love Him to distraction, and I feel that I am being loved by God. At those times when I meet with God deep within myself, I feel so happy that I do not know how to express it. Such moments are short, for the soul could not bear it for long, as separation from the body would be inevitable. Though these moments are very short, their power, however, which is transmitted to the soul, remains with it for a very long time. Without the least effort, I experience the profound recollection which then envelops me—and it does not diminish even if I talk with people, nor does it interfere with the performance of my duties. I feel the constant presence of God without any effort of my soul. I know that I am united with Him as closely as a drop of water is united with the bottomless ocean.

(411)

When I was attending Mass in a certain church with another sister, I felt the greatness and majesty of God; I felt the church was permeated by God. His majesty enveloped me and, though it terrified me, it filled me with peace and joy. I knew that nothing could oppose His will. Oh, if only all souls knew who is living in our churches, there would not be so many outrages and so much disrespect in these holy places!   (409)

OCTOBER 9

Once, the Image was being exhibited over the altar during the Corpus Christi procession [June 20, 1935]. When the priest exposed the Blessed Sacrament, and the choir began to sing, the rays from the Image pierced the Sacred Host and spread out all over the world. Then I heard these words: **These rays of mercy will pass through you, just as they have passed through this Host, and they will go out through all the world.** At these words, profound joy invaded my soul.   (441)

Once when my confessor [Father Sopocko] was saying Mass, I saw, as usual, the Child Jesus on the altar, from the time of the Offertory. However, a moment before the Elevation, the priest vanished from my sight, and Jesus alone remained. When the moment of the Elevation approached, Jesus took the Host and the chalice in His little hands and raised them together, looking

272 ⊛ REVELATIONS OF DIVINE MERCY

up to heaven, and a moment later I again saw my confessor. I asked the Child Jesus where the priest had been during the time I had not seen him. Jesus answered, **In My Heart.** But I could not understand anything more of these words of Jesus.

(442)

OCTOBER 10

Once after Holy Communion, I heard these words: **You are Our dwelling place.** At that moment, I felt in my soul the presence of the Holy Trinity, the Father, the Son, and the Holy Spirit. I felt that I was the temple of God. I felt I was a child of the Father. I cannot explain all this, but the spirit understands it well. O infinite Goodness, how low You stoop to Your miserable creature! (451)

I knew, more distinctly than ever before, the Three Divine Persons, the Father, the Son, and the Holy Spirit. But their being, their equality, and their majesty are one. My soul is in communion with these Three; but I do not know how to express this in words; yet my soul understands it well. Whoever is united to One of the Three Persons is thereby united to the whole Blessed Trinity, for this Oneness is indivisible. This vision, or rather, this knowledge filled my soul with unimaginable happiness, because God is so great. What I am describing I did not see with my eyes, as on previous occasions, but in a purely interior manner, in a purely spiritual way, independent of the senses. This continued until the end of Holy Mass.

This now happens often to me, and not only in the chapel, but also at work and at times when I least expect it. (472)

OCTOBER 11

When I entered chapel, I heard these words interiorly: **Every time you enter the chapel, immediately recite the prayer which I taught you yesterday.** When I had said the prayer, in my soul I heard these words: **This prayer will serve to appease My wrath. You will recite it for nine days, on the beads of the rosary, in the following manner: First of all, you will say one OUR FATHER and HAIL MARY and the I BELIEVE IN GOD. Then on the OUR FATHER beads you will say the following words: "Eternal Father, I offer You the Body and Blood, Soul and Divinity of Your dearly beloved Son, Our Lord Jesus Christ, in atonement for our sins and those of the whole world." On the HAIL MARY beads you will say the following words: "For the sake of His sorrowful Passion have mercy on us and on the whole world." In conclusion, three times you will recite these words: "Holy God, Holy Mighty One, Holy Immortal One, have mercy on us and on the whole world."** (476)

During Holy Mass I prayed fervently that Jesus might become King of all hearts and that divine grace might shine in every soul. Then I saw Jesus as He is depicted in the Image, and He said to me, **My daughter, you give Me the greatest glory by faithfully fulfilling My desires.** (500)

OCTOBER 12

On Friday during Mass when my soul was flooded with God's happiness, I heard these words in my soul: **My mercy has passed into souls through the divine-human Heart of Jesus as a ray from the sun passes through crystal.** I felt in my heart and understood that every approach to God is brought about by Jesus, in Him and through Him. (528)

O God, how I desire that souls come to know You and to see that You have created them because of Your unfathomable love. O my Creator and Lord, I feel that I am going to remove the veil of heaven so that earth will not doubt Your goodness.

Make of me, Jesus, a pure and agreeable offering before the Face of Your Father. Jesus, transform me, miserable and sinful as I am, into Your own Self (for You can do all things), and give me to Your Eternal Father. I want to become a sacrificial host before You, but an ordinary wafer to people. I want the fragrance of my sacrifice to be known to You alone. O Eternal God, an unquenchable fire of supplication for Your mercy burns within me. I know and understand that this is my task, here and in eternity. You Yourself have told me to speak about this great mercy and about Your goodness.   (483)

OCTOBER 13

Midnight Mass. During Holy Mass, I again saw the little Infant Jesus, extremely beautiful, joyfully stretching out His little arms to me. After Holy Communion, I heard the words: **I am always in your heart; not only when you receive Me in Holy Communion, but always.** I spent these holy days in great joy.
(575)

One time, I was in doubt as to whether what had happened to me had seriously offended the Lord Jesus or not. As I could not solve this doubt, I made up my mind not to go to Communion before first going to confession, although I immediately made an act of contrition, as it is my habit to ask for forgiveness after the slightest transgression. During those days when I did not receive Holy Communion, I did not feel the presence of God. This caused me unspeakable pain, but I took it as a punishment for sin. However, at the time of Holy Confession I was reproached for not going to Holy Communion, because what had happened to me was not an obstacle to receiving Holy Communion. After confession, I received Holy Communion, and I saw the Lord Jesus who said to me, **Know, My daughter, that you caused Me more sorrow by not uniting yourself with Me in Holy Communion than you did by that small transgression.** (612)

OCTOBER 14

Oh, what joy it is to empty myself for the sake of immortal souls! I know that the grain of wheat must be destroyed and ground between millstones in order to become food. In the same way, I must become destroyed in order to be useful to the Church and souls, even though exteriorly no one will notice my sacrifice. O Jesus, outwardly I want to be hidden, just like this little wafer wherein the eye perceives nothing, and yet I am a host consecrated to You. (641)

Holy Hour—Thursday. During this hour of prayer, Jesus allowed me to enter the Cenacle, and I was a witness to what happened there. However, I was most deeply moved when, before the Consecration, Jesus raised His eyes to heaven and entered into a mysterious conversation with His Father. It is only in eternity that we shall really understand that moment. His eyes were like two flames; His face was radiant, white as snow; His whole personage full of majesty; His soul full of longing. At the moment of Consecration, love rested satiated—the sacrifice fully consummated. Now only the external ceremony of death will be carried out—external destruction; the essence [of it] is in the Cenacle. Never in my whole life had I understood this mystery so profoundly as during that hour of adoration. Oh, how ardently I desire that the whole world would come to know this unfathomable mystery!   (684)

OCTOBER 15

On one occasion, I heard these words: **My daughter, tell the whole world about My inconceivable mercy. I desire that the Feast of Mercy be a refuge and shelter for all souls, and especially for poor sinners. On that day the very depths of My tender mercy are open. I pour out a whole ocean of graces upon those souls who approach the fount of My mercy. The soul that will go to Confession and receive Holy Communion shall obtain complete forgiveness of sins and punishment. On that day all the divine floodgates through which grace flow are opened. Let no soul fear to draw near to Me, even though its sins be as scarlet. My mercy is so great that no mind, be it of man or of Angel, will be able to fathom it throughout all eternity. Everything that exists has come forth from the very depths of My most tender mercy. Every soul in its relation to Me will contemplate My love and mercy throughout eternity. The Feast of Mercy emerged from My very depths of tenderness. It is My desire that it be solemnly celebrated on the first Sunday after Easter. Mankind will not have peace until it turns to the Fount of My Mercy.**   (699)

I spend every free moment at the feet of the hidden God. He is my Master; I ask Him about everything; I speak to Him about everything. Here I obtain strength and light; here I learn everything; here I am given light on how to act toward my neighbor. From the time I left the novitiate, I have enclosed myself in the tabernacle together with Jesus, my Master. He Himself drew me into the fire of living love on which everything converges.   (704)

OCTOBER 16

I will enclose myself in the chalice of Jesus so that I may comfort Him continually. I will do everything within my power to save souls, and I will do it through prayer and suffering.

I try always to be a Bethany for Jesus, so that He may rest here after all His labors. In Holy Communion, my union with Jesus is so intimate and incomprehensible that even if I wanted to describe it in writing I could not do so, because I lack the words. (735)

During Mass today, I saw the Lord Jesus, who said to me, **Be at peace, My daughter; I see your efforts, which are very pleasing to Me.** And the Lord disappeared, and it was time for Holy Communion. After I received Holy Communion, I suddenly saw the Cenacle and in it Jesus and the Apostles. I saw the institution of the Most Blessed Sacrament. Jesus allowed me to penetrate His interior, and I came to know the greatness of His majesty and, at the same time, His great humbling of Himself. The extraordinary light that allowed me to see His majesty revealed to me, at the same time, what was in my own soul. (757)

OCTOBER 17

When I experienced these sufferings for the first time, it was like this: after the annual vows,* on a certain day, during prayer, I saw a great brilliance and, issuing from the brilliance, rays which completely enveloped me. Then suddenly, I felt a terrible pain in my hands, my feet, and my side and the thorns of the crown of thorns. I experienced these sufferings during Holy Mass on Friday, but this was only for a brief moment.

This was repeated for several Fridays, and later on I did not experience any sufferings up to the present time; that is, up to the end of September of this year. In the course of the present illness, during Holy Mass one Friday, I felt myself pierced by the same sufferings, and this has been repeated on every Friday and sometimes when I meet a soul that is not in the state of grace. Although this is infrequent, and the suffering lasts a very short time, still it is terrible, and I would not be able to bear it without a special grace from God. There is no outward indication of these sufferings. What will come later, I do not know. All this, for the sake of souls...   (759)

I could not assist at the whole Mass today; I assisted at only the most important parts, and after receiving Holy Communion I immediately returned to my solitude. The presence of God suddenly enveloped me, and at the same moment I felt the Passion of the Lord, for a very short while. During that moment, I attained a more profound knowledge of the work of mercy.   (808)

*After novitiate the sisters take temporary vows for one year. These are repeated for five years. Then perpetual vows are taken. Sister Faustina took her temporary vows (which she calls annual vows) on April 30, 1928.

OCTOBER 18

December 12, 1936. Today, I only received Holy Communion and stayed for a few moments of the Mass. All my strength is in You, O Living Bread. It would be difficult for me to live through the day if I did not receive Holy Communion. It is my shield; without You, Jesus, I know not how to live.   (814)

This morning I had an adventure. My watch had stopped, and I did not know when to get up, and I thought of what a misfortune it would be to miss Holy Communion. It was still dark, so I had no way of knowing whether it was time to get up. I dressed, made my meditation, and went to the chapel, but everything was still locked, and silence reigned everywhere. I steeped myself in prayer, especially for the sick. I now see how much the sick have need of prayer. Finally, the chapel was opened. I found it difficult to pray because I was already feeling very exhausted, and immediately after Holy Communion I returned to my room. Then I saw the Lord, who said to me, **Know, My daughter, that the ardor of your heart is pleasing to Me. And just as you desire ardently to become united with Me in Holy Communion, so too do I desire to give Myself wholly to you; and as a reward for your zeal, rest on My Heart.** At that moment, my spirit was immersed in His Being, like a drop in a bottomless ocean. I drowned myself in Him as in my sole treasure. Thus I came to recognize that the Lord allows certain difficulties for His greater glory. (826)

OCTOBER 19

I have offered this day for priests. I have suffered more today than ever before, both interiorly and exteriorly. I did not know it was possible to suffer so much in one day. I tried to make a Holy Hour, in the course of which my spirit had a taste of the bitterness of the Garden of Gethsemane. I am fighting alone, supported by His arm, against all the difficulties that face me like unassailable walls. But I trust in the power of His name and I fear nothing. (823)

O merciful Jesus, how longingly You hurried to the Upper Room to consecrate the Host that I am to receive in my life.

Jesus, You desired to dwell in my heart. Your living Blood unites with mine. Who can understand this close union? My heart encloses within itself the Almighty, the Infinite One. O Jesus, continue to grant me Your divine life. Let Your pure and noble Blood throb with all its might in my heart. I give You my whole being. Transform me into Yourself and make me capable of doing Your holy will in all things and of returning Your love. O my sweet Spouse, You know that my heart knows no one but You. You have opened up in my heart an insatiable depth of love for You. From the very first moment it knew You, my heart has loved You and has lost itself in You as its one and only object. May Your pure and omnipotent love be the driving force of all my actions. Who will ever conceive and understand the depth of mercy that has gushed forth from Your Heart? (832)

OCTOBER 20

Today, when the doctor [Adam Silberg] making his rounds came to see me, he somehow didn't like the way I looked. Naturally, I was suffering more, and so my temperature had gone up considerably. Consequently, he decided I must not go down for Holy Communion until my temperature dropped to normal. I said, "All right," although pain seized my heart; but I said I would go only if I had no fever. So he agreed to that. When the doctor left, I said to the Lord, "Jesus, now it is up to You whether I shall go or not," and I didn't think about it anymore, although the thought kept coming to my mind: I am not to have Jesus—no, that's impossible—and not just once but for several days, until my temperature drops. But in the evening, I said to the Lord, "Jesus, if my Communions are pleasing to You, I beg You humbly, grant that I have not one degree of fever tomorrow morning." (878)

OCTOBER 21

In the morning, as I was taking my temperature, I thought to myself, "If there is even one degree, I will not get up because that would be contrary to obedience." But when I looked at the thermometer, there wasn't even one degree of fever. I jumped to my feet at once and went to Holy Communion. When the doctor came and I told him that I had had not even one degree of fever, and so had gone to Holy Communion, he was surprised. I begged him not to make it difficult for me to go to Holy Communion, for it would have an adverse effect on the treatment. The doctor answered, "For peace of conscience and at the same time to avoid difficulties for yourself, Sister, let us make the following agreement: when the weather is fine, and it isn't raining, and you feel all right, then, Sister, please go; but you must weigh these matters in your conscience." It made me very happy that the doctor was being so considerate for my sake. You see, Jesus, that I have already done whatever was up to me; now I am counting on You and am quite at peace. (878)

OCTOBER 22

During Holy Mass, I saw the Lord Jesus nailed upon the cross amidst great torments. A soft moan issued from His Heart. After some time, He said, **I thirst. I thirst for the salvation of souls. Help Me, My daughter, to save souls. Join your sufferings to My Passion and offer them to the heavenly Father for sinners.** (1032)

Monday of Holy Week. I asked the Lord to let me take part in His Sorrowful Passion that I might experience in soul and body, to the extent that this is possible for a creature, His bitter Passion. I asked to experience all the bitterness, insofar as this was possible. And the Lord answered that He would give me this grace, and that on Thursday, after Holy Communion, He would grant this in a special way. (1034)

I find myself so weak that were it not for Holy Communion I would fall continually. One thing alone sustains me, and that is Holy Communion. From it I draw my strength; in it is all my comfort. I fear life on days when I do not receive Holy Communion. I fear my own self. Jesus concealed in the Host is everything to me. From the tabernacle I draw strength, power, courage, and light. Here, I seek consolation in time of anguish. I would not know how to give glory to God if I did not have the Eucharist in my heart. (1037)

OCTOBER 23

Most sweet Jesus, set on fire my love for You and transform me into Yourself. Divinize me that my deeds may be pleasing to You. May this be accomplished by the power of the Holy Communion which I receive daily. Oh, how greatly I desire to be wholly transformed into You, O Lord! (1289)

When I received Holy Communion, I said to Him, "Jesus, I thought about You so many times last night," and Jesus answered me, **And I thought of you before I called you into being.** "Jesus, in what way were You thinking about me?" **In terms of admitting you to My eternal happiness.** After these words, my soul was flooded with the love of God. I could not stop marveling at how much God loves us. (1292)

OCTOBER 24

November 19. After Communion today, Jesus told me how much He desires to come to human hearts. **I desire to unite Myself with human souls; My great delight is to unite Myself with souls. Know, My daughter, that when I come to a human heart in Holy Communion, My hands are full of all kinds of graces which I want to give to the soul. But souls do not even pay any attention to Me; they leave Me to Myself and busy themselves with other things. Oh, how sad I am that souls do not recognize Love! They treat Me as a dead object.** I answered Jesus, "O Treasure of my heart, the only object of my love and entire delight of my soul, I want to adore You in my heart as You are adored on the throne of Your eternal glory. My love wants to make up to You at least in part for the coldness of so great a number of souls. Jesus, behold my heart which is for You a dwelling place to which no one else has entry. You alone repose in it as in a beautiful garden." (1385)

All the good that is in me is due to Holy Communion. I owe everything to it. I feel that this holy fire has transformed me completely. Oh, how happy I am to be a dwelling place for You, O Lord! My heart is a temple in which You dwell continually...   (1392)

OCTOBER 25

Oh, how painful it is to Me that souls so seldom unite themselves to Me in Holy Communion. I wait for souls, and they are indifferent toward Me. I love them tenderly and sincerely, and they distrust Me. I want to lavish My graces on them, and they do not want to accept them. They treat Me as a dead object, whereas My Heart is full of love and mercy. In order

that you may know at least some of My pain, imagine the most tender of mothers who has great love for her children, while those children spurn her love. Consider her pain. No one is in a position to console her. This is but a feeble image and likeness of My love. (1447)

After Holy Communion the Lord said to me, **If the priest had not brought Me to you, I would have come Myself under the same species. My daughter, your sufferings of this night obtained the grace of mercy for an immense number of souls.** (1459)

Today, when the chaplain [Father Theodore] brought the Lord Jesus, a light issued from the Host, its light striking my heart and filling me with a great fire of love. Jesus was letting me know that I should answer the inspirations of grace with more faithfulness and that my vigilance should be more subtle. (1462)

OCTOBER 26

Jesus, hide me; just as You have hidden Yourself under the form of the white Host, so hide me from human eyes, and particularly hide the gifts which You so kindly grant me. May I not betray outwardly what You are effecting in my soul. I am a white host before You, O Divine Priest. Consecrate me Yourself, and may my transubstantiation be known only to You. I stand before You each day as a sacrificial host and implore Your mercy upon the world. In silence, and unseen, I will empty myself before You; my pure and undivided love will burn, in profound silence, as a holocaust. And may the fragrance of my love be wafted to the foot of Your throne. You are the Lord of lords, but You delight in innocent and humble souls. (1564)

OCTOBER 27

I saw how unwillingly the Lord Jesus came to certain souls in Holy Communion. And He spoke these words to me: **I enter into certain hearts as into a second Passion.** (1598)

As I was praying to the living Heart of Jesus in the Blessed Sacrament for the intention of a certain priest, Jesus suddenly gave me knowledge of His goodness and said to me, **I will give him nothing that is beyond his strength.** (1607)

OCTOBER 28

Easter [April 17, 1938]. During Mass, I thanked the Lord Jesus for having deigned to redeem us and for having given us that greatest of all gifts; namely, His love in Holy Communion; that is, His very own Self. At that moment, I was drawn into the bosom of the Most Holy Trinity, and I was immersed in the love of the Father, the Son, and the Holy Spirit. These moments are hard to describe. (1670)

Write for the benefit of religious souls that it delights Me to come to their hearts in Holy Communion. But if there is anyone else in such a heart, I cannot bear it and quickly leave that heart, taking with Me all the gifts and graces I have prepared for the soul. And the soul does not even notice My going. After some time, inner emptiness and dissatisfaction will come to her attention. Oh, if only she would turn to Me then, I would help her to cleanse her heart, and I would fulfill everything in her soul; but without her knowledge and consent, I cannot be the Master of her heart. (1683)

OCTOBER 29

Jesus said to me, **Be at peace; I am with you.** Tired, I fell asleep. In the evening, the sister [Sister David] who was to look after me came and said, "Tomorrow you will not receive the Lord Jesus, Sister, because you are very tired; later on, we shall see." This hurt me very much, but I said with great calmness, "Very well," and, resigning myself totally to the will of the Lord, I tried to sleep. In the morning, I made my meditation and prepared for Holy Communion, even though I was not to receive the Lord Jesus. When my love and desire had reached a high degree, I saw at my bedside a Seraph, who gave me Holy Communion, saying these words: "Behold the Lord of Angels." When I received the Lord, my spirit was drowned in the love of God and in amazement. This was repeated for thirteen days, although I was never sure he would bring me Holy Communion the next day. Yet, I put my trust completely in the goodness of God, but did not even dare to think that I would receive Holy Communion in this way on the following day.

The Seraph was surrounded by a great light, the divinity and love of God being reflected in him. He wore a golden robe and, over it, a transparent surplice and a transparent stole. The chalice was crystal, covered with a transparent veil. As soon as he gave me the Lord, he disappeared.   (1676)

OCTOBER 30

God, You could have saved thousands of worlds with one word; a single sigh from Jesus would have satisfied Your justice. But You Yourself, Jesus, purely out of love for us, underwent such a terrible Passion. Your Father's justice would have been propitiated with a single sigh from You, and all Your self-abasement is solely the work of Your mercy and Your inconceivable love. On leaving the earth, O Lord, You wanted to stay with us, and so You left us Yourself in the Sacrament of the Altar, and You opened wide Your mercy to us. There is no misery that could exhaust You; You have called us all to this fountain of love, to this spring of God's compassion. Here is the tabernacle of Your mercy, here is the remedy for all our ills. To You, O living spring of mercy, all souls are drawn; some like deer, thirsting for Your love, others to wash the wound of their sins, and still others, exhausted by life, to draw strength. At the moment of Your death on the Cross, You bestowed upon us eternal life; allowing Your most holy side to be opened, You opened an inexhaustible spring of mercy for us, giving us Your dearest possession, the Blood and Water from Your Heart. Such is the omnipotence of Your mercy. From it all grace flows to us. (1747)

The most solemn moment of my life is the moment when I receive Holy Communion. I long for each Holy Communion, and for every Holy Communion I give thanks to the Most Holy Trinity.

If the Angels were capable of envy, they would envy us for two things: One is the receiving of Holy Communion, and the other is suffering. (1804)

OCTOBER 31

Today, I am preparing myself for Your coming as a bride does for the coming of her bridegroom. He is a great Lord, this Bridegroom of mine. The heavens cannot contain Him. The Seraphim who stand closest to Him cover their faces and repeat unceasingly: Holy, Holy, Holy.

This great Lord is my Bridegroom. It is to Him that the Choirs sing. It is before Him that the Thrones bow down. By His splendor the sun is eclipsed. And yet this great Lord is my Bridegroom. My heart, desist from this profound meditation on how others adore Him, for you no longer have time for that, as He is coming and is already at your door.   (1805)

Today, I feel an abyss of misery in my soul. I want to approach Holy Communion as a fountain of mercy and to drown myself completely in this ocean of love. When I received Jesus, I threw myself into Him as into an abyss of unfathomable mercy. And the more I felt I was misery itself, the stronger grew my trust in Him.

In this abasement, I passed the whole day.   (1817)

Today, I want to be transformed, whole and entire, into the love of Jesus and to offer myself, together with Him, to the Heavenly Father.

During Holy Mass, I saw the Infant Jesus in the chalice, and He said to me, **I am dwelling in your heart as you see Me in this chalice.**   (1820)

HUMILITY

November

HUMILITY IS A SUMMARY of sanctity, a counter-sign to our proud age. It means depending on God, like a small child depends on parents. It is the great characteristic of Jesus, Mary, and holy people like Blessed Faustina. This kind of profound humility has three dimensions: truth, totality, and transparency.

Humility expresses our free submission to the will of God, which is a delight to the Lord. Humility is foundational to all the other virtues, and is THE condition for receiving God's mercy.

FOR THIS MONTH:

Practice: Let simplicity and humility be the characteristic of your life—like a little child always trusting (55).

Prayer: Repeat often:
> Jesus, meek and humble of Heart,
> make my heart like Yours.

Promise: The torrents of grace inundate humble souls. The proud remain always in poverty and misery, because My grace turns away from them to humble souls (1602).

NOVEMBER 1

Spiritual Counsel Given Me
by Father Andrasz, S.J.

First: You must not turn away from these interior inspirations, but always tell everything to your confessor. If you recognize that these interior inspirations refer to your own self; that is to say, they are for the good of your soul or for the good of other souls, I urge you to follow them; and you must not neglect them, but always do so in consultation with your confessor.

Second: If these inspirations are not in accord with the faith or the spirit of the Church, they must be rejected immediately as coming from the evil spirit.

Third: If these inspirations do not refer to souls, in general, nor specifically to their good, you should not take them too seriously, and it would be better to even ignore them.

But you should not make this decision by yourself, either one way or the other, as you can easily be led astray despite these great favors from God. Humility, humility, and ever humility, as we can do nothing of ourselves; all is purely and simply God's grace.

You say to me that God demands great trust from souls; well then, you be the first to show this trust. And one more word—accept all this with serenity. (55)

NOVEMBER 2

Here are a few words from a conversation I had with the Mother Directress [Mary Joseph] toward the end of my novitiate: "Sister, let simplicity and humility be the characteristic traits of your soul. Go through life like a little child, always trusting, always full of simplicity and humility, content with everything, happy in every circumstance. There, where others fear, you will pass calmly along, thanks to this simplicity and humility. Remember this, Sister, for your whole life: as waters flow from the mountains down into the valleys, so, too, do God's graces flow only into humble souls." (55)

Humiliation is my daily food. ˙ understand that the bride must herself share in everything that is the groom's; and so His cloak of mockery must cover me, too. At those times when I suffer much, I try to remain silent, as I do not trust my tongue which, at such moments, is inclined to talk for itself, while its duty is to help me praise God for all the blessings and gifts which He has given me. When I receive Jesus in Holy Communion, I ask Him fervently to deign to heal my tongue so that I would offend neither God nor neighbor by it. I want my tongue to praise God without cease. Great are the faults committed by the tongue. The soul will not attain sanctity if it does not keep watch over its tongue. (92)

NOVEMBER 3

And again, I would like to say three words to the soul that is determined to strive for sanctity and to derive fruit; that is to say, benefit from confession.

First word—complete sincerity and openness. Even the holiest and wisest confessor cannot forcibly pour into the soul what he desires if it is not sincere and open. An insincere, secretive soul risks great dangers in the spiritual life, and even the Lord Jesus Himself does not give Himself to such a soul on a higher level, because He knows it would derive no benefit from these special graces.

Second word—humility. A soul does not benefit as it should from the sacrament of confession if it is not humble. Pride keeps it in darkness. The soul neither knows how, nor is it willing, to probe with precision the depths of its own misery. It puts on a mask and avoids everything that might bring it recovery.

Third word—obedience. A disobedient soul will win no victory, even if the Lord Jesus Himself, in person, were to hear its confession. The most experienced confessor will be of no help whatsoever to such a soul. The disobedient soul exposes itself to great misfortuncs; it will make no progress toward perfection, nor will it succeed in the spiritual life. God lavishes His graces most generously upon the soul, but it must be an obedient soul.

(113)

NOVEMBER 4

Today we are beginning the third probation. All three of us met at Mother Margaret's, as the other sisters were having their probation in the novitiate. Mother Margaret began with a prayer, explained to us what the third probation consists of, and then spoke on how great is the grace of the perpetual vows. Suddenly I began to cry out loud. In an instant all God's graces appeared before the eyes of my soul, and I saw myself so wretched and ungrateful toward God. The sisters began to rebuke me, saying, "Why did she break out crying?" But Mother Margaret came to my defense, saying that she was not surprised.

At the end of the hour, I went before the Blessed Sacrament and, like the greatest and most miserable of wretches, I begged for His mercy that He might heal and purify my poor soul. Then I heard these words, **My daughter, all your miseries have been consumed in the flame of My love, like a little twig thrown into a roaring fire. By humbling yourself in this way, you draw upon yourself and upon other souls an entire sea of My mercy.** I answered, "Jesus, mold my poor heart according to Your divine delight." (178)

Holy Hour. During this hour, I tried to meditate on the Lord's Passion. But my soul was filled with joy, and suddenly I saw the Child Jesus. But His majesty penetrated me to such an extent that I said, "Jesus, You are so little, and yet I know that You are my Creator and Lord." And Jesus answered me, **I am, and I keep company with you as a child to teach you humility and simplicity.**

I gathered all my sufferings and difficulties into a bouquet for Jesus for the day of our perpetual betrothal. Nothing was difficult for me, when I remembered it was for my Betrothed as proof of my love for Him. (184)

NOVEMBER 5

I want to hide myself so that no creature might know my heart. Jesus, You alone know my heart and possess it whole and entire. No one knows our secret. We understand each other mutually with one look. From the moment we came to know each other I have been happy. Your greatness is my fullness. O Jesus, when I am in the last place, lower than the postulants, even the youngest of them, then I feel that I am in my proper place. I did not know that the Lord had put so much happiness in these drab little corners. Now I understand that even in prison there can burst forth from a pure heart the fullness of love for You, O Lord! External things mean nothing to pure love; it cuts through them all. Neither prison doors nor the gates of heaven are strong enough to stop it. It reaches God Himself, and nothing can quench it. It knows no obstacles; it is free like a queen and has free access to all places. Death itself must bow its head before it.... (201)

I will thank the Lord Jesus for every humiliation and will pray specially for the person who has given me the chance to be humiliated. I will immolate myself for the benefit of souls, I will not count the cost of any sacrifice, I will cast myself beneath the feet of the sisters, like a carpet on which they can not only tread, but also wipe their feet. My place is under the feet of the sisters. I will make every effort to obtain that place unnoticed by others. It is enough that God sees this. (243)

NOVEMBER 6

I will hide from people's eyes whatever good I am able to do so that God Himself may be my reward. I will be like a tiny violet hidden in the grass, which does not hurt the foot that treads on it, but diffuses its fragrance and, forgetting itself completely, tries to please the person who has crushed it underfoot. This is very difficult for human nature, but God's grace comes to one's aid. (255)

Jesus told me that I please Him best by meditating on His sorrowful Passion, and by such meditation much light falls upon my soul. He who wants to learn true humility should reflect upon the Passion of Jesus. When I meditate upon the Passion of Jesus, I get a clear understanding of many things I could not comprehend before. I want to resemble You, O Jesus,— You crucified, tortured and humiliated. Jesus, imprint upon my heart and soul Your own humility. I love You, Jesus, to the point of madness, You who were crushed with suffering as described by the prophet [cf. Isaiah 53:2-9], as if he could not see the human form in You because of Your great suffering. It is in this condition, Jesus, that I love You to the point of madness. O eternal and infinite God, what has love done to You?...

(267)

NOVEMBER 7

Advice of the Rev. Dr. Sopocko.

Without humility, we cannot be pleasing to God. Practice the third degree of humility; that is, not only must one refrain from explaining and defending oneself when reproached with something, but one should rejoice at the humiliation.

If the things you are telling me really come from God, prepare your soul for great suffering. You will encounter disapproval and persecution. They will look upon you as a hysteric and an eccentric, but the Lord will lavish His graces upon you. True works of God always meet opposition and are marked by suffering. If God wants to accomplish something, sooner or later He will do so in spite of the difficulties. Your part, in the meantime, is to arm yourself with great patience. (270)

Once the Lord said to me, **My Heart was moved by great mercy towards you, My dearest child, when I saw you torn to shreds because of the great pain you suffered in repenting for your sins. I see your love, so pure and true that I give you first place among the virgins. You are the honor and glory of My Passion. I see every abasement of your soul, and nothing**

escapes My attention. I lift up the humble even to my very throne, because I want it so. (282)

NOVEMBER 8

Once, when I saw Jesus in the form of a small child, I asked, "Jesus, why do You now take on the form of a child when You commune with me? In spite of this, I still see in You the infinite God, my Lord and Creator." Jesus replied that until I learned simplicity and humility, He would commune with me as a little child. (335)

Concerning Holy Confession. We should derive two kinds of profit from Holy Confession:
1. We come to confession to be healed;
2. We come to be educated—like a small child, our soul has constant need of education.

O my Jesus, I understand these words to their very depths, and I know from my own experience that, on its own strength, the soul will not go far; it will exert itself greatly and will do nothing for the glory of God; it will err continually, because our mind is darkened and does not know how to discern its own affairs. I shall pay special attention to two things: Firstly, I will choose, in making my confession, that which humiliates me most, even if it be a trifle, but something that costs me much, and for that reason I will tell it; secondly, I will practice contrition, not only during confession, but during every self-examination, and I will arouse within myself an act of perfect contrition, especially when I am going to bed. One more word: A soul which sincerely wants to advance in perfection must observe strictly the advice given by the spiritual director. There is as much holiness as there is dependence. (377)

NOVEMBER 9

A certain moment, May 12, 1935. In the evening, I just about got into bed, and I fell asleep immediately. Though I fell asleep quickly, I was awakened even more quickly. A little child came and woke me up. The child seemed about a year old, and I was surprised it could speak so well, as children of that age either do not speak or speak very indistinctly. The child was beautiful beyond words and resembled the Child Jesus, and He said to me, **Look at the sky.** And when I looked at the sky I saw the stars and the moon shining. Then the child asked me, **Do you see this moon and these stars?** When I said yes, He spoke these words to me, **These stars are the souls of faithful Christians, and the moon is the souls of religious. Do you see how great the difference is between the light of the moon and the light of the stars? Such is the difference in heaven between the soul of a religious and the soul of a faithful Christian.** And He went on to say that, **True greatness is in loving God and in humility.** (424)

A moment later, I again saw the child who had awakened me. It was of wondrous beauty and repeated these words to me, **True greatness of the soul is in loving God and in humility.** I asked the child, "How do you know that true greatness of the soul is in loving God and in humility? Only theologians know about such things and you haven't even learned the catechism. So how do you know?" To this He answered, **I know; I know all things.** And with that, He disappeared. (427)

NOVEMBER 10

Nocturnal Adoration. I was suffering very much, and it seemed to me I would not be able to make my adoration, but I gathered up all my will power and, although I collapsed in my cell, I paid no attention to what ailed me, for I had the Passion of Jesus before my eyes. When I entered the chapel, I received an inner understanding of the great reward that God is preparing for us, not only for our good deeds, but also for our sincere desire to perform them. What a great grace of God this is!

Oh, how sweet it is to toil for God and souls! I want no respite in this battle, but I shall fight to the last breath for the glory of my King and Lord. I shall not lay the sword aside until He calls me before His throne; I fear no blows, because God is my shield. It is the enemy who should fear us, and not we him. Satan defeats only the proud and the cowardly, because the humble are strong. Nothing will confuse or frighten a humble soul. I have directed my flight at the very center of the sun's heat, and nothing can lower its course. Love will not allow itself to be taken prisoner; it is free like a queen. Love attains God. (450)

O Jesus, my heart stops beating when I think of all You are doing for me! I am amazed at You, Lord, that You would stoop so low to my wretched soul! What inconceivable means You take to convince me! (460)

NOVEMBER 11

During a meditation on humility, an old doubt returned: that a soul as miserable as mine could not carry out the task which the Lord was demanding [of me]. Just as I was analyzing this doubt, the priest who was conducting the retreat interrupted this train of thought and spoke about the very thing I was having doubts about; namely, that God usually chooses the weakest and simplest souls as tools for His greatest works; that we can see that this is an undeniable truth when we look at the men He chose to be His apostles; or again, when we look at the history of the Church and see what great works were done by souls that were the least capable of accomplishing them; for it is just in this way that God's works are revealed for what they are, the works of God. When my doubt had completely disappeared, the priest resumed his conference on humility.

Jesus was standing, as He usually did during each conference, on the altar and said nothing to me, but with His kindly gaze pierced my poor soul which no longer had any excuse.   (464)

Jesus, Eternal Light, enlighten my mind, strengthen my will, inflame my heart, and be with me as You have promised, for without You I am nothing. You know, Jesus, how weak I am. I do not need to tell You this, for You Yourself know perfectly well how wretched I am. It is in You that all my strength lies.

(495)

NOVEMBER 12

When a reluctance and a monotony as regards my duties begins to take possession of me, I remind myself that I am in the house of the Lord, where nothing is small and where the glory of the Church and the progress of many a soul depend on this small deed of mine, accomplished in a divinized way. Therefore there is nothing small in a religious congregation.

(508)

When my intentions are not recognized, but rather condemned, I am not too much surprised, for I know that it is only God who scrutinizes my heart. Truth will not die; the wounded heart will regain peace in due time, and my spirit is strengthened through adversities. I do not always listen to what my heart tells me, but I keep asking God for light; and when I feel I have regained my equilibrium, then I say more.

(511)

The day of the renewal of vows. The presence of God flooded my soul. During Holy Mass I saw Jesus, and He said to me, **You are my great joy; your love and your humility make Me leave the heavenly throne and unite Myself with you. Love fills up the abyss that exists between My greatness and your nothingness.** (512)

NOVEMBER 13

This Thursday, when we were having nocturnal adoration, at first I could not pray; a sort of dryness engulfed me. I could not meditate on Jesus' sorrowful Passion. So I lay prostrate and offered the most sorrowful Passion of the Lord Jesus to the heavenly Father in reparation for the sins of all the world. When I got to my feet after this prayer and walked to my kneeler, I suddenly saw Jesus next to it. The Lord Jesus appeared as He was during the scourging. In His hands He was holding a white garment with which He clothed me and a cord with which He girded me, and He covered me with a red cloak like the one He was clothed with during His Passion and a veil of the same color, and He said to me... **Fix your eyes upon Me and live according to what you see. I desire that you penetrate into My spirit more deeply and understand that I am meek and humble of heart.** (526)

After Holy Communion, I saw the Lord Jesus, who said these words to me: **Today, penetrate into the spirit of My poverty**

and arrange everything in such a way that the most destitute will have no reason to envy you. I find pleasure, not in large buildings and magnificent structures, but in a pure and humble heart. (532)

NOVEMBER 14

There will be no distinction between the sisters, no mothers, no reverends, no venerables, but all will be equal, even though there might be great differences in their parentage. We know who Jesus was, and yet how He humbled Himself and with whom He associated. Their habit will be like that worn by Jesus during His Passion, and they will not simply wear the robe [He wore]; they must also seal themselves with the marks He bore: suffering and scorn. Each one will strive for the greatest self-denial and have a love of humility, and she who will distinguish herself most in this latter virtue will be the one who is capable of leading the others. (538)

Work. As poor persons, the nuns themselves will do all the work in the convent. Each one should be glad when she is given some work which is humbling or which goes against her nature, as that will greatly help her interior formation. The superior will often change the sisters' duties, and in this way help them to detach themselves completely from the little details to which women have a great attachment. Truly, I often find it amusing to see with my own eyes souls who have forsaken really great things only to attach themselves to fiddle faddle; that is, trifles. Each sister, including even the superior, shall work in the kitchen for a month. Every one should take a turn at every chore which is to be done in the convent. (549)

NOVEMBER 15

O Holy Trinity, Eternal God, my spirit is drowned in Your beauty. The ages are as nothing in Your sight. You are always the same. Oh, how great is Your majesty. Jesus, why do You conceal Your majesty, why have You left Your heavenly throne and dwelt among us? The Lord answered me, **My daughter, love has brought Me here, and love keeps Me here. My daughter, if you knew what great merit and reward is earned by one act of pure love for Me, you would die of joy. I am saying this that you may constantly unite yourself with Me through love, for this is the goal of the life of your soul. This act is an act of the will. Know that a pure soul is humble. When you lower and empty yourself before My majesty, I then pursue you with My graces and make use of My omnipotence to exalt you.** (576)

Jesus, You know how ardently I desire to hide so that no one may know me but Your sweetest Heart. I want to be a tiny violet, hidden in the grass, unknown in a magnificent enclosed garden in which beautiful lilies and roses grow. The beautiful rose and the lovely lily can be seen from afar, but in order to see a little violet, one has to bend low; only its scent gives it away. Oh, how happy I am to be able to hide myself in this way! O my divine Bridegroom, the flower of my heart and the scent of my pure love are for You. My soul has drowned itself in You, Eternal God. From the moment when You drew me to Yourself, O my Jesus, the more I have known You, the more ardently I have desired You. (591)

NOVEMBER 16

O my Jesus, nothing is better for the soul than humiliations. In contempt is the secret of happiness, when the soul recognizes that, of itself, it is only wretchedness and nothingness, and that whatever it possesses of good is a gift of God. When the soul sees that everything is given it freely and that the only thing it has of itself is its own misery, this is what sustains it in a continual act of humble prostration before the majesty of God. And God, seeing the soul in such a disposition, pursues it with His graces. As the soul continues to immerse itself more deeply into the abyss of its nothingness and need, God uses His omnipotence to exalt it. If there is a truly happy soul upon earth, it can only be a truly humble soul. At first, one's self-love suffers greatly on this account, but after a soul has struggled courageously, God grants it much light by which it sees how wretched and full of deception everything is. God alone is in its heart. A humble soul does not trust itself, but places all its confidence in God. God defends the humble soul and lets Himself into its secrets, and the soul abides in unsurpassable happiness which no one can comprehend.   (593)

My Jesus, You see how weak I am of myself. Therefore, You Yourself direct my affairs. And know, Jesus, that without You I will not budge for any cause, but with You I will take on the most difficult things.   (602)

NOVEMBER 17

Today, I heard these words: **You see how weak you are, so when shall I be able to count on you?** I answered, "Jesus, be always with me, for I am Your little child. Jesus, You know what little children do."   (722)

I have understood that at certain and most difficult moments I shall be alone, deserted by everyone, and that I must face all the storms and fight with all the strength of my soul, even with those from whom I expected to get help.

But I am not alone, because Jesus is with me, and with Him I fear nothing. I am well aware of everything, and I know what God is demanding of me. Suffering, contempt, ridicule, persecution, and humiliation will be my constant lot. I know no other way. For sincere love—ingratitude; this is my path, marked out by the footprints of Jesus.

My Jesus, my strength and my only hope, in You alone is all my hope. My trust will not be frustrated.   (746)

NOVEMBER 18

Jesus gave me to know the depth of His meekness and humility and to understand that He clearly demanded the same of me. I felt the gaze of God in my soul. This filled me with unspeakable love, but I understood that the Lord was looking with love on my virtues and my heroic efforts, and I knew that this was what was drawing God into my heart. It is from this that I have come to understand that it is not enough for me to strive only for the ordinary virtues, but that I must try to exercise the heroic virtues. Although exteriorly a thing may be quite ordinary, it is the different manner [in which it is carried out] that only the eye of God catches. O my Jesus, what I have written is just a pale shadow of what I understand in my soul; these are purely spiritual things, but in order to write something of what the Lord gives me to know, I must use words with which I am totally dissatisfied, because they do not express the reality. (758)

Always and in all circumstances, yield the first place to others; especially during recreation listen quietly, without interrupting, even if someone tells me the same thing ten times. I will never ask questions about something that interests me very much. (789)

NOVEMBER 19

I must never speak of my own experiences. In suffering, I must seek relief in prayer. In doubts, even the smallest, I must seek only the advice of my confessor. I must always have a heart which is open to receive the sufferings of others, and drown my own sufferings in the Divine Heart so that they would not be noticed on the outside, insofar as possible.

I must always strive for equanimity, no matter how stormy the circumstances might be. I must not allow anything to disturb my interior calm and silence. Nothing can compare with peace of soul. When I am wrongfully accused of something, I will not explain myself; if the superior wants to know the truth, whether I was in the right or not, let her find out from others rather than from me. My concern is to accept everything with a humble inner disposition. (792)

I have experienced how much envy there is, even in religious life. I see that there are few truly great souls, ready to trample on everything that is not God. O soul, you will find no beauty outside of God. Oh, how fragile is the foundation of those who elevate themselves at the expense of others! What a loss!

(833)

NOVEMBER 20

Today, Jesus is bidding me to comfort and reassure a certain soul who has opened herself to me and told me about her difficulties. This soul is pleasing to the Lord, but she is not aware of it. God is keeping her in deep humility. I have carried out the Lord's directives. (1063)

That beautiful soul who is spreading this work of divine mercy throughout the world is, by his deep humility, very pleasing to God. (1083)

NOVEMBER 21

Today, as God's Majesty swept over me, my soul understood that the Lord, so very great though He is, delights in humble souls. The more a soul humbles itself, the greater the kindness with which the Lord approaches it. Uniting Himself closely with it, He raises it to His very throne. Happy is the soul whom the Lord Himself defends. I have come to know that only love is of any value; love is greatness; nothing, no works, can compare with a single act of pure love of God. (1092)

NOVEMBER 22

June 30, 1937. Today, the Lord said to me, **I have wanted to exalt this Congregation many times, but I am unable to do so because of its pride. Know, My daughter, that I do not grant My graces to proud souls, and I even take away from them the graces I have granted.** (1170)

It so happened that I fell again into a certain error, in spite of a sincere resolution not to do so—even though the lapse was a minor imperfection and rather involuntary—and at this I felt such acute pain in my soul that I interrupted my work and went to the chapel for a while. Falling at the feet of Jesus, with love and a great deal of pain, I apologized to the Lord, all the more ashamed because of the fact that in my conversation with Him after Holy Communion this very morning I had promised to be faithful to Him. Then I heard these words: **If it hadn't been for this small imperfection, you wouldn't have come to Me. Know that as often as you come to Me, humbling yourself and asking My forgiveness, I pour out a super-abundance of graces on your soul, and your imperfection vanishes before My eyes, and I see only your love and your humility. You lose nothing but gain much...** (1293)

NOVEMBER 23

Bring to me the meek and humble souls and the souls of little children, and immerse them in My mercy. These souls most closely resemble My Heart. They strengthened Me during My bitter agony. I saw them as earthly Angels, who would keep vigil at My altars. I pour out upon them whole torrents of grace. Only the humble soul is able to receive My grace. I favor humble souls with My confidence. (1220)

O humility, lovely flower, I see how few souls possess you. Is it because you are so beautiful and at the same time so difficult to attain? O yes, it is both the one and the other. Even God takes great pleasure in her. The floodgates of heaven are open to a humble soul, and a sea of graces flows down upon her. O how beautiful is a humble soul! From her heart, as from a censer, rises a varied and most pleasing fragrance which breaks through the skies and reaches God Himself, filling His Most Sacred Heart with joy. God refuses nothing to such a soul; she is all-powerful and influences the destiny of the whole world. God raises such a soul up to His very throne, and the more she humbles herself, the more God stoops down to her, pursuing her with His graces and accompanying her at every moment with His omnipotence. Such a soul is most deeply united with God. O humility, strike deep roots in my whole being. O Virgin most pure, but also most humble, help me to attain deep humility. Now I understand why there are so few saints; it is because so few souls are deeply humble. (1306)

NOVEMBER 24

O Lord, You who penetrate my whole being and the most secret depths of my soul, You see that I desire You alone and long only for the fulfillment of Your holy will, paying no heed to difficulties or sufferings or humiliations or to what others might think. (1360)

O my Lord, my soul is the most wretched of all, and yet You stoop to it with such kindness! I see clearly Your greatness and my littleness, and therefore I rejoice that You are so powerful and without limit, and so I rejoice greatly at being so little. (1417)

I strive for the greatest perfection possible in order to be useful to the Church. Greater by far is my bond to the Church. The sanctity or the fall of each individual soul has an effect upon the whole Church. Observing myself and those who are close to me, I have come to understand how great an influence I have on other souls, not by any heroic deeds, as these are striking in themselves, but by small actions like a movement of the hand, a look, and many other things too numerous to mention, which have an effect on and reflect in the souls of others, as I myself have noticed. (1475)

NOVEMBER 25

However, I asked my confessor what to do: whether I should continue to suffer this for the sake of sinners or ask the superiors for an exception by way of milder food. He decided that I should ask the superiors for milder food. And thus I followed his directions, seeing that this humiliation was more pleasing to God. (1429)

Today, the love of God is transporting me into the other world. I am all immersed in love; I love and feel that I am loved, and with full consciousness I experience this. My soul is drowning in the Lord, realizing the great Majesty of God and its own littleness; but through this knowledge my happiness increases... This awareness is so vivid in the soul, so powerful and, at the same time, so sweet. (1500)

I never cringe before anyone. I can't bear flattery, for humility is nothing but the truth. There is no cringing in true humility. Although I consider myself the least in the whole convent, on the other hand, I enjoy the honor of being the bride of Christ. Little matter that often I hear people say that I am proud, for I know that human judgment does not discern the motives for our actions. (1502)

NOVEMBER 26

When, at the beginning of my religious life, following the novitiate, I began to exercise myself particularly in humility, the humiliations that God sent me were not enough for me. And so, in my excessive zeal, I looked for more of them on my own, and I often represented myself to my superiors other than I was in reality and spoke of miseries of which I had no notion. But a short time later, Jesus gave me to know that humility is only the truth. From that time on, I changed my ideas, faithfully following the light of Jesus. I learned that if a soul is with Jesus, He will not permit it to err. (1503)

NOVEMBER 27

When we began to share the wafer, a sincere and mutual love reigned among us. Mother Superior [Irene] expressed this wish to me: "Sister, the works of God proceed slowly, so do not be in a hurry." In general, the sisters sincerely wished me great love, which is that which I desire above all. I saw that these wishes truly came from their hearts, except for one sister, who had a concealed malice in her wishes, although this did not cause me much pain, for my soul was pervaded by God. Yet this enlightened me as to why God communicates so little with a soul of this kind, and I learned that such a soul is always seeking itself, even in holy things. Oh, how good the Lord is in not letting me go astray! I know that He will guard me, even jealously, but only as long as I remain little, because it is with such that the great Lord likes to commune. As to proud souls, He watches them from afar and opposes them. (1440)

When I was apologizing to the Lord Jesus for a certain action of mine which, a little later, turned out to be imperfect, Jesus put me at ease with these words: **My daughter, I reward you for the purity of your intention which you had at the time when you acted. My Heart rejoiced that you had My love under consideration at the time you acted, and that in so distinct a way; and even now you still derive benefit from this; that is, from the humiliation. Yes, My child, I want you to always have such great purity of intention in the very least things you undertake.** (1566)

NOVEMBER 28

Today the Lord said to me, **Daughter, when you go to confession, to this fountain of My mercy, the Blood and Water which came forth from My Heart always flow down upon your soul and ennoble it. Every time you go to confession, immerse yourself entirely in My mercy, with great trust, so that I may pour the bounty of My grace upon your soul. When you approach the confessional, know this, that I Myself am waiting there for you. I am only hidden by the priest, but I Myself act in your soul. Here the misery of the soul meets the God of mercy. Tell souls that from this fount of mercy souls draw graces solely with the vessel of trust. If their trust is great, there is no limit to My generosity. The torrents of grace inundate humble souls. The proud remain always in poverty and misery, because My grace turns away from them to humble souls.** (1602)

Today, I went to confession to Father An. [Andrasz] I did as Jesus wanted. After confession, a surge of light filled my soul. Then I heard a voice: **Because you are a child, you shall remain close to My Heart. Your simplicity is more pleasing to Me than your mortifications.** (1617)

NOVEMBER 29

My daughter, I want to instruct you on how you are to rescue souls through sacrifice and prayer. You will save more souls through prayer and suffering than will a missionary through his teachings and sermons alone. I want to see you as a sacrifice of living love, which only then carries weight before Me. You must be annihilated, destroyed, living as if you were dead in the most secret depths of your being. You must be destroyed in that secret depth where the human eye has never penetrated; then will I find in you a pleasing sacrifice, a holocaust full of sweetness and fragrance. And great will be your power for whomever you intercede. Outwardly, your sacrifice must look like this: silent, hidden, permeated with love, imbued with prayer. I demand, My daughter, that your sacrifice be pure and full of humility, that I may find pleasure in it. I will not spare My grace, that you may be able to fulfill what I demand of you.

I will now instruct you on what your holocaust shall consist of, in everyday life, so as to preserve you from illusions. You shall accept all sufferings with love. Do not be afflicted if your heart often experiences repugnance and dislike for sacrifice. All its power rests in the will, and so these contrary feelings, far from lowering the value of the sacrifice in My eyes, will enhance it. Know that your body and soul will often be in the midst of fire. Although you will not feel My presence on some occasions, I will always be with you. Do not fear; My grace will be with you... (1767)

NOVEMBER 30

Conclusion of the Retreat.
Last Conversation with the Lord.

Thank you, Eternal Love, for Your inconceivable kindness to me, that You would occupy Yourself directly with my sanctification. **My daughter, let three virtues adorn you in a particular way: humility, purity of intention, and love. Do nothing beyond what I demand of you, and accept everything that My hand gives you. Strive for a life of recollection so that you can hear My voice, which is so soft that only recollected souls can hear it...** (1779)

O my Jesus, You know that there are times when I have neither lofty thoughts nor a soaring spirit. I bear with myself patiently and admit that that is just what I am, because all that is beautiful is a grace from God. And so I humble myself profoundly and cry out for Your help; and the grace of visitation is not slow in coming to the humble heart. (1734)

MARY

December

ON THE DAY OF HER PERPETUAL VOWS, Sister Faustina addressed
Mary and prayed:

> Mother of God, Most Holy Mary, my Mother, you are my
> Mother in a *special way* because your beloved Son is my
> Bridegroom, and thus we are both your children.... O Mary,
> my dearest Mother, guide my spiritual life in such a way that
> it will please your Son.   (240, emphasis added)

Mary heard Blessed Faustina's prayer. Later she revealed to
the young nun that God had ordained that Mary be *"in a
special and exclusive way your Mother"* (1414). She also admonished Blessed Faustina to cultivate three virtues in her life that
she would need in order to fulfill her mission: humility, purity,
and love of God.

FOR THIS MONTH:

Practice: Daily renew your consecration to the Blessed Mother.

Prayer: Ask for the grace to be a "special child" of Mary by praying the rosary daily.

Promise: Claim the promise of Mary to Blessed Faustina:
My daughter, at God's command I am to be, in a special and exclusive way your Mother; but I desire that you, too, in a special way, be my Child (1414).

DECEMBER 1

When I got off the train and saw that all were going their separate ways, I was overcome with fear. What am I to do? To whom should I turn, as I know no one? So I said to the Mother of God, "Mary, lead me, guide me." Immediately I heard these words within me telling me to leave the town and to go to a certain nearby village where I would find a safe lodging for the night. I did so and found in fact that everything was just as the Mother of God told me.   (11)

DECEMBER 2

Another time I heard these words, **Go to the Superior and ask her to allow you to make a daily hour of adoration for nine days. During this adoration try to unite yourself in prayer with My Mother. Pray with all your heart in union with Mary, and try also during this time to make the Way of the Cross.** I received the permission, though not for a full hour, but only for whatever time was left me after I had carried out my duties.
                                      (32)

I was to make this novena for the intention of my Motherland. On the seventh day of the novena I saw, between heaven and earth, the Mother of God, clothed in a bright robe. She was praying with Her hands folded on Her bosom, Her eyes fixed on Heaven. From Her Heart issued forth fiery rays, some of which were turned toward Heaven while the others were covering our country.   (33)

O Mary, my Mother and my Lady, I offer You my soul, my body, my life and my death, and all that will follow it. I place everything in Your hands. O my Mother, cover my soul with

Your virginal mantle and grant me the grace of purity of heart, soul, and body. Defend me with Your power against all enemies, and especially against those who hide their malice behind the mask of virtue. O lovely lily! You are for me a mirror, O my Mother! (79)

DECEMBER 3

The year 1929. Once during Holy Mass, I felt in a very special way the closeness of God, although I tried to turn away and escape from Him. On several occasions I have run away from God because I did not want to be a victim of the evil spirit; since others have told me, more than once, that such is the case. And this incertitude lasted for quite some time. During Holy Mass, before Communion, we had the renewal of vows. When we had left our kneelers and had started to recite the formula for the vows, Jesus appeared suddenly at my side clad in a white garment with a golden girdle around His waist, and He said to me, **I give you eternal love that your purity may be untarnished and as a sign that you will never be subject to temptations against purity.** Jesus took off His golden cincture and tied it around my waist.

Since then I have never experienced any attacks against this virtue, either in my heart or in my mind. I later understood that this was one of the greatest graces which the Most Holy Virgin Mary had obtained for me, as for many years I had been asking this grace of Her. Since that time I have experienced an increasing devotion to the Mother of God. She has taught me how to love God interiorly and also how to carry out His holy will in all things, O Mary, You are joy, because through You God descended to earth [and] into my heart.

(40)

DECEMBER 4

O Mary, Immaculate Virgin,
Pure crystal for my heart,
You are my strength, O sturdy anchor!
You are the weak heart's shield and protection.

O Mary you are pure, of purity incomparable;
At once both Virgin and Mother,
You are beautiful as the sun, without blemish,
And your soul is beyond all comparison.

Your beauty has delighted the eye of the Thrice-Holy One.
He descended from heaven, leaving His eternal throne,
And took Body and Blood of your heart
And for nine months lay hidden in a Virgin's Heart.

O Mother, Virgin, purest of all lilies,
Your heart was Jesus' first tabernacle on earth
Only because no humility was deeper than yours
Were you raised above the choirs of Angels
        and above all Saints.

O Mary, my sweet Mother,
I give you my soul, my body, and my poor heart.
Be the guardian of my life,
Especially at the hour of death, in the final strife.   (161)

DECEMBER 5

Exclamatory prayer: Mary, unite me with Jesus.   (162)

The first day of the retreat. I tried to be the first in the chapel in the morning; before the meditation I had a bit of time for prayer to the Holy Spirit and to Our Lady. I earnestly begged the Mother of God to obtain for me the grace of fidelity to these inner inspirations and of faithfully carrying out God's will, whatever it might be. I began this retreat with a very special kind of courage.   (170)

Three requests on the day of my perpetual vows. Jesus, I know that today You will refuse me nothing.

Mother of God, Most Holy Mary, my Mother, You are my Mother in a special way now because your beloved Son is my Bridegroom, and thus we are both your children. For your Son's sake, you have to love me. O Mary, my dearest Mother, guide my spiritual life in such a way that it will please your Son.   (240)

August 5, 1933, the Feast of Our Lady of Mercy. Today I received a great and incomprehensible grace, a purely interior one, for which I will be grateful to God throughout this life and in eternity...   (266)

DECEMBER 6

Christmas Eve. Today I was closely united with the Mother of God. I relived her interior sentiments. In the evening, before the ceremony of the breaking of the wafer, I went into the chapel to break the wafer, in spirit, with my loved ones, and I asked the Mother of God for graces for them. My spirit was totally steeped in God. During the Midnight Mass ["Pasterka" or Shepherds' Mass], I saw the Child Jesus in the Host, and my spirit was immersed in Him. Although He was a tiny Child, His majesty penetrated my soul. I was permeated to the depths of my being by this mystery, this great abasement on the part of God, this inconceivable emptying of Himself. These sentiments remained vividly alive in my soul all through the festive season. Oh, we shall never comprehend this great self-abasement on the part of God; the more I think of it, [unfinished thought].   (182)

A Moment Before the Blessed Sacrament. O my eternal Lord and Creator, how am I going to thank You for this great favor; namely, that You have deigned to choose miserable me to be Your betrothed and that You are to unite me to yourself in an eternal bond? O dearest Treasure of my heart, I offer You all the adoration and thanksgiving of the Saints and of all the choirs of Angels, and I unite myself in a special way with Your Mother. O Mary, my Mother, I humbly beg of You, cover my soul with Your virginal cloak at this very important moment of my life, so that thus I may become dearer to Your Son and may worthily praise Your Son's mercy before the whole world and throughout all eternity.   (220)

DECEMBER 7

Today [December 7, 1937] is the eve of the Feast of the Immaculate Conception of the Virgin Mary. During the midday meal, in an instant, God gave me to know the greatness of my destiny; that is, His closeness, which for all eternity will not be taken away from me, and He did this in such a vivid and clear fashion that I remained wrapped up in His living presence for a long time, humbling myself before His greatness.
                                                                (1410)

It is with great zeal that I have prepared for the celebration of the Feast of the Immaculate Conception of the Mother of God. I have made an extra effort to keep recollected in spirit and have meditated on that unique privilege of Our Lady. And thus my heart was completely drowned in Her, thanking God for having accorded this great privilege to Mary. (1412)

I prepared not only by means of the novena said in common by the whole community, but I also made a personal effort to salute Her a thousand times each day, saying a thousand "Hail Marys" for nine days in Her praise. (1413)

DECEMBER 8

The Feast of the Immaculate Conception. Before Holy Communion I saw the Blessed Mother inconceivably beautiful. Smiling at me, she said to me, *My daughter, at God's command I am to be, in a special and exclusive way your Mother; but I desire that you, too, in a special way, be my child.* (1414)

I desire, my dearly beloved daughter, that you practice the three virtues that are dearest to me—and most pleasing to God The first is humility, humility, and once again humility; the second virtue, purity; the third virtue, love of God. As my daughter, you must especially radiate with these virtues. When the conversation ended, she pressed me to her heart and disappeared. When I regained the use of my senses, my heart became so wonderfully attracted to these virtues; and I practice them faithfully. They are as though engraved in my heart. (1415)

This has been a great day for me. During this day I remained as though in unceasing contemplation; the very thought of this grace drew me into further contemplation; and throughout the whole day I continued in thanksgiving which I never stopped, because each recollection of this grace caused my soul ever anew to lose itself in God... (1416)

DECEMBER 9

I had permission to visit Czestochowa while on my journey. I saw the Mother of God [image] for the first time, when I went to attend the unveiling of the Image at five in the morning. I prayed without interruption until eleven, and it seemed to me that I had just come. The superior of the house there [Mother Serafin] sent a sister for me, to tell me to come to breakfast and said she was worried that I would miss my train. The Mother of God told me many things. I entrusted my perpetual vows to her. I felt that I was her child and that she was my Mother. She did not refuse any of my requests. (260)

Once, after an adoration for our country, a pain pierced my soul, and I began to pray in this way: "Most merciful Jesus, I beseech You through the intercession of Your Saints, and especially the intercession of Your dearest Mother who nurtured You from childhood, bless my native land. I beg You, Jesus, look not on our sins, but on the tears of little children, on the hunger and cold they suffer. Jesus, for the sake of these innocent ones, grant me the grace that I am asking of You for my country." At that moment, I saw the Lord Jesus, His eyes filled with tears, and He said to me, **You see, My daughter, what great compassion I have for them. Know that it is they who uphold the world.** (286)

DECEMBER 10

Mother of God, your soul was plunged into a sea of bitterness; look upon your child and teach her to suffer and to love while suffering. Fortify my soul that pain will not break it. Mother of grace, teach me to live by [the power of] God. (315)

Once, the confessor told me to pray for his intention, and I began a novena to the Mother of God. This novena consisted in the prayer, "Hail, Holy Queen," recited nine times. Toward the end of the novena I saw the Mother of God with the Infant Jesus in her arms, and I also saw my confessor kneeling at her feet and talking with her. I did not understand what he was saying to her, because I was busy talking with the Infant Jesus, who came down from His Mother's arms and approached me. I could not stop wondering at His beauty. I heard a few of the words that the Mother of God spoke to him [i.e., my confessor] but not everything. The words were: *I am not only the Queen of Heaven, but also the Mother of Mercy and your Mother.* And at that moment she stretched out her right hand, in which she was clasping her mantle, and she covered the priest with it. At that moment, the vision vanished. (330)

DECEMBER 11

August 5, 1935. The Feast of Our Lady of Mercy. I prepared for this feast with greater zeal than in previous years. On the morning of the feast itself, I experienced an inner struggle at the thought that I must leave this Congregation which enjoys such special protection from Mary. This struggle lasted through the meditation and through the first Mass as well. During the second Mass, I turned to our Holy Mother, telling her that it was difficult for me to separate myself from this

Congregation... "which is under Your special protection, O Mary." Then I saw the Blessed Virgin, unspeakably beautiful. She came down from the altar to my kneeler, held me close to herself and said to me, *I am Mother to you all, thanks to the unfathomable mercy of God. Most pleasing to me is that soul which faithfully carries out the will of God.* She gave me to understand that I had faithfully fulfilled the will of God and had thus found favor in His eyes. *Be courageous. Do not fear apparent obstacles, but fix your gaze upon the Passion of my Son, and in this way you will be victorious.* (449)

DECEMBER 12

Immaculate Conception of the Mother of God. From early morning, I felt the nearness of the Blessed Mother. During Holy Mass, I saw her, so lovely and so beautiful that I have no words to express even a small part of this beauty. She was all [in] white, with a blue sash around her waist. Her cloak was also blue, and there was a crown on her head. Marvelous light streamed forth from Her whole figure. *I am the Queen of heaven and earth, but especially the Mother of your [Congregation].* She pressed me to her heart and said, *I feel constant compassion for you.* I felt the force of her Immaculate Heart which was communicated to my soul. Now I understand why I have been preparing for this feast for two months and have been looking forward to it with such yearning. From today onwards, I am going to strive for the greatest purity of soul, that the rays of God's grace may be reflected in all their brilliance. I long to be a crystal in order to find favor in His eyes. (805)

DECEMBER 13

Once, the Lord said to me, **My daughter, take the graces that others spurn; take as many as you can carry.** At that moment, my soul was inundated with the love of God. I feel that I am united with the Lord so closely that I cannot find words to express that union; in this state I suddenly feel that all the things God has, all the goods and treasures, are mine, although I set little store by them, for He alone is enough for me. In Him I see my everything; without Him—nothing.

I look for no happiness beyond my own interior where God dwells. I rejoice that God dwells within me; here I abide with Him unendingly; it is here that my greatest intimacy with Him exists; here I dwell with Him in safety; here is a place not probed by the human eye. The Blessed Virgin encourages me to commune with God in this way.   (454)

August 15, the day of the renewal of vows. At the beginning of Holy Mass, I saw Jesus in the usual way. He blessed us and then entered the tabernacle. Then I saw the Mother of God in a white garment and blue mantle, with her head uncovered. She approached me from the altar, touched me with her hands and covered me with her mantle, saying, *Offer these vows for Poland. Pray for her.*   (468)

DECEMBER 14

On Friday evening during the rosary, when I was thinking about tomorrow's journey and about the importance of the matter which I was to present to Father Andrasz,* fear seized me at the sight of my misery and incapability, and of the greatness of God's work. Crushed by this suffering, I submitted

myself to the will of God. At that moment, I saw Jesus, in a
bright garment, near my kneeler. He said, **Why are you afraid
to do My will? Will I not help you as I have done thus far?
Repeat every one of My demands to those who represent Me
on earth, but do only what they tell you to do.** At that, a certain
strength entered my soul.   (489)

In the evening, when I was walking in the garden saying my
rosary and came to the cemetery, I opened the gate a little
and began to pray for a while, and I asked them interiorly,
"You are very happy, are you not?" Then I heard the words,
"We are happy in the measure that we have fulfilled God's
will"—and then silence as before. I became introspective and
reflected for a long time on how I am fulfilling God's will and
how I am profiting from the time that God has given me.(515)

*Father Sopocko, not sure of Sister Faustina's inspirations regard-
ing the establishing of a new community, wanted to refer the
matter to one more priest for consideration, and for that reason
he told Sister Faustina to give an account of all the commands she
received to her former confessor, Father Andrasz, S.J., in Cracow.

DECEMBER 15

On the evening of the last day [November 15] of the novena
at Ostra Brama, after the singing of the litany, one of the
priests exposed the Blessed Sacrament in the monstrance.
When he placed it on the altar, I immediately saw the Infant
Jesus, stretching out His little arms, first of all toward His
Mother, who at that time had taken on a living appearance.
When the Mother of God was speaking to me, Jesus stretched
out His tiny hands toward the congregation. The Blessed
Mother was telling me to accept all that God asked of me like
a little child, without questioning; otherwise it would not be

pleasing to God. At that moment, the Infant Jesus vanished, and the Mother of God was again lifeless, and Her picture was the same as it had been before. But my soul was filled with great joy and gladness, and I said to the Lord, "Do with me as You please; I am ready for everything, but You, O Lord, must not abandon me even for a moment." (529)

DECEMBER 16

All at once, I saw the Image in some small chapel and at that moment I saw that the chapel became an enormous and beautiful temple. And in this temple I saw the Mother of God with the Infant in her arms. And a moment later, the Infant Jesus disappeared from the arms of His Mother, and I saw the living image of Jesus Crucified. The Mother of God told me to do what she had done, that, even when joyful, I should always keep my eyes fixed on the cross, and she told me that the graces God was granting me were not for me alone, but for other souls as well. (561)

On the feast day of the Immaculate Conception of the Mother of God, during Holy Mass, I heard the rustling of garments and saw the most holy Mother of God in a most beautiful radiance. Her white garment was girdled with a blue sash. She said to me, *You give Me great joy when you adore The Holy Trinity for the graces and privileges which were accorded Me.* And she immediately disappeared. (564)

DECEMBER 17

One day, after our Mass, I suddenly saw my confessor [Father Sopocko] saying Mass in Saint Michael's Church, in front of the picture of the Mother of God. It was at the time of the Offertory, and I saw the Infant Jesus clinging to him as if fleeing from something and seeking refuge in him. But when the time came for Holy Communion, He [the Infant] disappeared as usual. Suddenly, I saw the Blessed Mother, who shielded him with her cloak and said, *Courage, my son, courage.* She said something else which I could not hear. (597)

In the morning, when the bell awoke me, I was so overcome by drowsiness which I could not shake off that I jumped into cold water, and after two minutes the sleepiness left me. When I came to meditation a host of absurd thoughts swarmed into my head, so much so that I had to struggle throughout the whole meditation. It was the same during prayer time, but when Mass began, a strange silence and joy filled my heart. Just then, I saw Our Lady with the Infant Jesus, and the Holy Old Man [St. Joseph] standing behind them. The most holy Mother said to me, *Take my Dearest Treasure,* and she handed me the Infant Jesus. When I took the Infant Jesus in my arms, the Mother of God and Saint Joseph disappeared. I was left alone with the Infant Jesus. (608)

DECEMBER 18

Mary is my Instructress, who is ever teaching me how to live for God. My spirit brightens up in your gentleness and your humility, O Mary. (620)

In the evening, when I was praying, the Mother of God told me, *Your lives must be like mine: quiet and hidden, in unceasing union with God, pleading for humanity and preparing the world for the second coming of God.* (625)

March 25, 1936. In the morning, during meditation, God's presence enveloped me in a special way, as I saw the immeasurable greatness of God and, at the same time, His condescension to His creatures. Then I saw the Mother of God, who said to me, *Oh, how pleasing to God is the soul that follows faithfully the inspirations of His grace! I gave the Savior to the world; as for you, you have to speak to the world about His great mercy and prepare the world for the Second Coming of Him who will come, not as a merciful Savior, but as a just Judge. Oh, how terrible is that day! Determined is the day of justice, the day of divine wrath. The Angels tremble before it. Speak to souls about this great mercy while it is still the time for* [granting] *mercy. If you keep silent now, you will be answering for a great number of souls on that terrible day. Fear nothing. Be faithful to the end. I sympathize with you.* (635)

DECEMBER 19

During a Mass celebrated by Father Andrasz, a moment before the Elevation, God's presence pervaded my soul, which was drawn to the altar. Then I saw the Mother of God with the Infant Jesus. The Infant Jesus was holding onto the hand of Our Lady. A moment later, the Infant Jesus ran with joy to the center of the altar, and the Mother of God said to me, *See with what assurance I entrust Jesus into his hands. In the same way, you are to entrust your soul and be like a child to him.*

After these words, my soul was filled with unusual trust. The Mother of God was clothed in a white dress, strangely white, transparent; on her shoulders she had a transparent blue; that is, a blue-like mantle; with uncovered head [and] flowing hair, she was exquisite, and inconceivably beautiful. She was looking at Father with great tenderness, but after a moment, He broke up this beautiful Child, and living blood flowed forth. Father bent forward and received the true and living Jesus into himself. Had he eaten Him? I do not know how this took place. Jesus, Jesus, I cannot keep up with You, for in an instant, You become incomprehensible to me.   (677)

DECEMBER 20

September, first Friday. In the evening, I saw the Mother of God, with Her breast bared and pierced with a sword. She was shedding bitter tears and shielding us against God's terrible punishment. God wants to inflict terrible punishment on us, but He cannot because the Mother of God is shielding us. Horrible fear seized my soul. I kept praying incessantly for Poland, for my dear Poland, which is so lacking in gratitude for the Mother of God. If it were not for the Mother of God, all our efforts would be of little use. I intensified my prayers and sacrifices for our dear native land, but I see that I am a drop before the wave of evil. How can a drop stop a wave: O yes! A drop is nothing of itself, but with You, Jesus, I shall stand up bravely to the whole wave of evil and even to the whole of hell. Your omnipotence can do all things.   (686)

DECEMBER 21

November 29, 1936. The Mother of God has taught me how to prepare for the Feast of Christmas. I saw her today, without the Infant Jesus. She said to me: *My daughter, strive after silence and humility, so that Jesus, who dwells in your heart continuously, may be able to rest. Adore Him in your heart; do not go out from your inmost being. My daughter, I shall obtain for you the grace of an interior life which will be such that, without ever leaving that interior life, you will be able to carry out all your external duties with even greater care. Dwell with Him continuously in your own heart. He will be your strength. Communicate with creatures only insofar as is necessary and is required by your duties. You are a dwelling place pleasing to the living God; in you He dwells continuously with love and delight. And the living presence of God, which you experience in a more vivid and distinct way, will confirm you, my daughter, in the things I have told you. Try to act in this way until Christmas Day, and then He himself will make known to you in what way you will be communing and uniting yourself with Him.* (785)

DECEMBER 22

November 30, 1936. During Vespers today, an unusual pain pierced my soul. I see that, in every respect, this work is beyond my strength. I am a little child before the immensity of the task, and it is only at the Lord's clear command that I am setting about to carry it out. On the other hand, even these great graces are a burden for me, and I am barely able to carry them. I see my superiors' disbelief and doubts of all kinds and, for this reason, their apprehensive behavior towards me. My Jesus, I see that even such great graces can be [a source of] suffering. And yet, it is so; not only may they be a cause of suffering, but they must be such, as a sign of God's action. I understand well that if God Himself did not strengthen the soul in these various ordeals, the soul would not be able to master the situation. Thus God Himself is its shield.

As I continued Vespers, meditating on this mixture of suffering and grace, I heard the voice of Our Lady: *Know, My daughter, that although I was raised to the dignity of Mother of God, seven swords of pain pierced my heart. Don't do anything to defend yourself; bear everything with humility; God himself will defend you.* (786)

I will spend this Advent in accordance with the directions of the Mother of God: in meekness and humility. (792)

DECEMBER 23

I am reliving these moments with Our Lady. With great longing, I am waiting for the Lord's coming. Great are my desires. I desire that all humankind come to know the Lord. I would like to prepare all nations for the coming of the Word Incarnate. O Jesus, make the fount of Your mercy gush forth more abundantly, for humankind is seriously ill and thus has more need than ever of Your compassion. You are a bottomless sea of mercy for us sinners; and the greater the misery, the more right we have to Your mercy. You are a fount which makes all creatures happy by Your infinite mercy. (793)

During Holy Mass, the little Infant Jesus brings joy to my soul. Often, distance does not exist—I see a certain priest who brings Him down. I am awaiting Christmas with great yearning; I am living in expectation together with the Most Holy Mother. (829)

December 23, 1936. I am spending this time with the Mother of God and preparing myself for the solemn moment of the coming of the Lord Jesus. The Mother of God is instructing me in the interior life of the soul with Jesus, especially in Holy Communion. It is only in eternity that we shall know the great mystery effected in us by Holy Communion. O most precious moments of my life! (840)

DECEMBER 24

December 24, 1936. During Holy Mass today, I was united in a particular way with God and His Immaculate Mother. The humility and love of the Immaculate Virgin penetrated my soul. The more I imitate the Mother of God, the more deeply I get to know God. Oh, what infinite longing envelops my soul! Jesus, how can You still leave me in this exile? I am dying of longing for You. Every touch of my soul by You wounds me immensely. Love and suffering go together; yet I would not exchange this pain caused by You for any treasure, because it is the pain of incomprehensible delights, and these wounds of the soul are inflicted by a loving hand. (843)

Christmas Eve 1937. After Holy Communion, the Mother of God gave me to experience the anxious concern she had in her heart because of the Son of God. But this anxiety was permeated with such fragrance of abandonment to the will of God that I should call it rather a delight than an anxiety. I understood how my soul ought to accept the will of God in all things. It is a pity I cannot write this the way I experienced it. My soul was plunged in deep recollection all day long. Nothing could tear me away from this recollection, neither duties, nor the business I had with lay people. (1437)

DECEMBER 25

Before the vigil supper, I entered the chapel for a moment to break the wafer spiritually with those dear to my heart. I presented them all, by name, to Jesus and begged for graces on their behalf. But that wasn't all. I commended to the Lord all those who are being persecuted, those who are suffering, those who do not know His Name, and especially poor sinners. O little Jesus, I fervently ask You, enclose them all in the ocean of Your incomprehensible mercy. O sweet little Jesus, here is my heart; let it be a little cozy dwelling place for Yourself. O Infinite Majesty, with what sweetness You draw close to us. Here, there is no dread of the thunderbolts of the great Jehovah; here, there is the sweet little Jesus. Here, no soul is afraid, although Your majesty has not lessened, but only concealed itself. After supper, I felt very tired and was in pain. I had to lie down. But I kept vigil with the Most Holy Mother, awaiting the arrival of the little Child.   (845)

When I arrived at Midnight Mass, from the very beginning I steeped myself in deep recollection, during which time I saw the stable of Bethlehem filled with great radiance. The Blessed Virgin, all lost in the deepest of love, was wrapping Jesus in swaddling clothes, but Saint Joseph was still asleep. Only after the Mother of God put Jesus in the manger, did the light of God awaken Joseph, who also prayed. But after a while, I was left alone with the Infant Jesus who stretched out His little hands to me, and I understood that I was to take Him in my arms. Jesus pressed His head against my heart and gave me to know, by His profound gaze, how good He found it to be next to my heart. At that moment Jesus disappeared and the bell was ringing for Holy Communion.   (1442)

DECEMBER 26

Sister C.* came in the afternoon and took me home for the holy days. I was happy to be reunited with the community. As we were riding through the city [Cracow], I imagined it was the town of Bethlehem. As I watched all those people hurrying about, I thought: who is meditating today, in recollection and silence, on this inconceivable mystery? O pure Virgin, You are traveling today, and so am I. I feel that today's journey has its symbolism. O radiant Virgin, pure as crystal, all immersed in God, I offer You my spiritual life; arrange everything that it may be pleasing to Your Son. O my Mother, how ardently I desire that You give me the Infant Jesus during the Midnight Mass. And I felt such a living presence of God in the depths of my soul, that it was only by sheer will-power that I restrained my joy in order not to show outwardly what was going on in my soul. (844)

Mary, Immaculate Virgin, take me under your special protection and guard the purity of my soul, heart, and body. You are the model and star of my life. (874)

*Sister Cajetan—Mary Bartkowiak. Born January 19, 1911, she entered the Congregation in 1933. She was with Sister Faustina in Warsaw and in Cracow. She was a witness at the information process in 1965-66.

DECEMBER 27

O Mary, today a terrible sword has pierced Your holy soul. Except for God, no one knows of Your suffering. Your soul does not break; it is brave, because it is with Jesus. Sweet Mother, unite my soul to Jesus, because it is only then that I will be able to endure all trials and tribulations, and only in union with Jesus will my little sacrifices be pleasing to God. Sweetest Mother, continue to teach me about the interior life. May the sword of suffering never break me. O pure Virgin, pour courage into my heart and guard it.   (915)

Since that time, I have been living under the virginal cloak of the Mother of God. She has been guarding me and instructing me. I am quite at peace, close to her Immaculate Heart. Because I am so weak and inexperienced, I nestle like a little child close to her heart.   (1097)

May 1, 1937. Today I felt the nearness of my Mother, my heavenly Mother, although before every Holy Communion I earnestly ask the Mother of God to help me prepare my soul for the coming of her Son, and I clearly feel her protection over me. I entreat her to be so gracious as to enkindle in me the fire of God's love, such as burned in her own pure heart at the time of the Incarnation of the Word of God.   (1114)

DECEMBER 28

August 15, 1937. Father Andrasz's instructions. "These times of dryness and stark awareness of one's wretchedness, which God has permitted, allow the soul to know how little it can do by itself. They will teach you how much you should appreciate God's graces. Secondly, faithfulness in all exercises and duties, faithfulness in everything, just as in times of joy. Thirdly, as regards the matters in question, be absolutely obedient to the Archbishop [Jalbrzykowski] although, from time to time, the matter can be brought to his attention, but peacefully. Sometimes, a little bitter truth is necessary."

At the end of the conversation, I asked the priest to allow me to commune with Jesus as I had done formerly. He answered, "I cannot give orders to the Lord Jesus, but if He Himself draws you to Himself you may follow the attraction. However, always remember to show Him great reverence, for the Lord is great indeed. If you are truly seeking God's will in all this and desire to fulfill it, you can be at peace; the Lord will not allow any sort of error. As to the mortifications and sufferings, you will give me an account next time of how you carry them out. Place yourself in the hands of the Most Holy Mother." (1243)

During one time of prayer, I learned how pleasing to God was the soul of Father Andrasz. He is a true child of God. It is rare that divine sonship shines forth so clearly in a soul, and this because he has a special devotion to the Mother of God.

(1388)

DECEMBER 29

August 15, 1937. During meditation, God's presence pervaded me keenly, and I was aware of the Virgin Mary's joy at the moment of her Assumption. Towards the end of the ceremony carried out in honor of the Mother of God, I saw the Virgin Mary, and she said to me, *Oh, how very pleased I am with the homage of your love!* And at that moment she covered all the sisters of our Congregation with her mantle. With her right hand, she clasped Mother General Michael to herself, and with her left hand she did so to me, while all the sisters were at her feet, covered with her mantle. Then the Mother of God said, *Everyone who perseveres zealously till death in my Congregation will be spared the fire of purgatory, and I desire that each one distinguish herself by the following virtues: humility and meekness; chastity and love of God and neighbor; compassion and mercy.* After these words, the whole Congregation disappeared from my sight, and I remained alone with the Most Holy Mother who instructed me about the will of God and how to apply it to my life, submitting completely to His most holy decrees. It is impossible for one to please God without obeying His holy will. *My daughter, I strongly recommend that you faithfully fulfill all God's wishes, for that is most pleasing in His holy eyes. I very much desire that you distinguish yourself in this faithfulness in accomplishing God's will. Put the will of God before all sacrifices and holocausts.* While the heavenly Mother was talking to me, a deep understanding of this will of God was entering my soul.   (1244)

DECEMBER 30

A vision of the Mother of God. In the midst of a great brilliance, I saw the Mother of God clothed in a white gown, girt about with a golden cincture; and there were tiny stars, also of gold, over the whole garment, and chevron-shaped sleeves lined with gold. Her cloak was sky-blue, lightly thrown over the shoulders. A transparent veil was delicately drawn over her head, while her flowing hair was set off beautifully by a golden crown which terminated in little crosses. On her left arm she held the Child Jesus. A Blessed Mother of this type I had not yet seen. Then she looked at me kindly and said: *I am the Mother of God of Priests.* At that, she lowered Jesus from her arm to the ground, raised her right hand heavenward and said: *O God, bless Poland, bless priests.* Then she addressed me once again: *Tell the priests what you have seen.* I resolved that at the first opportunity [I would have) of seeing Father [Andrasz] I would tell; but I myself can make nothing of this vision. (1585)

DECEMBER 31

When I was left alone with the Blessed Virgin, she instructed me concerning the interior life. She said, *The soul's true greatness is in loving God and in humbling oneself in His presence, completely forgetting oneself and believing oneself to be nothing; because the Lord is great, but He is well-pleased only with the humble; He always opposes the proud.* (1711)

GLOSSARY TERMS

Annual vows — vows of obedience, celibacy, and poverty taken after two years of spiritual formation called the novitiate. They are taken for a year at a time for five years, when formal perpetual vows are made. The perpetual vows are prepared for by a third period of spiritual formation, called the third probation, just prior to taking the final vows for life. Then each year, the vows are renewed as a devotional practice.

Calyx — a chalice, used to describe the shape of the heart.

Chaplet — a repeated prayer, using beads to keep track of the number, for example, the rosary.

Ciborium — a covered cup of precious metal, used to reserve the consecrated Hosts to be used for distribution of Holy Communion at Mass and also for distribution to the sick.

Confessor — a priest who is assigned to administer the Sacrament of Reconciliation (Penance).

Corpus Christi procession — "The Body of Christ" procession is a solemn liturgical procession with the priest carrying in the Blessed Sacrament from one chapel to another, honoring the Eucharistic Lord on the feast of *Corpus Christi*.

Degrees of humility — according to St. Ignatius of Loyola, there are three kinds of humility:
1. that which is necessary for salvation: to humble one's self *to obey* the law of God in all things.
2. that which is a *holy indifference* to riches or poverty, honors or dishonors, length of life.

3. The most perfect kind of humility, which is to desire to be more like Christ by choosing with Christ, poverty, insults, and humiliation.

Diary — written by Blessed Faustina under obedience to the Lord, her spiritual director, and her superior from 1934 to 1938 in six notebooks. The first was titled: *Divine Mercy in My Soul.*

Directress of Novices — the sister in charge of the spiritual formation of the young women (novices) aspiring to enter the religious community, during a two-year period called the Novitiate.

Father Andrasz — a Jesuit priest. He was the confessor for the convent of sisters outside of Crakow (location of the Novitiate) that first encouraged Blessed Faustina to follow the Lord's leadings.

Father Sopocko — the main spiritual director of Blessed Faustina in Vilnius, and a professor of Theology at Batory University, at times referred to as "the professor" or "Rev. Doctor."

Father Theodore — in the Cracow house, the chaplain, Father Theodore Czaputa, had weekly lectures to the sisters on ascetical subjects. These were familiarly called "Catechism."

Feast of Mercy — the first Sunday after Easter, asked for by Our Lord, as a special day of graces.

Holy Hour — an hour of worship and prayer spent before the Blessed Sacrament.

Holy obedience — Superiors in the Congregation may command "in the name of holy obedience" only professed sisters. A novice was not obliged to obey such a command. If the directress used these words, she was relying on the good will and virtue of the novice, who by subordinating herself to the command could be relieved of these painful experiences.

The Image — is the religious painting ordered by Our Lord as Blessed Faustina saw Him, with rays of Blood and Water emanating from the area of His Heart. It is called the Image or Icon because it represents Jesus who is the image (icon in Greek) of the Father (Col 1:15).

Iron belt — a kind of belt made of fine wire mesh, used as an instrument of penance. The Sisters could wear the belt with the superior's permission and only for a specified period of time.

Jubilee of Redemption — The year 1933 to 1934 was celebrated as the 1,900 year of our Redemption in Rome. In the year 1935, the celebration was extended to the world.

Mercy — is God's love poured out on the undeserving. It is love in action. It is the love of the Father creating us, the love of the Son redeeming us, the love of the Holy Spirit sanctifying us.

Monstrance — the Latin word means to show, like our English word "demonstrate." A monstrance is a decorative stand for showing the Blessed Sacrament for adoration.

Mother Directress — is the sister in charge of the formation of the novices (candidates for religious profession of vows), also called Directress of Novices.

Mother Superior — the sister in charge of the local house (convent) of sisters. The Mother Superior would be appointed for a fixed period of years.

Mystery of Mercy — a phrase used by Blessed Faustina and also by Pope John Paul II in his encyclical *Rich in Mercy* to describe the plan of God to have mercy on all (see Romans 11:32). "Mystery" is a term used to describe God's plan that is beyond what we can reason or even imagine (see 1 Cor 2:6-10; Col 1:27).

New Congregation — the religious community Our Lord wanted established to promulgate His mercy.

Nocturnal Adoration — On special feasts, the sisters would take turns throughout the night in adoration of the Lord Jesus in the Blessed Sacrament. It was a way to "watch and pray," keeping vigil with the Lord.

Pall — a large piece of black cloth with a white cross in the middle. According to the Congregation's ceremonial procedure, before taking perpetual vows the sisters prostrated themselves before the altar and were covered with the pall as a symbol of being dead to the world. In the meantime, other sisters recited Psalm 129, and the bells tolled as during a funeral. The officiating priest, usually a bishop, sprinkled the prostrate sisters with holy water and then said: "Rise, you who are dead to the world, and Jesus Christ will enlighten you."

Paten — a dish of precious metal on which the consecrated Host is laid during Holy Mass.

Perpetual Vows — see annual vows.

Secretary of Mercy — one of the names Our Lord called Blessed Faustina because she was to write down all He told her about His mercy. Other names were: apostle, witness, instrument, dispenser, mediator, intercessor of His Mercy.

Sisters of the Second Choir — At that time the Congregation was divided into two choirs, the so-called director sisters and coadjutor sisters (second choir). The membership to one or the other was decided by the Congregation's governing body on the basis of the candidate's intellectual level, age, and abilities. The director sister's task was to manage the Congregation and the penitents' homes. The coadjutor sisters did the manual work and served as helpers to the director sisters, especially in the area of physical labor.

Spiritual Director — a person, such as a priest, who guides the spiritual life of a person by helping to discern the action and presence of the Holy Spirit.

Third probation — see annual vows.

Turbile — a container on a chain, designed to hold burning charcoal on which incense is burned, as an act of worship. It is used during Holy Mass, adoration of the Blessed Sacrament, and in processions.

Tribunal of Mercy — is the way Our Lord referred to the Sacrament of Reconciliation (Confession), where the penitent receives mercy. It is in contrast to the legal court or "Tribunal of Justice."

Vows — solemn promises to God, to live a life of poverty, celibacy, and obedience, as recognized by the Church as a way to follow the gospel counsels. Vows taken for a period of testing are called temporary; vows taken for life are called perpetual. It is the custom to renew them annually.

Way of the Cross — a devotional practice in following the steps Jesus took carrying His cross to Calvary, originally on the actual sites in Jerusalem, later extended to the world. The usual pattern is fourteen stops from His condemnation by Pontius Pilate to His burial in the tomb.

Works of Mercy — are the deeds of mercy that put love into action. They are the ways in which mercy is described in practical terms by Our Lord in the Gospel of Matthew 25:31-46. These developed into the spiritual and corporal Works of Mercy (see general introduction on *our response of mercy to others.*)